ERIZA

by
Peter Molife

First printed in the United Kingdom, 2020

Published by Conscious Dreams Publishing
www.consciousdreamspublishing.com

Edited by Rhoda Molife
www.molahmedia.com

Cover design by Kennedy Madevu
Instagram: @kennedymadevu

ISBN: 978-1-912551-72-9

DEDICATION

For Zakar, Shona, Zuva and Andre

ACKNOWLEDGEMENTS

To my wife, Charity, and daughters Rhoda and Mussah – thank you for your steadfast support and encouragement.

To my nephews Christian Hunkeler and Brian Haukozi – thank you for reading the first draft.

To my brother David Musa – thank you for reading the final draft.

To Molah Media – thank you for your complete editorial dedication to this book.

To Oksana Kosovan – thank you for typesetting the book.

To Danni Blechner at Conscious Dreams Publishing – thank you for helping me to share *Eriza* with the world.

ONE

I n Chena they called her Eriza, pronounced *E-ree-za*. Her mother had long given up on the local folks calling her daughter by her proper name – Elizabeth. Those who tried only ended up calling her Erizabet.

Throughout the last three weeks before her departure, Eriza constantly daydreamt that, once settled in England, she would transform the structure of her parents' homestead so that the two mud huts would become a four-bedroom brick bungalow with corrugated zinc or asbestos roofing and an outside toilet. She wanted her uncle, Sekuru Fani, to live under the same roof as the rest of the family. His intricately thatched hut served as his private quarters, though all his meals were prepared and eaten in the family kitchen. But she had never felt comfortable with him being treated like an outsider. In her dreams, the rebuilt homestead would be fenced in, not to keep people out, but to banish her *mbuya's* – grandmother's – goats, that often made a meal of her washing, even her 'private' items. A year before, Mbuya Mukwesa, whose Christian name, Sophia, was only known clandestinely, had a good laugh when one of the goats was spotted chewing two of her granddaughter's special knickers. She had consoled Eriza by saying that it was a prank perpetrated by her ancestors' spirits. Eriza looked at her grandmother in bewilderment because, not long before the goat and knickers incident, she had read Aristotle and committed to memory a quote that said, 'The gods too are fond of a joke.' This confirmed her suspicion that the only difference between Greek and African philosophy was that the Greek was manually recorded, while the African was passed down the ages through oratory means. In Eriza's view, Mbuya Mukwesa had bettered Aristotle by saying that the ancestors enticed animals to carry out pranks on humans.

On this, the morning of her departure for England, Eriza was confronted by the knicker-chewing nanny goat at the entrance of the kitchen-cum-bedroom hut that she shared as a bedroom with her grandmother and Prudence, her niece. Eriza and the goat looked at each other. The goat pleadingly turned its head from side to side. She was not at all compelled to chase it away as she often did when any of the seven goats came to the kitchen door for bits of scrap food. Instead, she smiled. She suspected that the animal instinctively knew that it would not see her again. Then Mbuya Mukwesa spoke for them.

"It knows you are leaving today. Animals don't speak our language, but they damn well know our every move."

Mbuya then called out to wake her great-granddaughter, Prudence. Prudence was not too pleased based on the way she mumbled her response. In the kitchen-cum-bedroom, Naijo, Eriza's brother, was snoring incessantly. At that moment, the goat turned and wagged its short tail as it hoofed away to survey its pastures, which in August consisted of patchy areas of dry grass and remains of maize stalks from that year's harvest. The animal appeared to smell moisture in the air and see green grass in the distance. If her grandmother's wisdom was true, the goat was probably gazing in the direction of Eriza's journey that day. Eriza was now sure that the wagging was a goodbye rather than just flicks to chase off the flies that tormented its backside.

Wearing her *mapatapata* as usual, Eriza paced briskly towards the grass bathroom at the back of the kitchen. She wore the flimsy rubber slippers against the stern advice of her grandmother who believed that they offered no protection for her feet against the cold sand of the August morning air. She was convinced that the cold penetrated through the rubber, into her feet, through her legs and up into the chest to create havoc in the lungs. On completing her morning ablutions, Eriza heard the clatter of dishes in the kitchen competing with the not-so-friendly conversation between Mbuya Mukwesa and Prudence. The level of noise emanating from the dishes correlated with Prudence's mood. This morning she was definitely sour and everyone knew why.

Eriza felt for her. She decided that she would do one domestic chore that would have been Prudence's. In a way the chore was to allow her to leave her footprint in the sands of her home. It was the one chore she could take over that morning from Prudence, allowing herself one last grand tour of her home. This she would do by sweeping the whole homestead's yard. As she did so, a plume of dust rose from the ground and serenely soared in the calm morning air. Some of the dust settled on her. Just as well she still had on her shower cap that she always put on to protect her hair from smoke from the outdoor fireplace. The cap was somehow like a crown atop her pretty face with its smooth black complexion. The morning sun shone red rays through the dust and her bent body cast a shadow on the kitchen wall with reddish particles twinkling above it. Her shadow did not do justice to her well-shaped figure wrapped in a *zambia* from the waist down. The dust smelt good. She thought about how, tomorrow, her shadow would be replaced by that of Prudence.

"She will be all right," she said to herself, before straightening up. With the grass broom in her hand, she quickly walked over to the remains of last night's outdoor fire, with a shake of her behind that would have knocked out any young man who might have been looking at her. She thought about how that fire had warmed up the village folk who had come to bid her farewell. It was also around that fire that junior adults and children had enjoyed a farewell dinner of sadza, goat and chicken meat and vegetables, while the seniors spent the evening around the kitchen fire.

She was increasingly conscious of the fact that this was her last morning in Chena. She looked closely at everything around her, things she had taken for granted over the years. It dawned on her that when she returned, home would not be the same again. Some of the changes would be of her own making, but that little bush, that mingy dog and the whistles and voices of boys herding their parents' livestock to the pastures, would all have changed. She thought about how her parents were referred to by the other villagers. They assigned to them whatever title they chose to. She was told by her grandmother that when they had their first-born child, Chido, who became Prudence's mother, her parents were referred to as *Baba vaChido* – father of Chido and *Mai Chido* – mother of Chido. When Nigel her brother was born, her father was then referred to as *Baba vaNaijo*. The *g* and *i* in Nigel were discarded and, logically, the *g* became a *j*. Then Eriza came and her mother became *Mai Eriza*. At social gatherings, her parents were referred to as *Baba Mukwesa* and *Mai Mukwesa*. Then, people referred to them as *Sekuru na Mbuya vaPrudence*. It was only a matter of time before they were simply called Sekuru Mukwesa and Mbuya Mukwesa. That would mean that, to distinguish her grandmother from her mother, her grandmother would be *Mbuya Mukwesa vakuru* – the elder. Her mother would be *Mbuya Mukwesa vadiki* – the younger. She had never thought about all this evolution of titles and realised that these were some of the things she was leaving behind. But she refused to think about them not being there when she returned. Suddenly, she heard a familiar female voice.

"Have a good time where you are going, my grandchild."

Before Eriza could turn and answer, a male voice cut in, in a way which, to those who did not know this elderly couple, would have made them think the husband was being rude to his wife.

"Where Eriza is going is *Ingirandi* – England. I have been telling you this for a very long time." It was Sekuru Mhizha speaking to his wife, Mbuya Mhizha, in a stern but loving manner.

He started coughing badly and so couldn't finish his intended monologue. Both Eriza and Mbuya Mhizha looked quite concerned before Mbuya blamed the cold morning for her husband's harsh cough. Eriza then quickly gave them both her salutation.

"Marara here Mbuya na Sekuru?" – Did you sleep well Grandma and Grandpa?

With his coughing, Eriza was not sure how well they would have slept. The coughing subsided and he spat out the phlegm into his brown handkerchief. Normally he would have spat on the ground and covered it with soil before chickens made a snack out of it. However, Mbuya Mhizha had put her foot down and told him that he couldn't do it in front of other people.

"Zvinosemesa!" – It's nasty. That was Mbuya Mhizha's declaration as her body had convulsed at the sight of her husband's spit on the day of her edict on phlegm. Sekuru Mhizha, who normally did not take kindly to reprimands from his wife, had quietly conformed ever since. She had then handed him the handkerchief. Back then, it was white.

He was now able to complete his thoughts. "Tomorrow morning, and perhaps many more mornings after that, we will walk through your homestead and end up right here. We will imagine you standing where you are now. Everything will continue to change around us but this scene will be seared in our memories and yours too. And when you come back you won't see us pass this way again, but you will not forget us. You will remember how we stood here talking with you."

Sekuru Mhizha spoke while looking directly into Eriza's eyes, eyes that were already holding back tears because Sekuru expressed her silent sentiments perfectly. She managed to console him by saying that they still had many more Christmases to celebrate. He gave a hearty laugh and a gentle cough and swallowed the remnants of phlegm loosened as a result. At that moment, Sekuru and Mbuya Mhizha realised that Eriza, even though she was not their granddaughter, was going to miss them and that made their day – they knew she had them in her heart.

"Give our morning regards to your Mbuya. Is she sleeping?" Mbuya Mhizha knew very well that Mbuya Mukwesa was wide awake. Mbuya Mukwesa didn't want to engage in conversation with them because she had had enough of them the night before. All they would want to talk about was Eriza's departure, a subject that had already exhausted her.

Eriza also knew that her grandmother was feigning sleep, because a few minutes before that she was listening to the chatter between her grandmother and Prudence. Now, only the clatter of dishes could be heard. Mbuya always did that when she wanted to shut people out, and she, like Prudence now, connived with her feigned muteness. With a knowing smile, Eriza said she would pass on their regards and they walked on again – Sekuru Mhizha in front and Mbuya Mhizha about seven metres behind. This seven-metre gap was a constant between them. Their nineteen grandchildren had once occupied that gap but, after they'd all grown up, Mbuya Mhizha had never bothered to close it. Besides, Sekuru Mizha preferred to listen to his own thoughts rather than to the mutterings of his wife. The whole village loved them because their journey in the morning from their home to their eldest daughter's homestead just a mile away, and the return in the evenings, was another constant. It was as sure as the sunrise every morning and the sunset every evening. Most importantly, to see them walking meant they were still in good health and the community was stable.

Eriza watched them as they walked away along a narrow path. Mbuya Mhizha was short and plain. She always dressed in a long, brown skirt and a heavy, red jumper – a jumper that swayed from side to side in unison with her arthritic gait which made her roll from side to side with each step. Eriza could see that Mbuya Mhizha would not be making this journey for much longer. Perhaps it will be their daughter's turn to walk to them every morning. On the other hand, Sekuru Mhizha was a tall, lanky man who walked with a stoop. No matter the weather, he always wore a suit jacket. Soon they turned a corner and disappeared from her view.

She was about to return to the remains of last night's fire when she noticed the family dog, Hesvu, heading towards her with the entire male dog population of the village trotting behind her. Some of the dogs were licking wounds from the battles they had fought over her, right next to the then-blazing fire. Those dogs that had lost the scramble to pass on their genes through her had consoled themselves with the scraps of food and bones discarded by Eriza and Prudence earlier that morning. Hesvu trotted past Eriza without even casting a doggy glance in her direction; even her entourage of canine admirers were oblivious to Eriza. She recalled that the boys had at one point congregated around the dogs with a level of excitement that embarrassed her uncles – Sekuru Soromon and Sekuru Fani – more than any other adult around that fire. She wondered why boys showed more excitement than girls over the lovemaking of animals. Sekuru Fani kept on shouting at the boys to leave the dogs alone, but with such a bright moon the dog show was far more exciting than anything the adults around them could have offered. Eriza, who had helped to raise Hesvu's last litter, regretted that she would not be around to assist with the next batch of puppies.

She finally got to the ashes of last night's fire, but the memories of her last night in her country, and the people who bade her farewell, continued to float back into her thoughts. Some had sat on logs, others on stones and the women sat on a strong mahogany bench which was the workmanship of Sekuru Fani. Some of the younger boys deferred seats to the adults and either crouched in the spaces between the logs and stones or just stood and milled about behind those who were seated. Now and then, there was pushing and shoving from the teens as they competed for space around the fire. Young women were in and out of the kitchen helping Prudence to prepare her aunt's farewell dinner under the supervision of Mai Eriza. It had been an evening for everybody.

It was over this fire that Eriza, alongside most of the young people of the village, ate her last meal. Many wondered whether she would be able to eat sadza in England. Sekuru Fani, Sekuru Soromon and the other men in their thirties and forties who had shared in the evening's proceedings, drank a local brew. Its distinct aroma competed with the smell of smoke coming from the fire. The women protested over the beer-drinking but Sekuru Fani reminded them that Mbuya Mukwesa approved of social drinking of this nature. Eriza had remembered the day, some years ago, when her mother and grandmother engaged in a religious schism over alcohol. On that day, her mother had berated her own brother, Sekuru Fani, for drinking beer in the home when, by her actions and words, she had declared their home a Christian, alcohol-free zone. Mbuya Mukwesa, who was fed up with the 'Christian this and Christian that' of her daughter-in-law, countered her by reminding her that as far as she understood it, Jesus and his disciples often indulged in alcohol, especially on the night before the crucifixion, and indeed the day after, he had probably laid in God's arms with a little hangover. Eriza chuckled as she remembered the cynicism of her grandmother. From that day onwards, alcohol continued to be taken occasionally with Mbuya Mukwesa quietly cautioning Sekuru Fani not to overdo it.

As she stood over the ashes of last night's fire, Eriza saw a half empty metal cup of alcohol near the spot that Sekuru Fani had been sitting. She picked it and poured the contents out. She then picked up a stick and used it to scratch the ashes and unearth the remaining hot embers. Some chickens ran to her expecting some scraps of food. They were without their constant companion – a large cockerel. Based on the philosophical wisdom of her grandmother, Eriza mused that the chickens had figured out that their big male had been a part of the last supper. She ignored them and added dry twigs to the embers. The flames rose, and using a small metal sheet, she scooped the ashes into a metal bucket and threw them into the compost pit a few yards away. The chickens followed but she continued to ignore them. Then she added medium-sized logs onto the fire and remembered that Kudiwa, an eight-year-old girl, had been concerned that when in England, Eriza would be eating frogs – according to her history lessons. There had been a momentary silence before the crowd burst out laughing. Sekuru Soromon rescued the poor little girl by telling her that she should go and tell her teacher that it was the French who ate frogs.

One of the boys had then shouted, "What's the difference between the French and the British? They are all white."

The laughter had then given way to a universal disgust of the French. Eating frogs was unforgivable. It wasn't about animal rights. It's just that frogs were simply one of the most disgusting creatures on earth. Why would anyone eat them?

Eriza recalled Sekuru Fani looking at her and reminding her that in England, white people did not eat sadza. "They're like these whites here in our country," he'd said. Kudiwa's big, beautiful eyes had lit the night fire as much as the fire had lit hers, as she tried to envisage how Eriza would survive in England without sadza.

"Don't mind these whites here. They eat sadza and just pretend not to like it," said Sekuru Soromon, swaying his head from left to right and scratching the stubble of his beard.

"What will you eat then?" Kudiwa asked pitifully, ignoring Sekuru Soromon. It was as if she spoke with those huge eyes. People laughed at the deep concern in her words. She felt embarrassed.

"There's nothing special about what they eat. Cheese – you wouldn't think it was made from the same cow's milk that your Mbuya makes our delicious sour milk with," added Sekuru Fani.

"I enjoy potatoes, even though Fani thinks they taste like wax candles, to use his words, when they are boiled," interjected Sekuru Soromon.

"A person can acquire a taste for any food especially when they cook it. You, Soromon, you have been a kitchen boy for many years, even though you tell people that you were a chef in big hotels in the big town, so white people's food is in your blood now anyway," Sekuru Fani retorted. The crowd laughed. Sekuru Fani savoured moments like this, when he could deride his love rival, particularly when *Ceciria* – Cecilia – the subject of that rivalry, was in the vicinity.

Ceciria in turn milked these two men's rivalry over her, never declaring her love for either, but instead maintaining a balanced rapport with each, giving them hope of victory over the other. Mbuya disliked women like Ceciria because she said they were village prostitutes, especially as Ceciria accepted gifts from these two men.

"You can imagine the number of men that she takes all sorts of gifts from," she had muttered to Eriza one day when Sekuru Soromon strode past them, hand in hand with Ceciria.

Sekuru Soromon had let out a contemptuous laugh. The fire threw up a galaxy of sparks which melted into the bright moonlight, appearing to blend with the heavenly stars. He knew that, despite his vehement denials, he had indeed been a kitchen boy, albeit briefly, somewhere in the southern city of Bulawayo. It was widely believed that he had lost his job because he stole from the white couple he worked for. It was probably true, because whenever there was an argument about it, he would adamantly assert that no African could ever steal from a white person any more than a white person had stolen from him. Apparently, it was impossible to steal from a white person in Rhodesia because everything the white man was getting fat on was stolen from Africans anyway. According to Sekuru Fani, to take from a white man was to retrieve what had been yours anyway.

"Africans should get back their things from white people. White people go about saying, 'Thou shalt not steal', and yet they are the biggest thieves in this country."

He'd always rest his case on this point, and it resonated with whoever was listening. That is why he was Mbuya Mukwesa's political darling. She would echo this sentiment too and widen it to include the recovery of land taken by white men, especially her ancestral home of Kuwadzana.

Eriza recalled the moon that night. She, like the rest of the crowd, had continually looked up to the heavens. The moon shone brightly as it always did in the winter months, disguising the chilly nights. The stars had appeared to be dancing. The shadows of her well-wishers had sauntered around the fire as most people sought refuge from the tortuous smoke. In reality, as they gazed upwards, they were all thinking about Eriza's plane journey.

"This firewood's green!" Ceciria had suddenly shouted.

Eriza recalled how her grandmother had classified Ceciria's voice as that of a woman destined for a life of entertaining men. Indeed, her voice was aggressive, perhaps because of the smoke which seemed to go in her direction and with a veiled demand that one of her suitors should do something about it. With her shriek, Sekuru Fani had found an opening to boost his position with Ceciria.

"And yet just beyond those hills, there are so many dead trees, but the only thing is that they are in that white man's farm. That man Dick will shoot any of us if we attempt to pick up the logs for our fire," he'd said, looking at Sekuru Soromon, who he knew had friendly connections with some workers at Dick's farm. He had then violently shoved another log into the fire as he spoke. Ceciria mildly cautioned him to be careful when handling the fire. He liked the tone of her voice, especially as he thought he detected some sort of intimacy towards him in it.

The flames had then shot up. People could see each other's faces clearly again. Eriza saw that Sekuru Soromon was falling behind in the race for Ceciria that evening. He gazed into the fire intensely, in silence. Sekuru Fani's face was contorted because of the smoke, but it soon beamed, probably because he thought that Ceciria appreciated what he had said about Dick being a mean white farmer. But the thought that good firewood was in abundance not far away and a white man called Dick would rather see it rot than let it be used by his African neighbours, continued to bother him. He kissed his teeth not only to spite farmer Dick, but, like a rhino in heat, to gore at the emotions of Sekuru Soromon.

"At least Dick is better than Ndondo," said Sekuru Soromon.

No one bothered to question him about the merits and demerits of these two neighbouring white farmers. Everyone knew the doings of this particular white farmer they had nicknamed Ndondo. It was a very unsuccessful attempt on Sekuru Soromon's part to restore his hurt pride because of his connections with Dick's farm workers.

Eriza had been sitting among a group of women all of whom were dressed in headscarves and heavy jumpers to protect their heads and backs from the night chill. She was drifting between listening to the exchanges of the revellers to thoughts of her journey to London and then to the chatter of the women in her group. From time to time, Eriza had excused herself to go to the kitchen where most of the older women and men, including her parents, sat over a very friendly and warm fire. The women sat on the floor to the far right of the room on red reed mats and *zvikumba* – animal skins. The men sat on an earthen bench on the left side under a small window. In the far end of the room was a beautiful display of earthenware pots arranged in a pyramid. They were Mbuya Mukwesa's and were her most delicate and priceless possessions, some of which she had brought with her when she first moved to Chena some years ago. Some, she claimed, pre-dated her. They were truly exquisite, but the light from the kitchen fire and kerosene lamp did not do justice to the intricate designs on the pots.

Two men over on the bench had started smoking a harsh-smelling cigarette called Star. It was the cheapest brand and Sekuru Soromon had said that it was made from the scraps of Turkish tobacco. He said his friends at Dick's farm told him so. Mbuya Mukwesa disliked smoking and she soon chased them out of the kitchen. She did not mind snuff tobacco though, which one of the elderly ladies was savouring.

"But do you ever look at the mucus when you blow your nose?" Mbuya Mukwesa had nevertheless sniped at her.

The small kitchen crowd had laughed. Even the two men who were puffing away at their Star cigarettes outside joined in the laughter.

Mbuya Mukwesa was sitting on the exact spot where she slept. The flames illuminated her face clearly and anyone would have been hard-pressed to think that she was over eighty years old. Her skin was flawless. She always bragged about how the waters of her birthplace had kept her skin youthful and supple. However, she often commented to Eriza that she felt ancient, because she couldn't think of an animal that sat, ate and slept on the same spot every day. Her blankets, as well as those of the two girls, Eriza and Prudence, were religiously transferred every morning to Naijo's room, then brought back to the kitchen at bedtime. That was Prudence's job. It had been Eriza's before.

Despite the small talk in the kitchen, everyone's thoughts were firmly focused on Eriza and England. It was obvious because, as soon as she had entered the kitchen, one or two of the elders reminded her to carry her jerseys. This was without doubt a night for the local history books – Eriza's last night in Chena before departing for England. What that meant was that every sentence, every word, was significant. The questions were plenty, mostly because they were continuously repeated, by the same three women.

"When are you leaving for *Ingirandi*?

"When are you arriving in *Ingirandi*?"

Then came the order, "But you must come back."

They each asked the questions, one after the other, because each of them needed a personal response from Eriza. Everyone in the kitchen knew that it was their way of showing Eriza affection, but one man objected to this replication of questioning.

"Why are you troubling the child?" the man had complained. "You keep on asking her the same question. She gets tired. Eriza *mwan'gu*," – my child – the man said laughing, "imagine the questioning you will get about *Ingirandi* when you return in our lifetime."

However, Eriza had answered each of them patiently and politely. "Tomorrow afternoon I will leave from *Sosberi* – Salisbury – and then get to *Ingirandi* on the following day, and I will come back."

"*Ingirandi* is nearby then. It's like travelling from *Sosberi* to *Buruwayo*," one of the women had added, followed by a sort of mocking laughter from some of the men.

"It is called Harare and not that *Sosberi*." Mbuya Mukwesa had immediately corrected Eriza. "*Hingirandi* is far. How can you compare it with the journey from Harare to Buruwayo?" She sounded contemptuous of the woman's ignorance and at the same hinting at her own loathsomeness of England by saying *Hingiradi* when everybody else would say *Ingirandi*.

Mbuya Mukwesa however was permanently in conflict with all English names in her country, especially where the white man twisted the Shona name for his own convenience as they did by changing Mutare to Umtali. One could be forgiven for thinking that her middle name, Sophia, had been given to her as she faced the barrel of a gun – that is how much she hated it. No one had ever heard her say the name 'Rhodesia.' She always said *nyika yedu* meaning 'our country.' She knew that Rhodesia was called Zimbabwe, derived from *dzimba dzemabwe* – stone houses – from time immemorial. Her argument for not saying Rhodesia was that names given by white people were meaningless to her and white people could not be the ones to decide when the African name could be used. Until they were out of her country, she would stick with *nyika yedu* and then in time openly say 'Zimbabwe', as if the name Rhodesia never existed. And on the eve of her granddaughter's departure for England, she was no less anguished by the English hold on *nyika yedu*. Sometimes, she would prefer to refer to Harare as *guta* – city – rather than contaminate it with *Sosberi*.

On her last run to the kitchen that evening, Eriza had offered the elders tea. They and the children had already been served the main meal. These guests, sitting with her parents and grandmother, were touched, not because it was tea but because it was Eriza personally making it for them; it felt like the last rites. Their appreciation of the offer was camouflaged in pretences – mutterings about not having any more room in their stomachs after the meal. Mbuya Mukwesa was heard murmuring amid the excitement. Eriza, who knew her grandmother well, figured that she was complaining about Eriza spoiling the crowd.

Then the calls had come from outside.

"Eriza! *Mukoma* – Big sister – Eriza!"

The calling had sailed through the moonlight air into the kitchen, where the tea was beginning to boil in a big, green, open teapot with the tea leaves swiftly swirling, unseen, in the darkness of the vessel. The crowd outdoors had wanted a piece of her again, but first, she had to finish making this tea. She added milk then began to assemble an array of tin mugs on a tray with a basin of white sugar in the middle. Her father, who had been quiet throughout, mentioned that sugar was dangerous, upon which Eriza, who was going to England to train as a nurse, added that it caused an illness. She advised that they should drink their tea without sugar.

"Tea without sugar is not tea," an elderly, toothless man had said very gently.

"That's why you no longer have teeth," said his wife, laughing. "They told him at the hospital that he was eating too much sugar," she added.

Eriza's father had continued, saying that sugar caused a more serious disease than losing teeth, called diabetes. He knew Eriza hadn't been able to explain why sugar was dangerous because she had been interrupted by a woman urging her to add another teaspoon of sugar to the three she'd already shovelled into her cup.

"But only if you eat too much every day," Mai Eriza had interjected.

She was the only first-aider in the village other than one of the female teachers at Chena Primary, and did not like her husband usurping her position as the fountain of all medical knowledge. However, the villagers believed in Baba Eriza more than they did in his wife and further questions about diabetes were directed at him rather than to Mai Eriza.

The conversation had then been drowned out by the sound of teaspoons clanging against the metal cups, as they all stirred their tea cantankerously as if the tea, teaspoons and the metal mugs were in a fierce battle with themselves. Eriza could still, however, hear the toothless gentleman struggling to repeat the word diabetes. His gums couldn't handle the word, and Eriza nearly collapsed in giggles. What made it more hilarious, at least for Eriza and her parents, was that the old man thought that losing teeth was diabetes.

The significance of the link between sugar with this mysterious illness was immediately lost as they all began to sip their syrupy tea noisily, much to the chagrin of Mbuya Mukwesa. They were confused as to how diabetes manifested itself, especially in light of the old man's confusion about losing teeth and this illness. What they knew was that sugar was a highly regarded commodity in their community. At school, pupils were known to fight over allegations that their families were drinking tea without sugar.

Sugar, in all homes in country areas like Chena, was regarded as a measure of a family's affluence.

Eriza had decided to have the last word on matter. "You can have one teaspoon of sugar in your tea but not three, four teaspoons."

No one challenged her after that. Eriza had sensed that the drinking of this tea, as noisy as the slurps were, was akin to The Last Supper.

Mbuya Mukwesa had quietly drunk her bush tea in a china cup, with no sugar or milk. It dawned on her that her teeth still filled her mouth, and concluded that perhaps her god, the African god that is, had something to do with it. That god wanted every race to eat what came from their land. From Kuwadzana to Chena, her tea had always been from this bush. It refreshed her, but above all she believed that it was responsible for her good health, supplemented by her selective eating which excluded refined sugar. Eriza placed the small teapot with the remaining tea next to her grandmother because she knew that she would want a second cup.

Eriza had then excused herself again to go to the crowd outside. The fire was now smoke free, thanks to Sekuru Soromon who, after having made a joke about how some people's feet were so dry and dirty that they could be mistaken for fire logs, had gone to his house and returned with some prime logs of wood. He got his firewood from Dick's farm in the late evenings and never let anyone know about it. His friends from Dick's farm – the foreman, cook, garden boy and a few of other farm workers – helped him with his supply. It was via these friends that he knew about the goings-on in Dick's household, including the fact that Dick occasionally beat his wife, and that his wife had a boyfriend who came by when Dick was on call-up duty to patrol the Zambian-Rhodesian border against nationalist fighters. The fire glowed and Eriza could clearly see the faces of her guests whose voices sounded as if they were ignited by the flames. However, one voice had suddenly risen above all others because its owner was charting new emotional and physical territory.

"They eat *barcon!*" shouted Panashe in his soon-to-break adolescent voice.

Eriza couldn't believe that the discussion about English food was still going on. These people were hungry, more so after the kitchen crowd had been served.

"Panashe! Keep quiet! The food is coming," shushed Eriza.

By then Panashe's contribution to the matter had already generated laughter and giggles from a group of teenage girls. The look on Panashe's face had confirmed that the conversation was liable to degenerate into personal attacks between the teens. Indeed, Panashe had interpreted Eriza's response as her singling him out as a greedy boy. In his mind, that was clearly why the girls were laughing. As he was at that point in his life when he needed to ensure that he was of high market value to this same group of girls, being seen as greedy could prove to be a massive setback. Among this gaggle of girls was Francesca, who did not hesitate to correct Panashe's pronunciation.

"*Inondzi bacon,*" – It's called bacon – she'd said quietly.

Francesca desperately wanted to speak the Queen's English because she found the Rhodesian accent to be so savagely crude. At 13, she wanted African-English to have the distinct royal accent spoken by her English teacher at her mission school just outside Salisbury. Her name was Miss Myers, and she was from Newham in east London. Even Sekuru Fani who, like Mbuya Mukwesa, loathed English mannerisms in Africans, admired Francesca's spirit.

"And it's pig meat," she added quickly.

"That's Colcom!" Panashe shouted in laughter. Francesca's intervention was a setback to his effort to build a new image. The girls were making a fool of him and his response was not a retaliatory shot at them but unfortunately it was on the quiet chubby, girl called Alice. Colcom was a company that specialised in manufacturing processed pig meat. The boys had nicknamed Alice, Colcom, as she was fat. So Panashe continued laughing at his joke at Alice's expense. The crowd had totally ignored him as some among them had seen Alice crying a few days before after such cruel teasing. Nevertheless, he was rewarded by hearty laughs from his entourage of boys, over whom he exercised some sort of warlord status.

The impending exchange of insults was interrupted by a single file of girls led by Prudence, who carried a container of water and a dish to allow the guests to wash their hands before eating. Up until a few years ago, a dish filled with water was deemed sufficient, even though the last person to wash was obliged to use dirty water. Mai Eriza had stopped this practice after her first-aid course, and the whole village had followed suit. This first-aid-inspired change in eating habits replaced the age-old way whereby age groups ate from the same plate. Mai Eriza believed, and rightly so, that in a scramble to eat more than others, especially among teenage boys, dirty water dripped into the food from their hands. So, in her household it became one person to one plate of food.

Now the water was poured over each person's hands and caught in the dish. Prudence went to Sekuru Fani first, but he deferred to Sekuru Soromon, who was older than him. The girls behind Prudence carried a plate of food in each hand to hand over once a guest's hands had been washed. The boys began positioning themselves to receive their plates even though they knew that the older people would be served first. Nevertheless, when it was their turn, these boys followed the etiquette of eldest first, just as Sekuru Fani and Sekuru Soromon had done.

A few minutes into eating and there was nothing but the sound of chewing. Milling around just outside the circle of now diners were the dogs that had lost the battle for Hesvu's affections. They violently competed for scraps of food and at times their fights threatened to disrupt everyone. At the end of each fight, there was always one dog that would end up wailing while retreating into the leafless bushes nearby.

"Aha, you Panashe, a big boy like you! Putting your plate on the ground instead of taking it back to the kitchen! What example are you setting here?" Sekuru Fani reprimanded Panashe. "And besides, you eat too much," he added.

Panashe was again humiliated as the girls broke out in giggles. He glared at his entourage to see who among them dared laugh; fortunately, he was partially rescued by Prudence, who had just returned to check on the progress of dinner and offered to take his empty plate. Unfortunately, she asked him whether he was full. That generated more laughter. Most people found Prudence's question amusing because one never asked teenage boys whether they had eaten enough. Their stomachs were essentially bottomless pits. Panashe understood why the crowd found it funny, but since he knew that Prudence had given him a very full plate at the beginning, as far as he was concerned, those laughing were fools.

The quiet interlude following Panashe's and Prudence's conversation had given Comfort time to put forward his wishes to Eriza.

"Mukoma Eriza, w-w-will you b-b-be able to send m-m-me a Manchester United t-t-t-t-t-t-shirt?" stammered the little nine-year-old for what seemed like an eternity.

The crowd knew him and always gave him time to complete his thoughts. Besides, in the last week or so, he was spending a lot of time after school around the Mukwesa household and willing to do any and every errand for Eriza, who he saw as a big sister. Mbuya Mukwesa had quickly spotted that Comfort wanted to say something to Eriza, but his stammer kept getting in the way. Eriza sat facing Comfort with the fire between them. She saw the extent of his satisfaction for both having made his point through the stammer and for asking what he wanted from England.

"Is that all you want?" Eriza asked very kindly.

"Yes, Mukoma Eriza," Comfort responded quickly, and then added, "and pictures of Bobby Charlton and his brother Jack. It would make me very happy."

There was not a stammer this time. Everyone was spellbound. Few had ever heard him express himself so clearly. In a flash, Comfort had stammered out the prospect of any further confrontations about Panashe's love for food. He had set the stage for a new topic of discussion – football.

The older boys, especially Comfort's brother Raphael, known as *Rafero*, always grabbed centre stage with their zeal for football. Everyone was convinced that the cause of Comfort's stammer was Rafero's overbearing personality. As far as he was concerned, the only thing that would have been worthy of asking of Mukoma Eriza for was a picture of Wembley Stadium, where England had beaten Germany in the 1966 World Cup final. He would speak as if he was in possession of the final score itself – four to England and two to Germany. This was someone who only knew one local team – Dynamos – based in Salisbury, though that didn't stop him and the other boys from fantasising about how Dynamos would fare against Manchester United, their overseas dream team.

At boarding school, Rafero and the other boys in form four watched replays of the 1966 final, week in and week out. Rafero lived for those replays. He loved to talk about the goings-on at his school, especially if they had some something, anything, to do with football. As the village's role model was departing for England, this was of course an opportunity to speak about English football. So Rafero had fervently told the story of the impact of England's win as if Eriza's departure depended on it. He had regaled the crowd about how the maths teacher, Mr Ferris, had transformed the replays into an educational and motivational tool. The boys now referred to it as *baisikopu re bora* – the football show. Most of them, and even one girl, had become proficient at maths because of *baisikopu re bora.*

It transpired that Mr Ferris had decided to reward all those students who scored 100 percent in their weekly test with a Saturday afternoon show of the replay, as well as a replay of Portugal's Eusebio's phenomenal goals. All this took place in a small, dark room in the first floor of the school building. The idea was unsurprisingly popular with the boys. Within three weeks, more than half of the 46 boys were regulars at the shows. Quite a few girls were hundred percenters too, but they saw no added value to their maths performance because, whether they watched football or not, they were still on top in the subject. They therefore declined the reward of the replays. Then one day, a boy named Olysmus Mangwenya, who was nicknamed Pythagoras because of his mathematical skills, entered the scene. This was a surprise to all because he had never shown any interest in football. In addition, he had convinced his rather dull and not very pretty girlfriend, Kim Mazozi, to be a bit more proactive with her maths. It transpired that at one sitting in the darkroom, Pythagoras had realised a huge opportunity – one for the two of them to kiss and caress each other without being seen by teachers. After that, Kim then had a run of one hundred per cents with extra coaching from Pythagoras himself. Of course, the other boys never snitched. The smooching then graduated to Kim sitting on Pythagoras' lap. She then just managed to sit her final Cambridge 'O' Level exams in November of that year, before going home to deliver a little footballer in January of the following year. He was named Sebio. Two months later in March, the exam results came, and Kim got a distinction in maths but an 'F' and six 'Us' in her other seven subjects. No one would have believed Rafero's story if it wasn't for Sekuru Fani, who knew the Mazozi family that lived in the nearby town. He had enthusiastically confirmed Rafero's story because he had wondered why Kim's boy had such an unusual name. It was neither Shona nor Ndebele nor English. For Rafero on the other hand, the story was nothing short of compelling because it was borne out of his beloved 1966 World Cup final.

Sekuru Fani was about to launch into the topic of the Second World War and why Ian Smith, the Rhodesian Prime Minister, had bothered to fight against Hitler – *Hitra* in local saying – when Mai Eriza called everyone to the kitchen for one of her dreaded Christian prayers which always ended with, "Please Jesus, Son of God, deliver us from all sins. Amen." Not everybody could fit in the kitchen, but Mai Eriza insisted that people just piled up at the door.

❊ ❊ ❊

Many more of the tales told over the fire swirled around in Eriza's head as she added firewood to revive the morning fire. Even though some of the stories, like Rafero's, were exaggerated, one about guerrilla fighters trickling into surrounding villages made Eriza realise that she was leaving her country at a momentous time. That's when she missed Naijo being around. He was always in the know about the political goings-on in the liberation movement. He even knew that Che Guevara had left Cuba and fought in the Congo before going to Bolivia where he was eventually killed. He saw Patrice Lumumba, the liberator of the Democratic Republic of Congo, as Africa's Messiah. He loved to talk about how Lumumba had humiliated the Belgian king by telling him that one day the king will refer to 'us as *vous* and not *tu*.' Lumumba had also told the Belgian king that if he ever visited Congo again, which was most unlikely, he would come to Kinshasa and not Leopoldville.

Eriza recalled how her grandmother fussed about leaving some food for Naijo every weekend because 'he might just drop in to see us.' Mbuya Mukwesa believed that the new weapon to drive out Europeans from her country was education, and Naijo was getting that, so he deserved special treatment. Everyone was entitled to education, but it had to be delivered to young people in the right way, a way that would benefit their country.

As far as she was concerned, her grandson was being educated correctly because she had evidence that he was doing something to drive out the Europeans from her beloved Kuwadzana. This so-called evidence came from a conversation between Baba Eriza and a friend of his who had come to pay a visit some time ago. When her father had told the visitor that Naijo was studying law at university, the friend had responded by saying that Naijo was arming himself to fight the white man. Law was a weapon with which to fight Europeans. Mbuya Mukwesa had worked it out from that day – Naijo would drive the white man out of her land. Mbuya Mukwesa was sure to let everybody knew that Naijo was at *envesity* studying towards this one mission. Eriza chuckled to herself as she remembered one woman's explanation for Naijo's absence at the farewell dinner. Apparently, *envesity* students were taught at night. Eriza had laughed and answered, "University is not night school. Students are taught throughout the day and they read on their own at night if they want to." But of course, her explanation fell on deaf ears.

The morning fire was now burning fiercely, and Eriza heard Naijo coughing. She thought that he was getting up and looked forward to chatting with him over his morning cup of tea. Naijo had arrived in the dead of night after all the fanfare for his sister's send-off was done. He was still a first-year student in Salisbury. That Tuesday, he had caught the evening train from Salisbury Railway Station at nine o'clock and disembarked at the small railway siding of Mawiro at about ten to eleven. He had then walked the nine-mile journey to Chena, arriving at midnight. If he had travelled on a Friday, there would have been plenty of company from villagers travelling home for the weekend. But yesterday, he was very much alone on the dusty road from Mawiro to Chena.

❖❖❖

Naijo didn't expect anything unusual on the way except the sound of nocturnal animals. Fears of spooks on the road, which had dominated his childhood, lingered on in his mind but he was now certain that dead people's spirits did not wander about at night. Nor did their skeletal remains illuminate the bushes, nor did they race in front of nocturnal walkers enticing them to join in on their ghostly games, from which, if they did join, they would never return.

His childhood friend, Abisher, had once told him how much his uncle believed in the existence of these evil nocturnal beings. One day, seven years earlier, this same uncle had been accompanying his niece on the road from Chena to Mawiro to catch the same train that Naijo had used as it continued its journey to Bulawayo. They had reached a rocky hill where they saw two owls perched on two rocks – one on each side of the road. In the uncle's own words, it became so eerily quiet, as the two white owls gazed at them, as if daring them to proceed. He simply turned back home with his bewildered niece in tow. Not a word was exchanged between uncle and niece until the next morning. Naijo chuckled as he passed this notorious spot, looking at the two rocks for owls. He had no idea what his reaction would have been had he seen owls there that night.

❖❖❖

Normally, Hesvu announced Naijo's arrival but, last night, she had been busy with the male dogs. The homestead would have been quiet if it wasn't for the occasional bark from the canine romantic proceedings. Mbuya Mukwesa was still awake and when Naijo had entered the house, she had professed to have caught his scent from the time he got off the train – nine miles away.

"Ah! Mbuya," Naijo whispered.

Eriza then woke up.

"Hello Naijo. You have arrived too late. Why didn't you catch the bus? We were expecting you to."

"You know that I like to travel on the train and enjoy the walk from Mawiro," Naijo answered.

By now, Prudence was also awake.

"Put on the light Prudence," Mbuya hadn't so much asked as demanded. "We might be talking to a person who has been beaten by robbers," she added as if to justify her demand.

"Mbuya, robbers are in Salisbury," answered Naijo. He knew that his grandmother did not like people calling Harare by its colonial name of Salisbury. "Here in the dry settlements, there is nothing to rob."

"Sekuru, your meal is near the dying fire. The food is still quite warm." Prudence was still grumpy, having had a busy day. However, custom required that she served her uncle.

Naijo immediately pulled out a box of chocolates from his bag and handed it to Prudence. "Here you are. You can smile now and get me water to drink and to wash my hands," Naijo said teasingly.

"Thank you, Sekuru." Prudence gave him the broadest, brightest smile that she could marshal in the dim, kerosene-lamp-lit room.

She examined the box and confirmed that it was the right brand. Naijo had looked at her and noticed how much she reminded him of her mother, his sister Chido, who had died eleven years before. He felt Chido watching and smiling at the genuine care between uncle and niece. Naijo never turned his back on the spiritual world, even though it was under constant and heavy bombardment from the Christian homilies of his mother.

"Hmm, Prudence, you are becoming sophisticated, thinking of chocolate not as just chocolate, but in terms of a brand," Eriza observed laughing. "If it's Swiss, I want a bite!" she demanded jokingly.

Mbuya was lost and repeated over and over, "He? He?" with her head firmly on the pillow. They all ignored her as there was no point explaining some of these things of the modern world to her and Mbuya Mukwesa understood because she knew what it was like when the three of them were together.

As soon as Prudence served Naijo, he dived into his plate and ate silently.

"The food must be exceptionally tasty for you Naijo to eat without talking," Mbuya commented with a chuckle.

"I'm very hungry. I didn't bother to eat anything today because I knew Prudence would cook her best meal, and I am not disappointed," Naijo teased again.

"You're chewing loudly and disturbing the peace," said Eriza, falling straight into the role of annoying younger sibling. Naijo's response was simply to generate more and louder chewing noises. He stopped when Eriza kissed her teeth and then proceeded to thank Prudence profusely for such a hearty meal, just to torment Eriza.

"Naijo! Go to bed. We have a long day tomorrow," said Mbuya Mukwesa. Naijo didn't argue, and once in his bedroom, within ten minutes, he was snoring.

Mbuya muttered to herself, "Even in sleep he disturbs the peace." Now at peace, with her grandson safely at home, Mbuya retreated into her memories of her ancestral home of Kuwadzana. Eriza knew that, because she heard her say nostalgically, *"Oh Kuwadzana woye,"* before falling into a deep silence.

Allowing her mind to drift back to the events of the night before meant that her chores were effortless. The water in the bucket on the fire was now boiling and soon it would be time for a cup of tea and a chat with her brother. She had been worried that if Naijo had not come on this her day of departure, there would be no one to ease the apprehension she felt about her impending journey. First there was the leg from Chena to Salisbury Airport, then the ten-hour flight to Heathrow Airport – *Hifro*, according to her grandmother. Having said this, she was not short of goodwill gestures from her village. Mr Kanyemba, the headteacher of Chena Primary School, who owned a car, had offered to drive her to the airport. He was a reliable man, but Eriza, like her grandmother, was not so sure about the reliability of any piece of machinery or equipment.

When sitting 'O' Levels a few years before, a simple blue ballpoint pen had let her down three minutes before the end of her English Literature exam, just when she was about to explain why Shakespeare had used the word 'apparition' in *Macbeth*. Since then, she had come to terms with the fact that, though the hitch in the pen might have cost her an 'A' (she still ended up with a 'B'), God must have pre-ordained it, because she was still going to England. On top of that, she could visit Inverness in Scotland and engage with the ghosts that Shakespeare had imagined in *Macbeth*. With that, she brushed aside her fears about the reliability of Mr Kanyemba's car and the plane – for the time being anyway. As she bent over the fire to warm her hands, the local bus chugged past on its way to Salisbury. At that point she realised that, had it not been for Mr Kanyemba's generosity, she would have probably been squashed between some chickens and a wide-girthed village woman on a three-hour journey to Salisbury.

As the bus drove past their home, Eriza heard the door of the main house open. It was a familiar sound, one that announced that her father was up and that the voices of her parents would soon follow. But today, she only heard her mother's voice, praying. Being Catholic, Mai Eriza abundantly and solemnly invoked Mary, Mother of Jesus, to guide and keep Eriza on her journey. She heard the Latin phrase *sabat mater dolorosa* in her mother's Shona accent. Her mother always invoked it in prayer simply because the priest used it in Sunday prayers. Eriza knew that her mother didn't understand what it meant nor did she ever bother to ask the priest. Despite this, she knew the depth of the loss that her mother would feel over her departure.

Eriza had learnt the meaning in her first week at boarding school. Eriza's Latin teacher, Mr Wickens, a British veteran of World War Two, simply gave Eriza, in military precision, a direct translation: 'stood the mother, full of grief.' Eriza had then worked out, using her Catholic background, that it referred to Mary, Mother of Jesus, mourning the death of her son. She couldn't help but wonder whether her mother was not stretching things a little too much by comparing her sorrow to the grief Mary felt when Jesus was killed. After all she, Eriza, was neither Jesus, nor was she dead. Her mother never accepted that Jesus' death had been meticulously arranged by God to redeem humanity. She said she enjoyed washing in his blood but that did not stop his death from being an act of murder. What galled her most about this 'murder' of Jesus was the spear wound on his torso. She always put her right hand over her right flank, in the spot where she was sure that Jesus had been speared. At the same time, she would grit her teeth for full effect.

It was now almost 7 o'clock and Mr Kanyemba was expected at ten. Eriza heard her father say that she could only be guided if she was able to leave on time and, for that to happen, the prayer needed to end. She knew that her mother saw her father's rudeness and sarcasm as Lucifer's infringement which needed to be countered by imploring God to 'ignore all indignities thrust upon you because they are the devil's doings.' And with that, the prayer indeed came to an end. Baba Eriza got up and went to the small kitchen garden on the left of the front of the main house.

Mai Eriza left her bedroom as if she was running away from the devil. In no time, Baba Eriza heard the cupboard door in the sitting room slamming. He knew that morning's breakfast was to include eggs, because in that cupboard was the treasure trove of his wife's chicken eggs waiting to be 'shipped' to Francis at Mawira Siding.

She delicately placed a dozen eggs into a metal bowl, respecting their fragility when in contact with metal, but also the monetary value she was depriving herself. She then put one back, and another. It was clear in her mind that she didn't feel that her husband was entitled to two eggs that morning. But to make it not look so obvious, she also deprived herself of a second egg. Now with grace on her face, she headed to the kitchen where Mbuya Mukwesa was sitting on the floor solemnly, with the fire to her left equally gloomy.

"*Mangwanani* Mbuya," – Good morning grandmother – greeted Mai Eriza, starting the morning ritual with her in-law. She was hoping to shake off the gloom which engulfed Mbuya Mukwesa.

"*Aiwa tarara. Asi munhu haunyatsorara,*" – I didn't have a good sleep – she said.

"Don't you worry, your Eriza will be back. I'm going to cook these eggs for breakfast so that we get to Salisbury on full stomachs."

"*Ehee,*" Mbuya responded dismissively.

Mai Eriza knew that Naijo had brought home some bread. It was the usual way for people travelling back home from town to bring goodies, and bread was regarded as such. She called out to him to thank him for the parcel when he emerged. They then had a brief but very loving exchange of morning greetings.

Outside, Baba Eriza had teamed up with Sekuru Fani in front of the main house, watching the goats pick up bits of dry grass, but with an eye at the possibilities coming out of the kitchen. They talked about anything and everything but Eriza's departure. Soon Naijo joined them. They'd heard him the night before when he had arrived but, sensing that he was well, they left him to his grandmother and the girls.

"Breakfast is ready," announced Naijo

"*Hooo*. Thank you muzukuru," said Sekuru Fani. He had a weakness for bread and eggs and the smells coming out of the kitchen told him that he was in for a treat.

"Let's go then. It's not often that we beat Francis to the eggs!" joked Baba Eriza.

They all laughed.

"Just wash your hands. We've already prayed," commanded Mai Eriza.

The girls and Mbuya were puzzled. They all watched her as she did the cross, and then they knew. Mai Mukwesa did her personal prayer whenever she found her husband to be disagreeable.

She then put one fried egg on her husband's plate already loaded with slices of bread and vegetables. Eriza handed her father a cup of tea. Mbuya Mukwesa, who had been served first, declined a second egg.

Then Prudence said, "*Mbuya, masiira chikomana chenyu zai*" – Mbuya, you left the egg for your boy. Everyone laughed and Mai Eriza put the crispy, sunny-side-up egg on her husband's plate. Baba Eriza chuckled with pleasure, extending his thanks to his wife. They all gulped their tea except Mbuya, who drank just a quarter of her cup. They all knew why. She had no intention of stopping on the way to the airport.

TWO

Mr Kanyemba's car was a five-seat, brown Cortina sedan. Five occupants for the car was just the manufacturer's recommendation because the car had never seen anything less than eight. Today the tally would be seven – Eriza, her parents, grandmother, Prudence, Sekuru Fani and Naijo – plus one black suitcase on top of the car. The roof of the car was always loaded with passengers' wares, which could range from suitcases, as in the case of Eriza's journey, to bags of maize, peanuts and, sometimes, goats. The boot was full of his 'stuff'. He kept it locked and never opened it – as far as anyone knew. Neither was anyone else allowed to open it. People found that very strange. Of course, stories circulated in hushed voices about the likely contents of this boot. One rumour that held sway over all other rumours was that he kept tiny little humans which he unleashed now and then to acquire wealth for him. How? No one could explain, but a village headteacher driving a car was a sign of exceptional wealth.

The car was always clean because Mr Kanyemba's pupils washed it for him every morning, even during the weekends and school holidays, especially if he had not travelled to his home in KwaMtoko. None of the pupils ever ventured to open the boot. Word was the tiny figures would batter anyone who saw them to death, other than Mr Kanyemba of course. Every morning he woke up to a clean car, not knowing which of his pupils had washed it. It was widely known, a few weeks before, that Mr Kanyemba's car was Eriza's carriage to the airport. That morning, three boys had already washed it and as it was the August-September school holidays, they all had the time to polish the car too. Mr Kanyemba had recognised them as the quieter of his schoolboys. He was not surprised to see little Comfort just sitting there, ready to assist the big boys. And to think that he had already decided that if none of his pupils had come to clean it today, this was the one occasion he was going to clean it himself. He admired Eriza as much as the rest of the community did. That admiration was not because she was flying to study abroad, but because she never allowed her achievements as a girl in a male-dominated village to go to her head. She remained humble, continuing to help drive her parents' herd of cattle for dipping every Saturday right up to a week before her departure.

One by one they all piled into Mr Kanyemba's car. The seating arrangements were tricky. Being delicate, Mbuya could only sit in the front. But Mai Eriza sensed a risk. It had happened before. Mbuya Mukwesa had sat in the front seat of her distant nephew's car who had come to visit from Mutare some years ago. Unexpectedly she had grabbed the steering wheel to try to stop the car because she thought it was going too fast. The car had swerved. Fortunately, the speed was not as fast as she thought it was and the nephew quickly brought the car under control. Mbuya then proceeded to scold her nephew and said it was precisely because she foresaw this happening that she tried to stop it. She never flinched from her belief that she had saved the lives of five people in that car that day – her son, daughter- in-law, her nephew and his wife and, of course, herself.

That morning the likelihood of a repeat vigilante performance by Mbuya Mukwesa was heightened by the fact that her beloved Eriza would be in Mr Kanyemba's car. Mai Eriza was anxious and as she got into the car with her husband, she asked "*VaKanyemba mavaruma nzeve here?*" – Have you alerted Mr Kanyemba?

Baba Mukwesa had done so weeks ago. The conspiracy also involved Eriza sitting in the front seat between her grandmother and Mr Kanyemba with strict instructions to watch her grandmother's right hand. Everyone else squeezed in the back seat. Prudence sat between her grandmother and Sekuru Fani but was sitting forward. Naijo sat between his father and Sekuru Fani, and sat forward too.

Finally, the journey began in silence along the road that Eriza had walked to and from school since she was a little girl. No one noticed, but a tear fell down her cheek as they passed her old school.

Mr Kanyemba's pristine car finally arrived at the airport. The noise of the aircraft generated a range of emotions in the eight people who emerged from the car. Mbuya Mukwesa was filled with sheer apprehension that her beloved granddaughter would be cruising through the highways of the spirits and likely to be trespassing into the sacred world. Mai Eriza looked to the heavens expecting that her deep Christian faith would be rewarded by a glimpse of the biblical cloud that carried Jesus to heaven, and today it would be the vehicle for her daughter to a place here on earth. Sekuru Fani was still sorting out a conundrum in his head: whether getting on a plane was the same as getting on a train or bus. He thought about this as he pulled Eriza's suitcase from the roof of the car. One by one they emerged from the Cortina, making various grunts and noises as they stretched their limbs. They wasted no time walking into the airport building.

For Sekuru Fani, there were too many white faces, something he didn't like because one of them was bound to call him or Naijo, or Mr Kanyemba, or Baba Eriza, a 'boy' or something worse. It was demeaning and always made his blood boil in anger. Eriza's father on the other hand remained focused on the endless possibilities that awaited his daughter. He already had visions of Eriza graduating as a medical doctor, because as far as he was concerned, Eriza couldn't be going to England just to train as a nurse when there were two good training hospitals in Salisbury and Bulawayo. Mbuya Mukwesa, who was walking with Naijo, tightened her grip on his arm, and with that, he realised how much she would miss Eriza. But, as for himself, Naijo believed that it was only a matter of time before he joined his sister in England. He had ambitions of pursuing postgraduate studies in Law with the added bonus of reuniting with his sister.

Prudence on the other hand was being vocal about her feelings as she sobbed, holding on to Eriza. To Prudence, Eriza was not just an aunt, but a big sister and mother. When Prudence's mother had died, custom mandated that Eriza, as her mother's sister, would assume the full responsibility of motherhood. Though they had led their lives more like sisters than niece and aunt, on that day at Salisbury Airport, Baba Eriza was the first to notice that a mother-daughter bond had ripened between the two girls – the evidence was right there before him. Prudence no longer saw Eriza as *Mainini – young mother* – but as *Mai – mother*. This pleased Baba Eriza because, one, Prudence was finally feeling the warmth of a mother and, two, Eriza was now a woman.

Mr Kanyemba knew the departure procedures well and had made sure that Eriza had her passport and plane ticket in her hand and not in her suitcase. Eriza's thoughts were on the plane. She had never been in one before but had seen newspaper advertisements with all these glamorous white stewardesses and could only imagine what the inside of the plane must look like. She hoped she would meet the first local African hostess who had reached that milestone just a few years before. As a result of that milestone, many girls of her age had now widened their career horizons. She kept glancing at her watch, only for Mr Kanyemba to remind her jokingly that they had arrived well ahead of time. Despite all that supposed spare time, Mr Kanyemba led the way, with Sekuru Fani right behind him, towards departures.

❖❖❖

Sekuru Fani was still in conflict over the matter of the boarding procedure. He wanted to ask Mr Kanyemba but was embarrassed to, especially as he always wanted people to think that he knew more than he did. He was apprehensive about carrying Eriza's suitcase to the door of the East African Airways 5727 that was taking her to the first stop in Nairobi. He had no need to be, of course, as at check-in, Eriza's suitcase was taken over by a white girl, who slipped on a pair of gloves just to handle it. He wasn't expecting the boarding procedure to start here. No, not at all. The white girl checked the ticket, still gloved up, and for the next customer, who was white, removed the gloves. Mr Kanyemba commented that this behaviour would soon end in Zimbabwe. He spoke in Shona, but the name Zimbabwe made the whites around him turn and stare at all of them with penetrating hostility. Unknown to Eriza's entourage, the news had just reported that two white Rhodesian soldiers had been blown up by a landmine, or *chimbambaira* (the *nom de guerre* for a landmine meaning 'sweet potato') in the northern region of Karoi.

Mr Kanyemba led his party to some nearby benches where they all sat down. He then went to the kiosk with Naijo and bought drinks for everybody, with Naijo helping to carry them back to the thirsty group. Eriza sat between her mother and grandmother. She wanted to cry, but she knew that her grandmother would then demand that they drive back to Chena at once. So, she held back the tears by pretending to listen to the many words of wisdom, proffered once again, by all except Naijo, who sat

43

down on a bench beside his father facing the three women. He decided to lighten the mood with a running dress commentary on the three women.

"The daughter's face looks well-scrubbed with *Matirida* soap and greased with *vasrine*. She smells of perfume but the distinct odour of goats and smoke continue to linger mercilessly."

Eriza instantly sniffed her armpits, prompting Naijo to burst out in loud laughter and her father to stifle his chuckles. Her mother told her not to listen to Naijo's nonsense. In between snorts, Naijo continued.

"But she puts on a beautifully tailored two-piece cream suit over a light-brown blouse. She looks so beautiful that one would never know that the clothes were from Amato."

At that point Mbuya Mukwesa told him to shut up. His ramblings were distracting Eriza from listening to her words of wisdom, but Naijo continued laughing – even Sekuru Fani and Mr Kanyemba couldn't help but join in on the laughter. Amato was a shop in downtown Salisbury owned by an Asian family and with a reputation for selling rejects. He wanted to add that Eriza was wearing nylon stockings and high-heeled black shoes, but instead, he turned on his grandmother.

"...And sitting on her left is her grandmother dressed in black from top to almost bottom. I say almost because the black canvas shoes are tainted with a hint of brown, which makes them not quite black."

He was interrupted by the airport loudspeaker announcing boarding for a South African flight to Jo'burg, at which point it looked like every white person in the airport made a noisy beeline towards the departure gates. Francesca, Chena's mini-literary giant, would not have hesitated a bit to condemn the barbaric English accent of these whites. Some were busy comparing their holidays in Victoria Falls and Kariba, resorts which were out of bounds for African people – in their own country. Naijo, Mr Kanyemba and Baba Eriza, fully cognisant of the pain of being 'exiled' in one's country, resorted to the adage: "What you don't see you don't miss," as they watched the tourists file out towards their plane. Sekuru Fani was sullen.

"They don't realise that they have just put another nail into their own coffin."

He sucked his teeth but quickly cheered up as he remembered what a momentous occasion Eriza's journey was. It would be a pivotal chapter in the annals of his family's history and a salvo in the battle against 'these settlers.' The word 'settler' had been used at a secret meeting organised by one of the nationalist leaders in Chena. He liked it and looked forward to the day when he would say right into the face of one of these white people "You settler, OUT!" They or the police wouldn't be able to do anything about it. That will be the dawn of a new Zimbabwe, and the thought alone made him happy.

It was another half-hour before the departure announcement for Eriza's flight was made. These thirty minutes turned out to be the most anxious for Sekuru Fani. He had doubts over the validity of Mr Kanyemba's claim about Eriza's boarding procedure and indeed had questioned Mr Kanyemba several times as to whether he had listened carefully to the announcement. Besides, after watching the white girls at the check-in counter, he suspected that there was every possibility that they could conspire to make Eriza miss her plane. Much to his embarrassment, the announcement was eventually made, loud and clear.

Naijo, who was not interested in Sekuru Fani's fears, was the first to stand up and help his grandmother to her feet. With his right arm over her right shoulder, he knew that she needed his support now more than ever as Eriza walked in front of them towards the departure lounge. Eriza would have liked to hold onto her grandmother as she made her last steps through to the departure lounge, but with her grandmother moving so gingerly, she could not risk being late to board the plane.

Naijo called out to Eriza, "You are now crossing the River Rubicon but don't forget the Zambezi."

Eriza smiled. It was their special goodbye. Sekuru Fani was not at all happy at being told that he could not escort his niece to the doors of the aircraft. He was consoled when Mr Kanyemba suggested that they all go to the balcony and watch Eriza board her plane. Prudence was so tearful that her grandmother, Mai Eriza, had to hold her hand and lead her up the stairs behind Naijo and his grandmother. Mbuya Mukwesa was now chanting quietly. Naijo could clearly understand this to be a call to the ancestors to rally around Eriza. With his humour that was at times too much to bear, he referred to the chanting as, 'dressing Eriza in a bullet-proof vest.' It was a joke that only Eriza would have appreciated, but she had already been whisked away deep into the bowels of the departure lounge.

Mr Kanyemba could tell that both Baba Eriza and Sekuru Fani were wondering what the inside of the departure lounge looked like. So he decided to fill them in, especially as he had flown to Malawi on several occasions and knew this place quite well. He told them about the duty-free facilities provided in the lounge, but matters of excise duty were a bit beyond them, that is, until he mentioned that *doro rechirungu* – white man's alcohol – was a lot cheaper in the duty-free area. Sekuru Fani began to link duty-free business with the sales tax the government had recently introduced. He also knew that the sales tax was a war tax used to fund the killing of African people. White people were therefore more than happy to pay such a tax. The *Rhodesia Herald* newspaper even called it a 'tax to stop communism from crossing the Zambezi from the north'. That paper was a major propaganda tool for whites in Rhodesia, and Joseph Goebbels, Hitler's ally, would have envied it.

"It's only the whites who benefit from this duty-free business," Mr Kanyemba confirmed.

❊❊❊

Although Eriza walked calmly on the tarmac to board her flight to Nairobi, she was a bundle of nerves with her mind in complete turmoil. She forgot to stop on the tarmac and wave back to her relatives on the balcony as Mr Kanyemba had advised her to do. The aircraft engines noisily drowned everything out and that had disorientated her. Her seven people on the balcony had probably been waving frantically but to no avail. It was doubtful whether Mbuya Mukwesa would have spotted her in the queue anyway despite it being comprised mainly of white passengers heading to the aircraft. Eriza also had no idea that Sekuru Fani was surprised that she had not been given back her suitcase, especially as the whites all seemed to carry a case onto the plane.

Anyway, this was it. As she ascended the metal steps of the airplane, she could hear the 'clunk clunk' of her feet and, once at the top, she quickly remembered and stole one final glance at the balcony and said a final goodbye to her family. Then she turned to the plastic smile of the white air hostesses begrudgingly greeting her into the plane. She was all alone now, on her journey to England.

❊❊❊

That short hop to Nairobi remained a mystery to Eriza well into her pensionable years. The only thing she could recall with certainty was that she had turned down a cabin meal of beef, vegetables and rice. She may have been hungry, but the intense nausea would not have allowed her to eat. At least it had distracted her from the sea of white faces around her.

47

When she stepped off the plane in Nairobi and walked into the airport building, she was confused mainly because she was not sure what her next move should have been. There were too many airport announcements and passengers, even though it was night-time. Some walked hurriedly, some strolled leisurely and others sat, just as she had with her relatives in Salisbury Airport. She read notices about luggage collection but knew that she could not retrieve hers. The word *Uhuru* was everywhere with President Jomo Kenyatta's portraits hanging on what seemed like every other wall space. His eyes were penetrating and seemed to be watching every part of the building. She thought of the Mau Mau freedom fighters who were Sekuru Fani's heroes. Sekuru Fani always spoke about a Mau Mau leader named Didan Kimathi, who apparently battered the British in Kenya into submission and often wondered aloud when such a figure would emerge in Rhodesia. A Kenyan airport manageress, and by a unique coincidence with a name tag labelled Susan Kimathi, happened to be on walkabout. She approached Eriza with a huge smile and asked her a few questions before directing her to the British Airways desk. Eriza then relaxed a little as she walked purposefully to check in. She glanced back and wondered whether Susan Kimathi was Didan Kimathi's daughter.

Eriza was struck by the number of Indians in the airport. Even though some of the them were Pakistanis, in Rhodesia, all were referred to as Indians. An analogy of the India-Pakistan dichotomy was reinforced by the split up of the Federation of Rhodesia and Nyasaland in 1963. Despite that, many maintained that 'Zambians and us are still Africans.' The India-Pakistan war of 1971 made a huge difference to the delineation of Pakistanis and Indians to the people of Chena. Bangladesh had also been wrestled from Pakistan. There was a general admiration for the new nation of Bangladesh, and Pakistanis were seen in a very bad light – as defeated settlers.

Swahili could be heard all over the airport and was even spoken by some Indians. She also realised that the announcements were made in both Swahili and English, and in that order. Both Sekuru Fani and her grandmother would have loved to hear that the English language had been demoted in an independent Kenya. She stood in the queue and soon a Kenyan couple speaking in their mother tongue walked up behind her. She listened and heard some familiar words such as *nyoka* – snake – and *muzungu* – white person. The white girl at the desk attended to her with so much more respect, in contrast to the outright prejudice shown by the white girl at Salisbury Airport.

"Have a pleasant flight Miss Mukwesa," she said, with what Eriza could see was a genuine smile.

Two hours later, Eriza boarded her London-bound plane. She felt a lot more confident now than she did at Salisbury. There were a lot of passengers getting on the plane with her, but this time she felt Lilliputian as she walked with them towards the jet waiting under bright lights, on the runway of Jomo Kenyatta International Airport. She was surrounded by giant aircraft – Air India, Qantas, British Airways, Lufthansa, Air Pakistan, Aeroflot – and many more. Her plane was draped in the Union Jack. On nearing the stairs of the plane, she felt a sharp pang of guilt and sadness at the fact that she had forgotten to wave back to her relatives at Salisbury Airport.

The two-hour in-transit wait at Nairobi Airport had settled her stomach. As she walked down the aisle looking for her seat, F24, she thought back to the first leg of her plane journey. Was her initial anxiety triggered by the thought that she might never see her grandmother and parents again? Or was it fear of being trapped in a big piece of machinery? Now seated in her window seat, she seemed to have finally taken back control of her nerves. When the cabin crew began the detailed emergency procedures, she was surprised that though it was a repeat of the process en route to Nairobi, she could not recall a single word. She must have been catatonic.

As the plane ascended into the skies, she suddenly felt hungry and so gladly accepted the cup of tea and biscuits that came. Munching, she regretted having turned down her cabin meal earlier but she was sure she would have thrown up. It was also reassuring to see that she was no longer a lone African face, though solitude prevailed because the black faces spoke Swahili and seemed to discourage communication in English among themselves. They wrongly assumed that Eriza also spoke Swahili but was one of those who pretended to have lost their mother tongue once they were on a plane.

She drank her tea slowly as the captain announced that they were cruising at an altitude of 29,000 feet. Mt Everest came to mind; like a typical geography student, she knew more about faraway lands than her own country. On top of that, they had been taught to associate Mount Everest more with the conquerors – Sherpa Tenzing Norgay and Edmund Hillary – than with the Himalayas themselves. This reminded her of an argument that had erupted between the British-born geography teacher and two boys when she was in form four at boarding school. The teacher wholly attributed the achievement to Hillary, but the boys argued that Tenzing had led Hillary to the peak, so surely Tenzing should have been the one to be credited with the achievement? Willard, one of the two boys who later became a top military commander in the liberation war against the white Rhodesians, became belligerent because, at the time, Rhodesians were busy trying to credit the building of Great Zimbabwe to the Phoenicians so as to blight African architectural achievement.

Tenzing and Hillary were quickly forgotten in the argument when Willard wagged a finger at the teacher and shouted, "You people, this is the same thing you are doing with Great Zimbabwe."

The other boy whispered, "AK47. That they shall answer to."

The teacher objected vehemently to this referencing of military hardware, which was becoming synonymous with the liberation of southern Africa. He wanted them expelled from school but the headteacher, Mr Derwent, surprisingly, refused the request. Little did Eriza know that the argument would be settled many years later in 1980 with Willard hoisting the Zimbabwean flag on the Tower of Great Zimbabwe, and the geography teacher flying one way, on a British Airways flight from Harare to London. As she mused over the time at her school, she nearly missed the announcement that food was to be served.

The late cabin dinner was rice and chicken mixed with vegetables, and at that moment, nothing in the world could have tasted better for Eriza. She ate heartily, washing every few forkfuls down with an orange drink. The dessert was downed in three spoons, even though she had no idea what it was. The tea was dreadful, but she drank it anyway.

After dinner, the Swahili tones around her hushed, the plane cruised at an altitude of 38,000 feet, but Eriza was still very much awake. Without bothering to check her watch, she figured that her family back in Chena were now long in bed. She thought about her father, but it was her grandmother that continued to dominate her thoughts. The day would have been tiring for Mbuya Mukwesa, but Eriza was sure that she was the one who was more likely to still be awake.

❊ ❊ ❊

On the way from Chena to the airport, Mbuya Mukwesa had asked Mr Kanyemba to stop at her ancestral home, though it was now a white man's farm. In her day, it was known as Kuwadzana, but 'they' had renamed it Central Estates. Mr Kanyemba had obliged. Kuwadzana was in a valley and in August, with the trees bare, standing on the side of the tarred Salisbury to Bulawayo road on which they were travelling, they could see far into the farm. After a walkabout along the side of the road for just twenty or so yards, their shoes were covered in red dust from the rich soils of the Highveld. This was the inspiration for Naijo's reference to his grandmother's canvas shoes as carrying an offering from the ancestors.

Beyond a barbed wire fence and trees lay a field of green winter wheat being irrigated. The sprinkler spray and the bright August sunshine threw a rainbow over the field. Naijo, who often teased his grandmother about Kuwadzana, asked her whether her people would have kept the land so green during a very dry winter. She ignored him, but with hostility nevertheless, while wondering why there was a rainbow with no sign of rain, but the ways of the spiritual wisdom had told her that one should not comment on unusual phenomena. The spirits would simply disorientate such a person and laugh at them as they walked in circles for hours at a time, just to teach them to respect their world.

"Somewhere in this field is our burial mound. Many generations of the Mukwesas and Muchaidas are buried here.' She had been born a Muchaida.

She paused with her glassy eyes unblinking and zooming in on a mound, and then pointing with a shaky finger, she said softly, but her voice breaking, "That is where your great-grandfather, Muchaida lies, but I do not think he is resting."

She swallowed the lump of bitterness that had swelled in her throat and remained quiet. Everyone gave her space as they walked solemnly behind her. For her, the rainbow, even though it was the product of the gadgetry of new farming methods and the forces of nature, represented the presence of her people in Kuwadzana. In fact, she was certain that the rainbow was a sign from the spirits that Eriza's passage to London was assured.

Naijo, like the rest of the entourage, knew that the stopover in Kuwadzana had more to do with Eriza's departure for England than their grandmother's sentiment for her childhood home. She wanted Eriza to bid farewell to her ancestors. That was why when they had all settled back in the car she had muttered, *zvaitwa* – it has been done.

Eriza was right. As she settled back into her seat, and the plane sliced through the cold air high above the Abyssinian Mountains in Ethiopia, her grandmother lay awake in Chena. As usual, in the stillness of every rural night, and as was the case ever since she moved to Chena, her mind drifted back to Kuwadzana. Tonight in particular, she had to plead with the spirits to guide Eriza safely to London. Even though the spirits had 'confirmed' this with the rainbow in Kuwadzana, reinforcement through her night-time spiritual communication with her ancestral home was still needed. Mbuya Mukwesa felt a pang of hunger at the precise moment that Eriza was eating her cabin meal but she had to wait until the morning. At the same time, as Eriza ate, she knew that her grandmother would have grudgingly liked it too.

THREE

Eriza had been told several times over that her grandmother was born Rudo Muchaida in Kuwadzana in the early part of the mid-1870s. Her precise birth year was unknown. All she knew was that she was born just before the first white settlers made a mass appearance in what is now known as Salisbury. Mbuya Mukwesa believed herself to be the first person to see a white person in Kuwadzana.

As a young girl, her daily routine started with reviving the kitchen fire. That was then followed by a short trip to fetch water. It was on one of these mornings, with an earthenware water pot on her head, that she had this first sighting. She'd had the feeling that she was being followed and so had stolen a look behind her. She was terrified to bits, she would always say, when she saw this strange, white figure. Rumours abounded that such strange, white beings were about and had already been sighted in the south. Their description fitted so well with that of the dangerous, evil spirits of legend, and their appearance heralded pestilence to the nation. She couldn't run with the water pot perched on her head. Neither could she throw it down and run because its destruction would have led to a major domestic incident. So instead, she threw the water out, held on tightly to her pot and ran for her life. The being did not chase her. It just stood there. She didn't scream for help and she had never been able to understand why. Though she had reported the sighting, her credibility was questioned because so many other girls from her village had fetched water that morning and hadn't seen anything unusual. No one took her seriously and her sighting became nothing more than a bedtime fable for a while. However, she was sure that her people were in denial of the impending danger because the consequences of her story being true were unimaginable.

Not long afterwards, more sightings of white beings were reported. Then cartloads followed. They put tall, wooden pegs into the ground and hung pieces of cloth at the top end anywhere they chose. Some of them started digging randomly. Soon all girls were accompanied by elders to fetch water and firewood because word had gone round that the male species of the white beings were kidnapping children.

One day, one of the white men came to the river to scoop some water up in a cup when Mbuya Mukwesa and some other girls were there. He held this strange stick that looked like a little brush onto which he smeared some potion, which he then brushed across his teeth. There was white foam all over his mouth. He then drank the water from the cup and spat out more of the foam. They were sure he was having a fit, but then again, a person having a fit would have fallen to the ground. But this white one? No – nothing happened. He seemed perfectly fine. Soon, more and more of them started the foaming business, as well as washing themselves in the waters above the spot where they fetched drinking water. As the days went by, the white men became even more strange and the people of Kuwadzana became increasingly angry. But before things came to a head, the white men suddenly moved on.

❊ ❊ ❊

Mbuya Mukwesa and the rest of Kuwadzana thought that the whole episode was done, and their lives would return to normal again. But no. Some people in Kuwadzana had become friendly with these invaders. They now dressed like them and moved like them and tried to convince the others to do the same. There were two in particular who accompanied a group of the whites, carrying guns, as they went from village to village declaring that the villages were now called Rhodesville and were to be taken over by the biggest of all these beings. There was uproar. Shortly afterwards, the people of Kuwadzana heard that the strong kingdom in the south had been destroyed by these white men. It was clear to all that these white people were indeed not good.

Mbuya Mukwesa recounted that there were secret gatherings in the forests and mountains which were attended by their fathers and older brothers.

"We were told nothing." She always emphasised the solemnity of secrecy required in those crucial days with a hushed tone.

"You can tell us now Mbuya. The war ended 70 years ago." Naijo had seen that the memory of those petrifying days still weighed on her heavily.

"There is another war coming soon and the secrets of this war will be much like the secrets of the last war," she'd responded with a cautionary look at Naijo before continuing with her narration.

The boys of the village were no longer boys who looked after cattle and goats, but instead they had become young men who spied on the movements of the white beings. They were told not to speak to them but to just watch them, especially at night, then report what they had seen to a designated elder.

Then, it happened. Just like that. Even though rumours of war were rife, it still caught everyone unawares. It was like thunder. That is why they called it *hondo yechindunduma* – war of rebellion. Women and children were taken to mountain hideouts and caves that had been stocked with food and water. It was then that they understood why their fathers and brothers were away for so long before the war had actually started.

It was a time of terror, but African gallantry was at its best. Spears flew into the white laagers. In turn, the whites blew up dynamite in the caves. Many perished. The cave in which Mbuya Mukwesa and some girls had been hidden was also blown up just before their father joined them, but there was a passage which led to the other side of the mountain with a steep fall into a valley through which a river flowed. They then took refuge in the thick forest, a no-go area, because it was secret land where ancestral ceremonies and rituals were conducted. In times of danger though, the area was also a place of refuge. Away from the safety of the forest, it was mayhem. The white man ran amok, killing women and children, looting and burning their homes. The revenge for the African rebellion was brutal. Vast swathes of land were scorched and those who survived, like Mbuya Mukwesa, were expected to starve to death or die from disease.

"We'd never seen that kind of illness before – the blisters and pus all over before death," she'd said with pain etched all over her face. "Some said it was caused by the smoke from the guns. Others thought it was because the white man had deliberately poisoned the water, and some said it was caused by breathing in the same air as them. Then a white man who had wandered into the forest said, in broken Shona, that the illness was *simori pox* – small pox – coming from their breath and blood. We ran away from him, scattering in all directions."

At this point, Mbuya's eyes had darted around the room to get across the desperation her people had felt.

"He stood there, speaking words we didn't understand. But it sounded like the disease was expected to finish off any remaining stragglers and then drift into other parts of the country to meet with little resistance from the immune system of the African population." She continued, her eyes focused frightfully at the little window of the kitchen, as if the white figure was likely to appear from there. Her mother, Mai Muchaida, was one of those finished off by the *simori pox*. "Even cattle were bewitched by these white men. That year, the land lay barren because planting was impossible." She opened her palms to emphasise the emptiness of the time.

Naijo filled the gaps in Mbuya Mukwesa's account with the story of Cecil Rhodes. Rhodes had a dream of building a railway line from Cape Town to Cairo, carving through the African landscape. The story goes that Rhodes was a sickly boy and was an easy target for bullies in his country. He was doomed to be a failure but his life was revived by sailing to Africa. He then saw the destruction of African life and land as an atonement for his misery in England. Soon after the destruction of Mbuya Mukwesa's childhood land, Rhodes wrote his will stating that his remains were to be interred on one of the most sacred places in her land, so as to blight the spiritual landscape of the vanquished.

At the time, Mbuya Mukwesa was not familiar with these inner demonic ambitions held by the leader of the white race in her country. Years later, when Naijo went to teach at a school near Matopo, the holy place that Rhodes had defiled with his dead body, he visited the site and worked out how best to untomb Rhodes and make his body available to the British to discard. When he visited Chena one school holiday, he told Mbuya Mukwesa about Rhodes' grave. To Naijo's surprise, she'd not made a single comment at this piece of news.

Very few men survived and one of them was Mbuya Mukwesa's father, Sekuru Muchaida. He alone lived to regale his fellow villagers with tales of the bravery of their people as they faced the carnage unleashed by the white man. He remained with his depleted family in their ancestral home in Kuwadzana until 1938 even though they were declared squatters by the 1934 Land Apportionment Act that had made Kuwadzana a white man's area. By that time, she was now Mai Rudo Mukwesa, having married Sekuru Mukwesa, and had reluctantly become a Christian with the name 'Sophia'. That year they were told that they would be moved to Chena with their two sons. These two boys had been *christianed* at the same time as she had been. The eldest, Thomas, was impetuous. He vowed to return to Kuwadzana one day and slay Goliath like David had done in the Bible. The younger son was Lazarus. He hated the name, even the vernacular version of 'Razaru', and preferred being called Choto. As Thomas refused to go to school, Choto was groomed by his father to learn to read and write. At the age of ten, he succeeded in getting a sub-standard A. He was so proud to write his name in the sands of Kuwadzana: *CHOTO L. MUKWESA*. He went on to carve it on big trees. When they left Kuwadzana, these carvings became a testimony – '*PANO PAMUSHA PA CHOTO L MUKWESA*' – This is the home of Choto L Mukwesa.

Only those who were willing to be agricultural labourers of the white owners could stay, but it was without rights to the land. Both her husband and father refused the offer of such servitude. Her father, already a widower, then died two weeks before the entire community of Kuwadzana was uprooted and trekked to Chena with whatever they could carry, which was not much.

Each family was allowed just three cows and the remaining herd remained with the new white owner of Kuwadzana, now named Sendere. They couldn't be bothered to say Central Estates, the name given to that section of Rhodesville. The white owner paid nothing for the cattle he retained, nor were her people compensated for their land. In fact, no one was compensated for this huge expanse of land, apart from six-pence as stamp duty to their government. Mbuya Mukwesa and her people headed south from Kuwadzana on a dusty path that only about half a century earlier had been the route followed by Cecil Rhodes' occupation force heading north to settle in Harare, which they renamed Salisbury. What bothered her most was that her father's burial was incomplete, and his spirit remained at large rather than be reunited with those of his ancestors.

Eriza did not know her grandfather, Sekuru Mukwesa *mukuru* – older – who had lived until 1944. All she knew was that he had trained as a carpenter and had found employment attending to Italian prisoners of war sent to Rhodesia to build bridges. He apparently reported back to his family that they, the African workers, were treated like the convicts, rather than the Italian prisoners. After six weeks, he returned home and never went back. He had died two years after his return. Mbuya Mukwesa never spoke much about her husband. She said that her black attire was enough to show her sorrow for his loss and that of her father. However, she spoke of her father often.

So, Chena could never be home for Mbuya Mukwesa. In all her years there, she barely had a full night's sleep, with her mind drifting back to Kuwadzana as she lay on her bedding on the kitchen floor. The night somehow shone a light on the sacred memories of Kuwadzana seared in her psyche. With time, some details of her glorious youth faded. She struggled to remember who was who, but she was convinced that one day she would return, though she conceded loudly in the middle of the night of Eriza's departure that, 'the place would not be the same.'

Other times, she would joke with her daughter-in-law whose Christian zeal perplexed her. Nevertheless, she would beg her to tailor her prayers to release the Moses in her Bible to come and liberate them from Chena and lead them back to Kuwadzana. She would laugh at her own sarcasm, much to the chagrin of Mai Eriza. One day Mai Eriza quietly asked Mbuya Mukwesa whether she had ever considered that it was her Christian faith that sustained the family. Mbuya Mukwesa's response was that she admired her strong faith, but she still had to figure out whether it was indeed Mai Eriza's faith or her own belief that it was the ancestors, with some input from God, who were responsible for the well-being of the family.

"I think several people doing a job is better than one," she had said in reference to her god plus the spirits, whereas Jesus was on his own. Their different religious beliefs made them the best of friends though, to the extent that Mbuya Mukwesa had even gifted Mai Eriza with much, including two cows. Nothing got between the appreciation between mother and daughter-in-law, not even Baba Eriza; Mbuya Mukwesa sided with her daughter-in-law whenever her son tried to pull rank. She also said that it would be a domestic disaster if she was seen to be siding with her son when husband and wife disagreed.

"*Hapazodyiwi rinopisa,*" she would say – There would be trouble in the home.

Eriza recalled being told about *Babamukuru* – elder father – Thomas, who she had never known. Mbuya Mukwesa did not like to talk about him at all. Baba Eriza was even worse – he became mute whenever the subject of his big brother came up. Mai Eriza and Sekuru Fani also observed the code of silence on Babamukuru Thomas. But on the eve of Eriza's departure, Mbuya Mukwesa had spoken of him.

"Don't be like your Babamukuru who left one morning to go to Mawiro to sell a half-bag of peanuts and never returned," she said sternly.

"What happened to him, Mbuya?" Eriza had asked curiously, hoping that this would be the day she would finally find out about Babamukuru.

❖❖❖

"We heard that he went to *Buruwayo*. Your grandfather and father travelled there to bring him back, but they missed him by a day. They were told that he had moved on to Winera in South Africa. There was no point waiting for letters from him because he couldn't read or write. He was good at *aritmatic* though." Mbuya stopped with a faraway look in her eyes. Eriza saw the pain in those eyes.

"Maybe he's dead now because in Winera there are *tsotsies* – crooks – who will kill just for a penny. On top of that, white people shoot Africans at a whim. I heard your father and Sekuru Fani talking about that place where hundreds of people were shot, and I could see my son among the dead. But hopefully, he'll come back like that boy from the family of Magwede who came back with his *makaradi* – mixed-race – children." Mbuya's face relaxed at the thought. "Go and do what you need to do now *muzukuru* – my grandchild," she added with a smile that failed to betray her pain.

Eriza got the hint and did not ask any more questions. She walked away from her Mbuya as she too was becoming emotional.

Eriza was lost in her grandmother's odyssey as her plane crossed the Mediterranean Sea. She expected some turbulence or something to indicate that it was flying over a large body of water. The no smoking and the 'fasten seatbelt' signs lit up but the plane continued to glide smoothly. She was a little confused when the captain announced that they were soon to land in Rome.

Within 15 minutes, the plane had indeed landed. The stopover was to last three hours, but people like her with Rhodesian passports could not leave the plane. She didn't mind anyway and was glad to peer through the windows as she walked up and down the aisle. As she did so, she thought back to her brother Naijo bidding her farewell at the airport in Salisbury with his reference to crossing the Rubicon River. She thought back to the Roman history she had assiduously absorbed in secondary school, and how much she admired the manner and style of Julius Caesar. Perhaps her plane had landed on the very spot where Caesar had dazzled his fellow Romans with his oratory skills before the fatal Ides of March.

"*Et tu brute*," she muttered, as if she were Caesar.

What a betrayal she thought. Then her mind moved on to another betrayal that her mother could not get over – that of Jesus by Judas. She giggled when she remembered how Naijo referred to their mother as being in the 'JJ mode' when she was pensive and solemn. Mai Eriza strongly believed that her devotion to Catholicism would be rewarded with a pilgrimage to Rome. At that very moment, Eriza wanted to exchange places with her mother. If she were there, she would not only visit the Vatican, which she imagined to be paradise on earth itself, but also realise that Rome and Palestine were two different places. With that, Eriza mused over the other misconceptions about Jesus and Christianity that featured in the many discussions between her mother and grandmother as they sat under the shade of the *msasa* tree at the back of their kitchen.

❁ ❁ ❁

They'd often sit there on reed mats, shelling peanuts. Her grandmother wore her black headscarf. Over her shoulders was a black shawl which fell to her waist. The dress covered her outstretched legs to her ankles, and the outfit was completed by a pair of black canvas shoes. The ankles themselves always looked dry unless Naijo applied some Vaseline over them, teasing his grandmother that someone might try to pick them up thinking that they were tiny logs of firewood. Eriza's feet resembled her grandmother's, and even though they were not half as dry, Naijo teased her that she might as well start greasing her feet now to avoid the fate of her grandmother. Eriza could only kiss her teeth.

Mai Eriza wore all colours of headdress except black. She was especially fond of those with a flowery pattern. Her dresses and skirts were always long, and her chosen footwear was also a pair of canvas shoes purchased at Tomas' shop at the railway siding of Mawiro, nine miles away. When these two women sat under the tree or anywhere for that matter, they always did so at an angle to each other, never directly facing each other. Neither one of them nor anyone else could explain why.

One day, under the *msasa* tree, Mai Eriza was reading the Bible quietly while Mbuya Mukwesa was fidgeting with her fingers not knowing what to say. She didn't believe in Christianity, especially because it was a weapon of the white man which they used to subdue her people, but the story of Jesus interested her.

"Jesus Christ must have been Moses' grandson," she said.

"No Mbuya," Mai Eriza replied impatiently, "they were *Israraitsi* – Israelites – who could have been related but were many generations apart."

"But I get the impression that Jesus took over when Moses died. And don't they say he was Jesus of Nazareth, King of the Jews?" Mbuya Mukwesa replied hesitantly.

Eriza had discovered that most of what her grandmother knew about the Bible had been acquired at the 'brainwashing meetings', as she called them, that she'd attended before being renamed Sophia. She was left with the impression that the Israelites collaborated in the killing of Jesus because he was a Jew. The impression spilled over to embrace Herr Hitler – *iye Hitra* – she would say – that Hitler. Out of that she held the view that the Germans were Israelites because of *mazana nemazana nemazana emaJuta avakaponda* – the thousands and thousands and even more thousands of Jews that Hitler murdered.

"*Ndizvo zvinondzi na Naijo horokosti achitiwozve takaitwawo iyowo horokosti nevarungu. Aiti mazana akawanda chaizo evanhu vedu vakakandwa mugungwa. Ndatokanganwa kuti zita racho regungwa rinonzi ani. Harisiriro rimwe ramunoti iye Moses akavura nedanda ma Israrites akamaya kuyambuka?*" – That's what Naijo calls the holocaust which he also says we suffered at the hands of white people. Some of us were thrown in the sea. I can't recall the name of the sea but I think it's the same one which Moses opened up with his stick and across which the Israelites scampered into the promised land.

"But," she sighed, "it has nothing to do with us and we should not lose sleep over it, unless the white man who took Kuwadzana was an *Israraiti* or Jew."

"Moses led the *Israraitsi* out of slavery from Egypt which is here in Africa. But Jesus was born in Bethlehem in Canaan which was the promised land to which Moses delivered the *Israraitsi*," said Mai Eriza. "They call the sea they crossed the Red Sea – *Gungwa Dvuku*," she added. She did not bother to mention Joshua, because it would have entailed a lengthy explanation of his relationship to Moses, confusing Mbuya Mukwesa further.

"Yes!" Mbuya Mukwesa exclaimed. "That is the sea our people were thrown into because red is blood and survivors became slaves. We are treated like slaves here in our own country. The moment one is not allowed to be where they want to be, it is slavery. I can't go and live in Kuwadzana and that is where I want to be," blurted Mbuya Mukwesa.

Mai Eriza was about to reply but Mbuya Mukwesa continued. She wanted to know where the Arabs fitted in all this because Naijo had told her that Jews and Arabs are the same people but differ violently on religion. And *Ijipiti* – Egypt – is home to the Arabs so the Jews were enslaved in *Ijipiti* by Arabs long ago."

Mai Eriza knew that Mbuya Mukwesa was mixing things up but she herself did not quite understand the link between Arab Egypt and ancient Egypt.

"The British people did the same too. They enslaved our people to America and now they enslave us here," Mai Eriza decided to talk about something she was certain of. "They call our people negroes over there in

America. That's what Naijo told me. I think they should call themselves Africans even there in America, because, as Naijo says, if you met with them on the road, there is no difference between us."

"Are they going to come back here?" Mbuya Mukwesa asked.

"They have their homes there in America. Africa is just as foreign to them as America or England is foreign to us," Mai Eriza answered assertively. "Besides, they are no longer slaves. It was their ancestors who were taken there as slaves, as Naijo was saying," she added, so that Mbuya Mukwesa was clear that mother and son also talked about these things.

"I will always want Naijo, Eriza and Prudence to go back to Kuwadzana. That is their home, not here. That white man and his children will never own Kuwadzana. Never." Mbuya Mukwesa was becoming visibly agitated.

"Yes Mbuya," replied Mai Eriza, sighing heavily.

"You and your husband don't care, I know. Did you know that Magaya, whose great-grandfather ran away from the Portuguese many years ago, is talking about going back? They call the place Mozambique."

"Mbuya, there's fighting there. What is he going back there to do? He will only get himself killed," Mai Eriza said. "Here, Magaya is a Christian and what he does for God, like that other Mozambican, Bernard Mzeki, he does for his people too."

But Mbuya Mukwesa was of the opinion that Mzeki should not have gone about telling people to abandon their God for the God of the white man, and she certainly did not blame her people for killing him. Besides, if Sekuru Fani was telling the truth, Mzeki was killed because he was trying to stop Africans from killing white people who had not only occupied their land, but also slaughtered their brothers and sisters during the Chindunduma War.

Even though Mbuya Mukwesa could not see herself becoming a Christian, she was nevertheless fascinated by some of the stories in the Bible. Growing up, Thursday was a day of rest and it did not please God to toil the land on that day. Christians choosing Sunday to rest was not a big deal for her. Those who were not Christians could toil on Sunday so long as they had their own special day for their God. She knew that *masabata* – Seventh Day Adventists – put down tools on Friday evening and spent Saturday with God. She also thought that people must have a day to socialise, whether God decreed it or not.

Then there were the stories of Moses and Jesus which she believed to be epic scenes of human suffering and endurance which had nothing to do with religion. All that grandfather Moses and grandson Jesus did was to stand up against assailants like these white men who drove her out of Kuwadzana. Chena was the biblical Egypt and Kuwadzana was Canaan and all that was needed was a Moses among her own people to lead them back.

Each night she was reminded of the last days of Christ the liberator because of the rooster. For her, the crow heralded dawn and the beautiful morning sunshine but the sun shone in the wrong place. She longed, every morning, to see the sun rise in Kuwadzana. The rooster had engaged St Peter in an act of denial of Jesus, according to her daughter-in-law's homilies and here in Chena, it announced to her another day in a land from which only night offered a reprieve. In some ways, the Bible was full of inspiring stories and her second biggest regret was that she could not read it herself. The first biggest regret was of course that white men had been allowed to take over *nyika yedu* – our land.

Unlike Mbuya Mukwesa, Mai Eriza could read and the Bible was her favourite book. She found the Old Testament too violent and if left to her, she would have had it expunged. Eriza and Naijo used to call out to each other *ex nihilo* – from nothing – when they saw their mother reading the Old Testament. Their mother never found out that they were teasing her about her desire to recreate the Bible. She said she couldn't be anything but a Catholic because Catholicism retained the flavour of Christ. Priests, like Jesus, saw the work of the Lord as their calling.

In their front room hung a portrait of Pope Pius XII. The 'Sodom and Gomorrah-like' behaviour of some Catholic priests in the villages was not going to shift that picture of Pius XII at all. She brushed aside the rumour that the untimely disappearance of her Irish Diocesan priest, Father Patrick, was linked to a 16-year-old girl becoming pregnant at the mission. She was also aware that a village to the west of the Catholic Centre had a few *makaradi* and several Friesland cattle, just like those bred at the farm that belonged to the Catholic Centre. It was clear therefore that some of the priests were conducting affairs with wives of absent migrant workers and the local chief would order them to pay damages with their Friesland cows. Now and then, the farm manager offered to sell heifers and bullocks to the villagers, but Baba Eriza, as much as he wanted to, never bought one. He knew that his wife was an upright woman and would not allow the presence of a Friesland beast in his herd to compromise her integrity. He also knew that in some ways his wife, as well as some of the other Catholicised men and women in the village, were being hypocritical because they clearly tolerated the sins of the clergy because, after all, 'they were educating the community,' they said. What a price to pay to learn to read and write. He suspected that even pastors of other denominations competing with the Catholics were not immune from the sacrilege of deceit but at least they did not play hyenas in sheep's clothing.

For Mai Eriza, parables and Jesus' miracles were the essence of a true religion and there was something about Catholicism that made them authentic. Though she lived in hope of one day visiting the sites of Jesus' miracles, she realised that such a pilgrimage would demand a hefty financial commitment. That would have meant selling at least nine of the fifteen cattle her family owned. Her husband was always telling people that his in-laws had demanded ten cattle for him to marry Mildred (Mai Eriza's Christian name). So, Mai Eriza was sure that he would not support what he would no doubt term a conspiracy between the Church and his wife to go to Palestine just to see 'places'. On top of that, the Church had 'made' them have a white wedding, adding another expense to the whole holy matrimonial business. The Church's argument was that dwelling in a traditional union alone was an impediment to entry into paradise. He had capitulated, and their church wedding set new standards for matrimonial bliss in Chena. Even Mbuya Mukwesa loved it, though grudgingly so. That was all of 12 years ago.

One parable, that of The Good Samaritan, inspired Mai Eriza to move around the village checking on neighbours and making her mark in the community. It was this same parable that made her sign up for the first-aid training course offered by her diocese. After qualifying as a first-aider, she urged people to understand that 'cleanliness was very much nearer to godliness'. At church, she urged people to go on 'The Road to Damascus' and like St Paul, be blinded before they could see again in the light of God. Every Good Friday she and her children joined with other Catholic parishioners on a pilgrimage of sorts to the mission centre where the story of the crucifix was enacted. It was on one such pilgrimage that Naijo, at the age of nine, fell into a ditch as they walked back home. His explanation was that he had been blinded in the manner of St Paul. That was when the family realised that they had a serious joker in their midst.

Everything about or associated with Jesus was sacrosanct for Mai Eriza, including the donkey on which Jesus humbled himself by riding on the first stage of his journey to be crucified. She would cry openly whenever a donkey wandered into their village with its mouth all wired up to starve it to death, even though this was the long-established method of putting down the unwanted animals. She cursed the unknown human who had brought suffering to the donkey that had strayed right into her yard. According to her thinking, it would have wandered her way because God guided it there knowing that she would not let it down. She called upon God to let loose on that cruel person with the ten plagues that he had visited upon the Egyptians even though this was an event of the Old Testament that she so vehemently objected to. On that occasion Baba Eriza, who naturally cared for the welfare of animals, heroically tried to save the animal even though he knew that the damage had already been done. Eriza was ten then and had never seen her mother so distraught. They found the donkey dead the following morning on a lush green area near a well. Mbuya Mukwesa had commented on how it had chosen to die surrounded by what it had been denied – pasture and water.

As Eriza thought about her mother and family, she suddenly realised that it was her mother's work as a first-aider that had motivated her to go into nursing, and maybe medicine later on. She gazed down at the lights of Rome at three in the morning. Were it her mother looking through the window, the sight would have been declared a miracle. Eriza chuckled to herself.

The takeoff from Rome was so smooth that she fell into a deep sleep. Even the captain's voice announcing the plane's arrival at Heathrow did not rouse her. She was gently awakened by a hostess who gave her the trademark smile. Nothing from Nairobi through Rome had given her the impression that these white air hostesses were like Rhodesian women. It made Eriza feel welcomed into the land of the white man.

FOUR

Her letter from Colchester Royal Infirmary, like her Rhodesian passport, bore her full names: *Elizabeth Rudo Mukwesa*. She readily responded to *Miss Mukwesa* but she was so used to being called Eriza that when the immigration officer asked for her name at customs, even though it was right in front of him, she simply answered "Eriza".

"Your full name please," he asked again.

"Elizabeth Rudo Mukwesa," she answered. It sounded so alien to her, but she immediately realised that Eriza would have to be put to bed while in England.

The immigration officer looked at her passport, then at her, and back at her passport for at least four rounds, with a stern expression on his face. He appeared to be on the verge of interrogating her, but the contents of the letter clearly left him no room to do so. It said that she would be met at the airport by the hospital's senior sister and two other nurses. It also made it clear that she had been accepted onto a nurse's training course complete with accommodation and a stipend. After what felt like an eternity, he stamped her passport violently, grunted, handed her passport and grunted again. She correctly realised that the second grunt was a signal for her to go.

She remembered Mr Kanyemba telling her that after going through immigration, she would need to collect her suitcase. He told her to follow everyone else coming out of immigration, as they too would be collecting their luggage. It made sense to follow the crowd, but being Eriza, she wanted to confirm she was indeed headed in the right direction, so she read the various signs around carefully before following one that said *baggage.*

"Once you get to the baggage area," he'd said, "you need to look out for a sign with your flight number and there you will see a conveyor belt with all the luggage from your plane. Just look out for your suitcase."

Eriza had never known that suitcases came in all these shapes and sizes, colours and styles. She only knew the tattered, brown, hardbacked contraptions that she'd seen stockpiled on the bus to Salisbury. She saw one covered in lots of different labels, so much so that it was impossible to tell what its original colour was. I guess it meant that the owner must have travelled to many countries. How lucky for them. Eriza was so engrossed in the suitcases and the stories behind them that she nearly missed her brown contraption. She dragged it off the belt and, having spotted the *exit* sign earlier, she headed in that direction for the next leg of her journey.

"Just walk tall and straight and confidently through *nothing to declare,*" Mr Kanyemba had said. She did just that and soon found herself walking out into a sea of white faces.

They were indeed there, holding a banner which read *Elizabeth Mukwesa.* She smiled at the banner before she smiled at the three white women holding it up. As she walked calmly towards them, she wasn't sure if they knew who she was. The older of the three women smiled back and so did the other two nurses, but she couldn't help but wonder whether British white women behaved like Rhodesian white women who didn't shake hands with Africans. She walked straight into them.

"I'm Margaret. Sister Margaret Thompson."

The Senior Sister introduced herself, reaching for Eriza's hand. They did shake hands then. Sister Margaret took it a step further and hugged Eriza. Eriza hugged her back but she was stiff. Rhodesian whites would never have done this, nor would they have allowed an African to hug them. The other two nurses completely dispensed with handshakes and went straight for the hugs. Eriza was so taken aback that she did not hear the names Sinead and Trish. On top of that, she couldn't believe that these were the same people who, back home in Rhodesia, wanted Africans dead.

"Let me help you with your case Elizabeth," Sinead offered, oblivious to Eriza's shock. At the same time, Eriza's handbag fell off her shoulder and Sister Margaret picked it up, no hesitation, and handed it to Eriza along with a pat on her back.

"Thank you," Eriza said, with a nod and a smile, looking straight into Sister Margaret's eyes.

She fleetingly thought of Mbare in Salisbury. There, neither man nor woman *ever* gave their luggage to strangers, no matter how friendly they presented themselves to be. You would never see it again. So, naturally, her hold on the case stiffened a bit when Sinead grabbed it. Sinead felt Eriza's resistance, but she put it down to the fact that Eriza was also contending with her wayward handbag.

"Girls, let's get some coffee and give Elizabeth time to…," Sister Margaret said. "I'm just going to the loo. Do any of you want to come with me to the toilet?"

Eriza joined her. She didn't realise it was an invitation to her rather than to Sinead and Trish. In the airport washroom, Eriza freshened up but before that, she spent a few minutes examining her surroundings. She was impressed by the size of the washroom and the number of toilet cubicles. The smell of detergent told her that the toilet had been recently cleaned. She proceeded to brush her teeth over the small wash basin. When she came out, Sister Margaret was waiting for her.

"We have just about fifty minutes until we get on the bus," said Sister Margaret, still smiling. "We could go by train but tube trains are quite busy in the mornings and we would have to change at least three times before we catch the main train at Liverpool Street to Colchester." She paused as she looked at Eriza, thinking that Eriza had no understanding of the underground train system.

On the other hand, Eriza knew exactly what Sister Margaret was talking about and she was a little annoyed at herself for not having said first "Let's go on the underground." After all, travelling on the tube was on her list of things to do and write home about. How exciting for her people to receive a letter detailing the nature of travelling in an underground train? She could hear Sekuru Mhizha declaring, unchallenged, that it was the same as being in a mine shaft.

"Trish and Sinead must be waiting for us now." Sister Margaret led Eriza to where the two girls were sitting. They were in animated conversation, oblivious to two Asian women who were cleaning the floors, but it was clear that the conversation had nothing to do with Eriza. The two Asian women reminded Eriza of President Amin of Uganda, who was removing plane-loads of them from Uganda. She did not quite understand Amin's problem, but had no time to consider this further as Sister Margaret hesitated before calling out to them.

"Come girls, let's join the queue for some food."

They walked towards an eatery where the service was cafeteria style. Sister Margaret picked up a tray. Eriza did the same and walked behind her while Trish and Sinead in turn walked behind Eriza. It dawned on Eriza that she still wasn't sure who was Sinead or who was Trish. She decided to bide her time until she found an opportunity to work out who was who, instead of embarrassing herself. The two girls were speaking excitedly about a 'he', who, from the sounds of it, was Sinead's boyfriend.

"But, Sinead, you're not giving yourself time to know him," Trish entreated. Eriza turned back quickly and got it. Trish was the girl right behind her. She was slim and tall with black hair and wore blue jeans. Sinead was short, wearing black trousers and a white t-shirt. Her face was kind, probably more so because she had offered to carry Eriza's suitcase. The conversation between the two girls made her think about her own love life. Her 'he' was David. He was the same age as Eriza and like her brother Naijo, was at the local university where he was in the first year of studying agriculture.

"Pick whatever you want Elizabeth," Sister Margaret said softly.

Eriza accepted her offer with a smile. She stuck to the more familiar foods – two scones and a cup of coffee. David liked scones and she was going to eat one for him. The longing for David took her by surprise and she chuckled to herself when she rationalised that eating a scone for him was a way to let him know that she had arrived.

On the National Express bus to Colchester, Eriza sat with Sister Margaret, who asked her about her family. She couldn't believe that Eriza had just two siblings, one of whom was deceased. She decided to put it in another way.

"Your father would have had other wives with their own children, wouldn't he?"

"No, he has just one wife, my mother," Eriza laughed. "My grandmother, uncle and niece also live with us."

Defeated, Sister Margaret focused on being a tour guide. "We're now driving on the A12. It's built on an old Roman road and Colchester had a Roman garrison."

"Ah! Camulodunum, that's the Roman name for Colchester. This is where Julius Caesar came, saw and conquered," she said.

"You know a bit of our history then," Sister Margaret said.

"Yes, but more Roman than British," said Eriza. "I was fascinated by Caesar when I read that he was born by caesarean," she added.

"You know Elizabeth, I have been a nurse for years and years and this is the first time since my training that I have heard a trainee nurse mention Caesar in conversations about childbirth." Sister Margaret was impressed. She turned to Sinead and Trish. "Did you know about Julius Caesar and caesarean babies?" she asked, very excited.

"Yes," Trish said with her blue eyes on Eriza, "he was not just a soldier and emperor but also a surgeon. He delivered a lot of babies."

Eriza's lower jaw dropped in disbelief as she looked at Trish. She had heard that white people had different eye colours from Africans. In Rhodesia most Africans never got close enough to white people to confirm this. Eyes were supposed to be windows to one's soul, and no one really wanted to see the soul of a white Rhodesian.

The August mid-morning summer sun was shining brightly. Wheat combine harvesters were busy on the Essex farms and the view from the bus was just like the scenes depicted in paintings of the English countryside. She noticed the plume of dust as the harvester cut, threshed and poured grains of wheat into a tractor-drawn trailer. Bales of straw dropped out of the harvester at intervals, complete with a string tied neatly around the middle. Birds were flying above the whole operation and feeding on the wheat grain and insects flushed out by the harvesters. She stared intensely at the scene of what appeared to be a dog chasing a rabbit. In Chena, such scenes would have been orchestrated by young men hunting rabbits with their dogs. But as they got closer, she realised that it was a fox in hot pursuit of its rabbit lunch. She was absorbed, and the three nurses allowed her to be. For a while, anyway.

"I grew up on a sheep farm in Yorkshire," Sinead finally disrupted the reverie.

"Did you use sheepdogs to look after your sheep?" Eriza asked with excitement. "Our geography teacher always showed us films of sheep farming in England and watching the dogs driving sheep or sniffing out some in heavy snow was fascinating."

"Yes, once the dog is trained like our Roy was, a sheepdog can round up sheep easily. But it must be a special breed of dog. You can't train a bulldog to do it," Sinead answered. Eriza laughed at the mention of the word bulldog.

❈❈❈

It was November 1965 and Eriza was preparing for her standard six exams. That year, white Rhodesia thought that it could escape the 'wind of change' that was blowing political independence across African countries by declaring Rhodesia independent without Queen Elizabeth II's royal assent. In the bickering that ensued, the word 'bulldog' had caused a diplomatic uproar. All arguments had been exhausted to dissuade Ian Smith, the Rhodesian prime minister, from going Unilateral Declaration of Independence (UDI). His opinion was if British-American settlers could declare themselves independent, as they had done in 1776, he could not see why British-Rhodesian settlers could not do it in 1965. In 1776, George III had sent troops to crush the Boston Tea Party but had failed dismally. So, it was also expected that in 1965, Elizabeth II would send paratroopers to quell the Salisbury Cabal and the operation would not be as dismal as George III's, yet she didn't. And surely it couldn't be that she feared suffering the same humiliation her ancestor had. Word was about that the British Prime Minister, Harold Wilson, saw white Rhodesians as kith and kin. Africa was furious. The Zambian High Commissioner to London consequently called

Britain 'a toothless bulldog'. You would have thought he'd walked into 10 Downing Street and shouted the insult right into the face of Prime Minister Harold Wilson, because the ensuing furore had reverberated across the world. Of course, the Third World countries applauded the Zambian High Commissioner. Even though Zambia was forced to recall him, he returned to a hero's welcome in Lusaka. Meanwhile, Ronald Webster, the Chief Minister of Anguilla, had declared the little island's independence, and Britain had the audacity to send a warship. Eriza remembered her father, who had borrowed her atlas to find out where Anguilla was, commenting that the island was smaller than one of the British frigates sent to quell the uprising.

"And this Mr Webster is African," Mr Mukwesa said, "that's why Britain will not send an army to stop Smith… kith and kin."

❖❖❖

While Eriza was absorbed with the tale of the bulldog, Sinead and Trish were venting about their hospital rotations. Sister Margaret listened attentively but did not interject. As they prattled on, Eriza spotted a road sign to Basildon. It reminded her of the letters David wrote to her on Basildon Bond writing pads and posted in Basildon Bond envelopes. Eriza and David had become A Level sweethearts after four years in the same boarding school during which time they'd barely noticed each other. This was despite the fact that, since form one, they'd both been in the top sets for all subjects.

Their first real romantic encounter took place in the unlikely setting of the exam hall. It was the final GCE O Level English Literature paper, the tenth of 11 exam sittings, in the third week of exams. David, who was left-handed, sat at a desk to the left of Eriza. In the stillness of the exam room, he had a good view of everything going on to his right. It had dawned on him that each time he needed to answer a question, one look at Eriza was all it took to reveal the answer. In actual fact, to him, Eriza was even more beautiful under the pressure of writing exams.

Towards the end, he noticed that Eriza was in some sort of 'pen crisis'. He glanced quickly around the big hall and saw the invigilators all piled up in one corner. He dropped his spare pen and kicked it towards Eriza. She looked at David with an appreciative smile and his eyes caught full sight of the glory of her beauty. She dropped her broken pen and picked up David's then completed her sentence, '...*a sudden and dramatic appearance.*'

"Stop writing. Put your pens down and remain quiet," Mr Evans, the deputy head and exam officer instructed.

Eriza wanted to write more to explain the demise of Macbeth. She looked at David, who was looking the other way, but who knew that Eriza was smiling at him. Once outside, Eriza ran after David to hand over the pen.

"You can keep it," David said nervously.

"Thank you, but I have more in the dorm," said Eriza, still pointing the pen towards David. He noticed her hand was shaking.

"OK. Latin tomorrow," he said and took the pen.

"Yes, Latin," she replied with a generous smile.

Neither of them cared much about getting caught up in the excitement that followed the completion of each exam paper.

Eriza walked to the girls" dorms while David remained standing in front of the hall staring at her. Wilfred, one of his more 'exuberant' friends, and one who never seemed to miss a step, startled him.

"What do you see over there that I can't see?" he asked.

"I don't like it when an exam is as easy as this one," David replied.

"You are a mad man. That was tough!" Wilfred exclaimed before he ran off to join a more boisterous set of boys and where the consensus was that Shakespeare was a lunatic to write prose they could not understand. Chinua

Achebe, of *Things Fall Apart*, wrote about conflict which they understood, so the questions on this book had given them hope of passing the exam.

David headed to the boys' dorms. He was irritated by Wilfred's intrusion because by the time he'd run off to the noisy bunch, Eriza had disappeared, thus depriving him of one last gaze at her backside and shapely legs. The consensus was that if a girl was not pretty, that could be overlooked if the backside and leg work made up for that lack. There was no doubt that Eriza was beautiful on all these accounts, but it was essential that he examined the other attributes. He was more than satisfied with what he'd seen. Unbeknownst to each other, they both looked forward to the following day's Latin paper.

David was nicknamed 'Centurion' because of his phenomenal grasp of the Latin language. He always got full marks on tests. Eriza was good too but not as good as David. Nevertheless, the following morning they both left the exam room on a high. The grand finale was saluted by the boys shouting *finito* as they ran out of the hall to go to their dorm rooms for their luggage. As required by the school exam procedures, all form four and upper six students were bused off home at the end of their final sitting. Buses were already waiting. Eriza and David bid each other farewell quietly as they boarded separate buses. Wilfred, who had noticed the chemistry between Eriza and David, went to sit next to David, something he never did. He was determined to tease him about what he'd witnessed, and he showed him no mercy. Meanwhile, all David could think of was Eriza, and as Eriza headed to Chena, all she could think of was David.

Eriza and David longed for each other intensely during the long summer holiday and the tension was amplified by the wait for their exam results. David spent hours and hours composing the conversation they would have when they met again. His mother noticed his frequent moments of solitude and concluded that the wait for the results was getting to him. Meanwhile Eriza, in her silent bedtime prayers, implored for David to return to form five. She did the same at church when the priest asked the congregation to humbly make their personal requests to God through Jesus, and even lit a candle for him at the Chena mission church one Sunday.

Throughout Eriza's reverie about her boyfriend, Sinead and Trish had moved on to complaining about the hospital routines, with Sister Margaret defending the regime. By now, she had heard enough and felt compelled to enlighten these two girls about some of the misconceptions they held about hospital administration. Fortunately, the increasingly agitated debate was cut short by their arrival in Colchester.

The walk from the bus station to the hospital was short. At the hospital, Sinead and Trish took Eriza to her accommodation. Eriza immediately fell in love with it. It was a flat, Flat H, which she would share with two other trainee nurses, Debbie and Chris. After the introductions, both girls showed her around the flat and allocated her space in the kitchen cupboards. She had her own bedroom where the bed was already made... at midday. After her tour, Sinead told her to seek them out in Flat K if she needed anything before she and Trish ran off.

Debbie and Chris spoke in soft tones which promised Eriza that they would be kind flatmates. They shared an uncanny resemblance to each other. But Eriza, still smarting from the racial prejudice of Rhodesia, did not immediately warm to the girls. Chris offered her a cup of coffee and all three of them sat at the small kitchen table.

"We've just finished our first year," Debbie said. "It's quite enjoyable even though it can be very heart-breaking and traumatic when you lose a patient."

"Don't let Debbie dent your nursing enthusiasm," Chris interrupted. "I always tell her that a hospital is for sick people and some are bound to die. Anyway, how long was your flight?" Chris quickly changed the topic.

"I would say about 13 hours including stopovers in Nairobi and Rome." Eriza was quite startled by the time she had spent travelling. She hadn't thought about it until now.

"My sister is a charge nurse in Zomba in Malawi. I visited her last year and the flight was really long." Chris was warming up to Eriza more and more. "Have you been to Malawi?" she asked Eriza.

"No," Eriza answered as she too warmed up to Chris.

"But it must be near to your home. Just like here to Wales," Debbie said. Both Eriza and Chris smiled.

"Debbie. You can travel by train or car to Cardiff in the morning and be back by teatime. Not so with Malawi and Rhodesia," Chris said.

"There isn't a border between us and Malawi," Eriza explained.

"My sister likes your country, Elizabeth, but she says that there is too much of what the locals call a 'colour bar', you know, like apartheid in South Africa," Chris said, looking at Eriza for confirmation, and also trying to reassure her that there was nothing of the sort among them.

"Yes, there is," Eriza responded. She thought about whether she should tell them that a scene like the one they were enjoying at that very moment would be unheard of in Rhodesia.

"Elizabeth, we have to go so let's talk later," Chris said.

"OK. Thank you. And leave the cups to me," Eriza said as she stood up with her cup.

"You don't have to," Debbie protested as Chris dashed to her room in a flash.

"No really. It gives me a chance to begin to know how things work," Eriza explained. Debbie took one look at Eriza's innocent eyes and could not object.

"Sure, go ahead," she responded.

Debbie left, leaving Eriza standing in the middle of the kitchen by herself. It suddenly hit her hard that she was far away from home but a descent into panic was averted when she saw an African nurse through the kitchen window. She wore a white uniform and her hair was styled in an elaborate pinup on the top of her head, or was it a wig? Her attention was diverted by a phone ringing in the corridor. She wasn't sure what to do until Chris answered it. Eriza's eyes then scrambled to get another glimpse of the African nurse but only managed to catch a flash of the back of her white uniform as she turned a corner.

Time to herself, even in a strange land, was soothing. Her room had a brownish carpet with matching curtains on the single window. She checked the white bed linen. Satisfied that it was clean, she sat on the bed and slowly scanned her room. There was a desk, a wardrobe, a dressing table and a bedside table with a lamp on top. She suddenly felt the urge to use the toilet and quickly jumped off the bed and headed to the corridor. The toilet was clean but, out of habit after six years at boarding school, she wiped the toilet seat before sitting on it. She ventured through the open bathroom door to wash her hands. The floor and walls were covered in white tiles. There was a bathtub with a shower hanging over it. The afternoon light was coming through the bathroom window and Eriza could see that the bath was well-scrubbed. She took this as a clear invitation to bathe and it thrilled her to think that she had graduated from washing from a bucket, in a grass-walled bathroom, to a delightfully tiled bathroom in just over 30 hours.

With that, she went back to her room and rummaged through her suitcase. She pulled out her new dressing gown which was a gift from Naijo but was most certainly chosen by his girlfriend. Naijo could not have managed to pick out such a pretty, cream-coloured gown complete with a matching toilet bag and bathroom slippers. She slid her feet into the fluffy footwear and headed back to the bathroom. There, in the glow of the full-sized mirror, she admired her body for David. She knew just what would make David long for her.

She rinsed the tub, turned the tap on and let the water mix with her Radox bath salts. She gazed at the foam filling the tub before immersing herself, allowing the scented water to slide over every bit of her body. It was exhilarating. She knew that time was on her side – at 1:30 in the afternoon, surely the bathroom would be hers for a while. David came to mind again, as did her people in Chena. Thoughts of her grandmother took prominence. She missed her more than anyone else. Eriza smiled and she splashed water on to her face. It was out of pleasure and at the memory of her last bath in Chena, about 20 hours ago.

That last morning in Chena, she'd taken her bath after the elaborate breakfast. Her feet, legs, arms and face were dusty from sweeping the yard and ash. She had carried a bucket full of warm water with her right hand and a towel, an old dressing gown, flannel and small bar of Palmolive soap with her left hand. She took off her clothes in the privacy of the grass-walled bathroom. Out of habit she bent down and scooped a few handfuls of water on to her feet to wash off the dust and ash. She then rubbed the bar of soap on to her flannel and gently washed her face. The scent of soap engulfed the grass bathroom, suffocating the smell of dust and smoke. She heard the goats' hoofing outside. It was not unusual for them to walk around the bathroom, prying. Today, though, a crisis was about to loom when one of the goats started to push the bathroom's wooden door. With her eyes itching from the soapy water from the flannel, she kicked the door to scare the animals away. They ran off as Prudence shouted at them.

Naijo and Sekuru Fanu retreated to Sekuru Fani's hut where they cleaned themselves up for the journey. Mai Eriza went back to the main house for her ablutions. They missed out on Eriza's bathroom scene with the goats. Baba Eriza returned to the kitchen garden to pass the time waiting for Mr Kanyemba

Eriza laughed loudly as she remembered Prudence being in the same predicament last year. It was hilarious as Prudence called out helplessly for Eriza to close the door, clinging to the fragile grass wall, totally naked. She was not concerned about that; her fear was being attacked by the goats. Fortunately, Eriza rescued her before her father, who'd heard the screaming from a nearby field, got to the house.

Just as he had done before, Baba Eriza had run from the garden when he'd heard Prudence's shouting, arriving to hear his daughter and granddaughter laughing.

"They wanted to see you before you left," Prudence giggled.

"Stop joking so loudly," he reprimanded, "I thought you'd been attacked by a snake," he continued, a little relieved.

"*Imbudzi Sekuru*," – It's only goats, granddad – Prudence explained over Eriza's sniggering.

Eriza then looked up at her father, who she could see above the grass wall, and they both started laughing loudly.

"Don't laugh, Sekuru," said Prudence, even though she herself was giggling. Baba Eriza continued to snigger as he returned to his task.

❖❖❖

Eriza sunk herself deeper into the bath and was enveloped in the warmth and silky-smooth feel of the Radox-infused water of her Colchester bath. Thoughts of that summer after O Levels and the wait for the results crept back. The results were the only thing that could have interfered with her budding romance with David. They were published in February each year and at the beginning of March those who had achieved a first class returned, if they wished, to lower sixth form. Some, like Christopher, a gifted physics student, who were considered by the school authorities to be too ill-disciplined, were sent telegrams as soon as the results were known, which simply said *Pass and go.* Christopher's *Pass and go* was given even with As in 11 subjects. Throughout that three-month summer wait for the results, all Eriza had hoped for was that David would return to do sixth form too. She had no doubt that she would be back with a first class based on her termly performances throughout the year.

For everyone, the results were relayed by a phone call and the only accessible phone for Eriza was at the post office in Mawiro. On the day the results were due, Eriza walked the nine miles to Mawiro with Naijo, who was waiting for his A Level results. Naijo made the call and when she heard him say the words 'in three days', she almost urged him to enquire about David. She quickly held back because Naijo didn't know about David and her intentions with him. He would have teased her mercilessly. It turned out to be the longest three days of her life, with her emotions veering between elation at her excellent exam results and anxiety about whether David would be back or not.

There was a knock on the bathroom door. It startled her and she tried to silence the splashes of the bath water with her hands. Before she could respond to the knock, Chris called out to her saying that they were off to town but had left some cooked food for her in the kitchen.

"Thank you," she called back, acknowledging the kindness.

She knew it wasn't going to be sadza but wished it were. The water was now lukewarm, and she could have come out of the tub at that point, but with the departure of her flatmates, she decided to half-empty and refill it with more hot water and radox. She was soon engulfed in soap suds, bar the nipples of her breasts which caught her eye. With that, Eriza felt a tingly sensation, one that gave her a sense of déjà vu. She had felt that same sensation under David's right hand on her breast, in Salisbury's Cecil Square Park, that April during her first school holiday as a sixth former.

Eriza loved to relive the events between early March and mid-April of that first term of lower sixth. Today, in a bathtub in England, she suddenly realised, that the period coincided with the Christian 40 days of Lent. She wondered whether she had sinned in doing what she had done during that holy time just over two years ago. Fasting also meant abstaining from all pleasures of life, but until now, she had never questioned her time with David in the park as going against the dictates of Lent. To her, the pleasures of love were a necessity of life and could not be considered as acts of aggression against Lent. Besides, they had only kissed and held each other, but as this was her first time kissing a boy, it was a major milestone in her life – almost as monumental as Eve enticing Adam to that fruit, as told in the Bible.

FIVE

In Chena, girls going through puberty were inducted into the adult world through instilling in them the fear of getting pregnant if they did as little as allow a boy to touch them. It would take a few more years for a girl to bust this myth. For Eriza, that realisation came even quicker because, by being at boarding school, she saw many school 'couples' kissing, with no reported pregnancies. Nevertheless, her Catholic upbringing, which had tempted her to consider the nunnery at 12 years old, still cautioned her against having a boyfriend...until the encounter with David.

As she rationalised things in her head, the penny dropped on one particular issue: Naijo was born in December and he was neither premature nor overdue, and it certainly wasn't through a holy conception. It could only have been as a result of a blatant disregard of the rules of Lent by her parents. Eriza threw water on her face as if to wash the thought out of her mind. As the luxuriously warm water ran down her face, she let her mind take her back to the journey from Chena to lower sixth form.

❖ ❖ ❖

This time around, transport to school was *indodha iyasibonela* – each person to herself or himself – from Salisbury. New students were now coming from all over the country, so it would have been impossible to coordinate their travel arrangements to transport them all at once from Salisbury. In addition, the intake into lower sixth was small; in Eriza's class, there were now only six of them out of 65 students at the start of form one. The remainder of the total intake of 34 students came from other schools in the country.

For Eriza, the return to school that year was unforgettable from the moment the VaMusiyamwa bus arrived in Salisbury and turned the corner towards the railway station. Through the bus window she saw David walking along Railway Avenue with his trunk in tow. Eriza covered her face as she sat in the bath because she was still embarrassed by her reaction. She couldn't recall exactly what she'd done when she saw David but all she remembered were the other passengers staring at her in amusement. To them, David was of no consequence nor was there anything spectacular happening in Railway Avenue to warrant whatever reaction Eriza had displayed.

"They must have thought I was mad," she said to herself and chuckled.

❖ ❖ ❖

The bus drive was about three minutes away from its railway station stop but it seemed like eternity to Eriza, more so because David was walking in the opposite direction. Her mind was working out different strategies to retrieve her suitcase from the top of the bus then pursue and catch up with him. Every second counted.

"*Sekuru, ndingawanewo box rangu nekukurumidza?*" – Uncle, can I get my suitcase urgently please? – she requested of VaMusiyamwa with an embarrassed smile, betraying her fear that he might want to dig into the cause of Eriza's urgent matter.

"*Zvadii muzukuru?*" – What is the rush for my niece? – VaMusiyamwa asked, not waiting for an answer as he added a compliment. "You did well in your exams so let me speak to you in English," he laughed. He then turned to his bus conductor, ordering him to retrieve Eriza's suitcase from the top of the bus.

"But Eriza, your bus to school is from Mbare. You want the Mazungudze bus. You can get it from the Charge Office to Mbare." VaMusiyanwa spoke authoritatively while sitting casually in his driver's seat and surveying the happenings around him through the windows and mirrors. With that, VaMusiyanwa had given Eriza the vital information she needed to take action. David must have been walking to the Charge Office.

When she caught up with David, he was sitting on his metal trunk and reading a newspaper. She startled him with a very tender call of his name. Eriza was in control of herself but David was not. He stood up, shaking with excitement, unable to say a word, then adjusted his clothes before extending his right hand to meet Eriza's for a handshake. She was about to put her suitcase down but quickly reminded herself that she was in Salisbury. They stood hand in hand, speechless and smiling, wanting to kiss. However, such public displays of affection were frowned upon and besides, some of the wayward Salisbury boys would have loudly jeered them while others plotted to stealthily take off with their suitcases.

She climbed out of the tub and dried herself with a bath towel, another gift from Naijo via his girlfriend. She then wrapped it around her body but on catching a glimpse of herself in the huge mirror, she unwrapped the towel allowing her body to momentarily react again to her first intimate encounter with David. She then put on her dressing gown before finally heading across the corridor to her room. Her room. She couldn't quite believe that she had her own room as she searched her suitcase for her toiletries. She saw her jar of Vaseline which was going to be fine for her legs but not for her face; what she needed was a cream that would keep her complexion smooth so long as it didn't lighten it. One thing she was not going to be was a 'dual citizen', that is, one of those women with a white face and a black body. Next was deodorant, her favourite part, and she smiled as she fished out one from the very bottom of her suitcase. As the fragrance engulfed her room, she recalled how quickly the seven weeks of that first term had flown by and how suddenly the Easter break had arrived. On that last day of term, David had taken her by surprise.

❖ ❖ ❖

"I would like to take you window shopping tomorrow in Salisbury," he'd declared in his deep voice. The fact that they were sitting in the silence of the library had made his voice sound even deeper.

"You're too loud David and OK we can go," Eriza replied as she hushed him with a smile.

She was excited, especially because she'd not visited the city in all the days she had been at boarding school. For four years, it had always been Chena, Salisbury then school at the beginning of each term, and then school, Salisbury, a short stop at Amato shop, then Chena. This had led to an ever-widening social gap between her and her township classmates, especially when it came to shopping. Now the time to close that gap had finally come. Unfortunately, none of these classmates would be present to bear witness to her change in status as none had joined the academic elite of fifth form. The more outrageous ones had long disappeared after their poor exam results way back in form two, never to be heard of again, and the remainder were silenced by their GCE results. In fact, there were now just two girls standing in fifth form. Her fellow female survivor, Kumbirai, was also from a strong rural background and had already started studying medicine at Salisbury University as Eriza landed in England.

What that meant was that later, in upper six, they were the only two candidates for the positions of head and deputy head girl. The school staff had a very tough decision to make, so much so that the head decided to interview both girls at the same time and ask them to appoint each other to the positions. They pointed at each other for the top slot and the headteacher defied all logic by settling the appointment in a novel way.

"Elizabeth, since you pointed at Kumbirai before she pointed at you, she becomes the head girl and you will be her deputy," he said smiling.

"With that wisdom of Solomon," said the Welsh-born deputy headteacher, "you girls are free to go. You can see me tomorrow for your badges."

He marvelled at this rare display of judicial wisdom from his boss, especially as this was a man who came to work every Monday morning with a hangover and a strong scent of alcohol that clung to him for the rest of the week.

Eriza and Kumbirai were as amused as the other four members of staff who served as the interview panel. They subsequently heard the two girls laughing and knew that the best decision had been made.

"Pakumanya, Kumbi, anotanga kusimuka haawanzowina," – You see Kumbi, I've always told you that starting off the blocks first doesn't necessarily mean that you will be the winner – Eriza said as they crossed the courtyard, unaware that the headteacher's window was open.

"Ndiko kuzadzikisa kwaunoita njere dzaSoromon?" – Is that your confirmation of the wisdom of Solomon? – replied Kumbirai as they both laughed.

Only the three African members of the panel understood the conversation between Eriza and Kumbirai and they couldn't help chuckling too. The head and his deputy, being white, didn't understand the Shona language so could not follow the girls' jokes.

Though she was looking forward to going back home on that first day of the Easter break, Eriza's thoughts were firmly focused on her trip to the city with David. Spending time with David and going into the big department stores would finally put her on equal footing in shopping etiquette with the now-vanquished township girls. As she sat in the bus with David beside her, she felt her heart racing and the blood heating up inside her veins. Oh how she wished those girls could see her now. In fact, there was a younger version of their type, Emma, a girl in form one, sitting a few seats in front of them. She talked excitedly about shopping in Barbour's Rhodesia just as Eriza's classmates had done every year for four years.

I will be there too today, Eriza thought to herself.

She was sure Emma would have been chastised by Mbuya Mukwesa for saying 'Barbour's Rhodesia' when she could have simply said 'Barbour's'. Nevertheless, Eriza was uncomfortable at her envy of this little girl. It wasn't her fault she was city-wise. Eriza should have taken the opportunity to wisen up years ago.

Instead of getting off the bus in Mbare, they got off at Railway Avenue, just opposite the railway station. Their train tickets allowed David to store his luggage in a cloakroom at the station, making it easier for him when he had to catch the nine o'clock night train to his hometown of Bulawayo. He had offered to store Eriza's suitcase with his so that they were both free to stroll easily through the city streets. For Eriza, this was a welcome change from dragging her suitcase from the school bus to shop at Amato. There she would buy a few items for her mother, who, like most rural residents, steadfastly believed that Amato was the only shop in Salisbury which offered the best deals. That was because Amato himself made them believe that they could bargain to the lowest prices in the country. But Amato was more than just about bargain prices for them. They could shop freely and be served by African shop attendants who respected them, and Amato himself was quite welcoming. It was his wife and daughters who were snobbish but one only had to put up with them at the cash registers.

By 9:30 in the morning, the two love birds had hit First Street, walking in the opposite direction to Amato towards the hub of the big city. The anticipation didn't stop Eriza from looking back at Amato with a fleeting nostalgic urge to do her shopping there. David noticed but ignored it and drew her attention to the Citroen car that drove past them along First Street. It was the talk of the town among the boys who were certain that those wheels would get them any girl in town. Eriza smiled because she could see herself in the passenger seat enjoying the smooth ride under the glorious April sunshine with David at the wheel.

And what a glorious April morning it was, considering that the month came with unpredictable weather. In any one day, the temperatures could drop as low as that felt during the winter months of May and June, then a few hours later, rise to the expected highs of summer. Not infrequently, the days were like this with clear, blue skies that poured out shimmering, bright sunshine which brought the mannequins behind the huge display windows to life. Then all would be randomly punctuated by an annoying drizzle that even the plants didn't seem to want much. As they strolled along the pavement outside Barbour's, it was in one of these crystal-clear windows that Eriza caught a glimpse of their reflections; she was taken aback by how beautiful and happy they both looked.

They walked into the famous store. The scent of new clothes and perfumes filled the air. Young white shop assistants darted about busily, deftly avoiding all contact with their African customers. The few African shop assistants that were around were employed to see to African customers up until the sale or exchange of goods; that was handed over to the white assistants. Once the sale was done, they could step in again, bag the purchases and hand them over to the African customers. For the white customers, it was smiles all around and their only encounter with a black face was at the door, on their way out, unless they had made a big purchase which needed to be carried out of the shop. Some white women even refused having their shopping packed by the African shop assistants but curiously, they expected the bags to be carried to their waiting cars by the same black hands. As Eriza watched all of this, she knew she was being closely watched, especially around small items. Even though her four years in secondary school had enlightened her about a Rhodesia in which Europeans basked in the 'privileges' of racism, she couldn't understand how one could enjoy shopping in this atmosphere.

However, finally being inside this famed department store with David superseded her feelings about the social injustice of the set-up. David nudged her and whispered 'diversity' as he pointed across the shop floor. It was the key word of the last term's school debate. Willard, who to the chagrin of his former geography teacher had returned for sixth form, fired his AK47-style literary salvo with the word 'diversity'. He was a skilled debater. After a few minutes of wizardry with his words, some borrowed from Socrates and Plato, he stunned the debating hall.

"African and European diversity in Africa is a threat to African identity, freedom, dignity and rights."

The eloquence was superb. While the white staff shuddered, the African members of staff and students were thrilled. The atmosphere in the school hall was heavy with excitement.

"This is what Willard was talking about last week," said Eriza as her eyes followed David's finger

David led Eriza to a white mannequin. Well, all the mannequins were white. He started to laugh. He then told Eriza about an incident in one of the department stores in Bulawayo. A cousin of his had come from the village to spend the school holiday with him. They were about nine years old then. One day, David's mum had taken them to shop in the city. His cousin saw these mannequins and was puzzled. Were they dead or alive? He plunged his index finger into the face of one and waited for a reaction. None came. So, he slapped it in the face. Two white women suddenly appeared. One slapped the boy and the other grabbed his arm, dragged him out of the shop calling out to the young African security man to take over. David called out to his mum who was on the other side of the store, deeply absorbed in her shopping. He too was assaulted by the same white woman, presumably for calling out, then handed over to security. They were now accused of trying to steal.

The conclusion to this shocking tale never came because little Emma from the bus appeared from nowhere and interrupted things. She looked genuinely pleased to see two fifth formers and was very deferential to them.

"Ah Mukoma Eriza, you're here too. Are you going to buy me something? My sister Ruth said to say hi to you. You know her Mukoma. She left our school in form two. She said you are very nice." Emma stopped suddenly when she realised that she had not given Mukoma Eriza time to respond.

Eriza remembered Ruth. "Are you Ruth's sister?" she asked anyway.

Ruth was one of the location girls who tormented every rural girl at school. When she did not come back for form three two years ago, her absence was very much felt, and appreciated, throughout the school. She had been horrible to her classmates.

"Yes Mukoma," Emma answered, with an air of expectation for compliments about her sister.

Ruth certainly annoyed Eriza and funnily enough, Emma's behaviour in the bus had reminded her of Ruth even before she had realised the connection. But for some reason, Eriza soon warmed to Emma.

"Are you shopping Emma? Where are your friends? Be careful here in town." Eriza surprised herself with the big-sisterly attitude towards Emma.

"Don't worry Mukoma. I know the town quite well. I'm going to Greatermans where my mother works," Emma replied, walking towards the exit.

"She's quite a nice and confident girl," David whispered to Eriza.

"Surprisingly so, especially with Ruth as an older sister. You remember Ruth?" Eriza replied, as she watched Emma who was already chatting with friends at the door, telling them that Eriza and David were in the shop.

"Yes, I remember her. She was always in some argument with somebody..."

Before David could finish his sentence, they were besieged by three girls and two boys – Emma's friends from the shop entrance. One by one they filed past Eriza and David, grinning at them with knowing curiosity.

"These form ones! All they want is for us to see that they have seen us together," David chuckled. He smiled back at them and they seemed pleased with the response.

"When we're back in school in three weeks' time, I bet they will rush up to us just to say, 'Mukoma, we saw you in Barbour's,' then run off again," laughed Eriza, mimicking the way young teen girls spoke.

They both laughed. Suddenly, David excused himself and walked briskly to one end of the shop, out of Eriza's view and made a very discreet and quick purchase of a necklace for her. She also wanted to make a discreet purchase, but David came back too quickly, so she abandoned the fountain pen she was about to hand over to the shop assistant.

First Street was now crowded with Easter shoppers. The sun continued to blaze and the plants and flowers lining the street created a cacophony of exuberant colours. Eriza pointed at the foliage and hinted to David that Cecil Square was supposed to be even more beautiful than First Street. For David, Cecil Square Park was on the agenda anyway. For four years, at the end of each term, he had spent time with his school friends in this park to pass the time before catching his train to Bulawayo. During those junior years, he saw a few senior boys from his school with their girlfriends stealing treasured moments. The park's acres of manicured lawns, profusion of tropical flowers and shoulder-high bushes were idyllic pastures for a schoolboy and schoolgirl to express their profound and everlasting love, punctuated with kissing and touching of breasts. Their minds were collectively but independently set on Cecil Square, bringing their shopping to an unceremonious end. They just threw cursory glances through some shop windows as they walked to the Square.

The ten-minute walk felt like five. There they found 'their spot' in the park. They had the opportunity to talk about their families and found that they shared very similar values. David lived in Bulawayo but his parents were Shona and had moved to Bulawayo as youngsters. They wanted him to go to school near Salisbury, so he could keep in touch with the Shona culture. David spoke Ndebele fluently though and that day in the park, he sometimes fell back to it, forgetting that Eriza didn't understand. Eriza cautioned him with a cough each time he did, though it turned out that David could only confidently express his love in Ndebele.

"Niyakutanda kakulu wena Eriza."

She understood the expression as a total commitment of love and she amused David by responding in Ndebele – *Siyabonga*.

True to the tradition of sixth formers, in their spot in Cecil Square, they awkwardly ventured just in the perimeters of the world of physical intimacy, marking the start of a long and undying love for each other. They kissed and Eriza allowed David the freedom of her breasts. At first it was very awkward, and more so for David who wanted to touch both breasts at the same time. In the sub-culture of African teen boys, palming a girlfriend's breasts was considered more romantic than kissing her. And David, at 18, had not yet graduated from that romantic vision. However, they soon found that sitting on the park bench and holding each other with Eriza's head on David's chest was more tranquil.

Suddenly, they heard sniggering behind them. It was the same bunch of form one pupils from Barbour's but there were some new faces too. While Eriza was clueless, David knew, as he had done it too. It was standard practice for first formers to track down couples in the park so they could catch some action. Some, like now, would announce their arrival with sniggers so that you would know that they had seen you. Others waited after school reopened to ambush you, *en masse*, at break time and whisper, "*Mukoma*, we saw you in the park," before running off in a flurry of annoying cackles.

The interruption, though unwelcome, was timely. They were both hungry and anyway, it was almost time to collect Eriza's suitcase and head for Mbare so that she could start her journey to Chena. The aroma of meat pies hit them and David bought two from a bakery next to the square. Of course, they'd eaten pies before, but eating them together as they did now made them even more tasty. They took bites off each other's as they walked back to First Street. Pedestrians continued to criss-cross the neat streets attended to by the City of Salisbury Amenities Team. A younger boy from their school deliberately dropped an empty packet of toffee sweets right in front of them and the pavement cleaner. David made him pick it up and dump it in a bin just a few feet away from them. There was much tut-tutting from passers-by and even the boy's friends showed their disapproval by distancing themselves from him.

Eriza and David picked up their pace and Eriza hinted that she had some unfinished business which she needed to complete alone. David missed the cue and just urged her to quicken her pace so that she wouldn't miss her bus. A year later, when they repeated their romantic shopping trip, she reminded him of how clueless he'd been.

"I'd wondered whether you wanted to dump me at the bus stop so that you could have time with another girlfriend," she laughed at the memory.

As Eriza finished dressing, she said to herself, "Well, eventually he learnt." She looked out through her window at the bright green and neatly cut lawn between the nurses' flats and the hospital building. It was lined with even brighter green bushes on either side. Nurses walked back and forth between the flats and the hospital. She spotted two quite happy African girls and secretly wished they were from home, and more so from Chena so she could speak Shona. It hadn't even been a day in England, and she was already missing the warmth of her mother tongue. At that moment, she remembered the offer of food from her flatmates. She wasn't hungry but had to show respect for her flatmates' kindness by eating it.

She went into the small, shared kitchen. There was no food on the counter so she looked inside the small fridge. There was a bottle of milk, butter, cheese and some bits and pieces of food scattered over the two shelves, but nothing resembling cooked food. She peered into the oven, through its glass door and saw a plate of food. Reaching in, she pulled it out and lifted off the top plate to reveal bacon, two fried eggs and French toast. She liked fried eggs more so because her mother never allowed them to eat eggs. That was because Mai Eriza had a business arrangement with Francis over her eggs. Francis was the in-store tailor in Tomas. He also had a side-venture selling boiled eggs to boozers on the train station compound – and Mai Eriza was his supplier of fresh eggs.

She lit the oven and shoved the china plate back to warm up the food, then she took a knife and fork from the drawer and washed them, though she wasn't sure why. That didn't stop her from wondering how clean the plate with her food was. She soon dismissed the thought because any germs would be dead by the time she'd reheated the food but as a precautionary measure, she kept the plate in for five minutes longer than she had planned.

Eriza settled down to eat on the kitchen table, facing the cupboards. There were four of them and she remembered that one had been allocated to her. She liked the yellow paint on the kitchen walls and vinyl tiling on the floor. The food was going down well but would have gone down even better washed down with a cup of tea. There was no sign of tea bags on the kitchen counter and she didn't want to go searching through the cupboards. After finishing her first meal in England, she headed over to the kitchen sink under the window to wash up. She scowled at the sink – it looked clean, but she always suspected that these metal ones were deceptive, so she ran hot water over it while rubbing it hard with a wire gauze. She then washed the two plates with dishwashing liquid and a sponge then placed the plates on a metal rack on the side of the sink. Eriza glanced back at the table just to be sure that she had not left any mess.

In Chena, she would have washed the plates in metal bowls filled with water. Then, using a small slab of Matilda soap on a piece of cloth, she would have rubbed the two plates before rinsing them with clean water in another bowl and placing them on a wooden rack to drain dry. Her mother had always implored her to make sure that the bowl was thoroughly clean before putting clean water in it to wash dirty dishes. She remembered that the pressure to do so intensified after her mother had graduated from the first-aid course. It was rumoured that she did so at the top of her class of fifteen, even beating the two female primary school teachers. She was even less happy with air-drying dishes outside because unseen particles of dirt landed on the clean dishes, as taught at the first-aid seminars. Her solution to this problem was to use a clean, damp cloth to wipe the clean dishes before putting them back in the kitchen.

It was now 5 o'clock in the evening so, in Chena, it would be six. She looked through the kitchen window again as water dripped down her hands into the sink. The trees were flush with leaves here while in Chena delicate buds were just peeking out of branches: the beginning of spring.

Eriza took another look around the kitchen. She couldn't help but kneel to touch the vinyl flooring. It would have made a nice replacement for the earthen floor in their kitchen in Chena. Walking back to her room, she was not sure what to do next until she saw her suitcase on the bed and decided to unpack.

❉ ❉ ❉

A day after her arrival in England she sent a telegram home. It was brief.
Baba naAmai,
Ndasvika zvakanaka.
Eriza

Dad and Mum,
I arrived safely.
Eriza.

❉ ❉ ❉

Mawira Post Office was efficient. Within 36 minutes of its transmission to Mawira, it was delivered to Baba and Mai Eriza and Chena was ablaze with the news. Even Sekuru and Mbuya Mizha left their daughter's home early to spend a little bit more time with Mbuya Mukwesa before proceeding to their own home on the eastern side of the village. Mbuya Mukwesa sat alone on the ground, in front of the kitchen with the telegram on her lap as the August sun beamed down on her. With that piece of paper, she felt as if she was sitting with her granddaughter. Meanwhile, at the Catholic Mission, Sekuru Fani was besieged the minute word of the telegram and the content therein had arrived. He abandoned everything and rushed home. When Mbuya Mukwesa gave him the telegram to read the news for himself, he was surprised to read just five words – words so meagre compared with what he had been told by a few people he had met on the way.

"The girl got there fine but she said it's very cold and she's happy that I told her to carry her jersey," said one woman who had been at Eriza's farewell. Sekuru Fani had simply smiled.

Mai Eriza and Prudence were at the primary school PTA meeting about a mile away when the telegram was delivered. Baba Eriza was of two minds: should he wait for them to return or send for them? He opted for the latter and Comfort was on hand to run to the school and tell them to come home.

He saw Prudence outside the main building and stuttered. "Mu-ko-ko-koma, Se-se-se-se-Sekuru said there is a telegram," he blurted.

Prudence rushed inside to find her grandmother and whispered to her, "Mainini Eriza sent a telegram."

Mai Eriza loudly excused herself, announcing, "Our girl has arrived in England safely. I have to go home."

"You rush off. We shall say a short prayer to thank God," Mistress Takudzwa, a schoolteacher and PTA secretary said, making a note in her minutes.

For the rest of the day, people turned up at the family home to hear more than the telegram could say. In fact, it mattered little that they did not get more, because they simply made up the rest, only to later argue over the veracity of each other's version.

SIX

The following day, Eriza's journey to becoming a nurse began. The first week was dedicated to orientation. There were forms to fill in, uniforms to order, endless introductions and training sessions. A total of 23 girls had been recruited in that year's intake. And what a cohort they were. There were just five white girls in her group, including an Irish girl called Mary, who she recognised as living in the flat opposite hers. The others were all African, well sort of, depending on one's socio-political leanings. They came from Nigeria, Ghana, Kenya and the Caribbean islands of Grenada, Saint Lucia, Jamaica and Trinidad. Jamaica, she had heard of, but the other islands, never. Naijo would probably have heard of them; as her brother was not here to school her, she would have to go and look these islands up herself. What amazed Eriza was that if it weren't for their accents, which immediately lit up any conversation, one would never have thought that they had come from places over 5,000 miles away from Africa.

It turned out that Sister Margaret was some sort of chief nurse who spent most of her time in an office coordinating the training activities of nurses. In the early days of Eriza's training, Sister Margaret spoke with her regularly, taking interest in her progress. However, once she had settled in, she saw less and less of the Sister, which was fine with her.

The training schedule, which was handed to each of them on the first day, started in week two. Eriza was dismayed to find that the first six weeks were predominantly taken up with cleaning and washing the floors of the wards. They were also to be taught how to set up medicine and dressing trolleys. Only after this six-week preliminary training was complete could they be unleashed onto the wards, where practical training was combined with teaching sessions led by a doctor and senior nurse. As far as she was concerned, there were not enough of these sessions. She really looked forward to these times when she learnt about the diseases that afflicted patients. Cancer, in particular, horrified her. It manifested itself in so many ways, anywhere in the body, spreading to other organs so ferociously and painfully that no medicine could halt its invasion or alleviate the ensuing pain. It intrigued her that the human heart cells never succumbed to cancer though.

They then spent three months on each specialist ward, with the first being on the children's ward. There, Eriza saw some very sick children. Some were on drips, lying listlessly as parents sat at their bedside, their faces etched with worry. The experience allowed her to fully understand the extent of her mother's fear at the time of the outbreak of whooping cough in Chena.

She was a six-year-old girl then. Her big sister and hero, Chido, and Naijo, though found wanting in manners by their mother, both protected her fervently. The medical team deployed to the village visited every household, giving advice to families on how to keep away the dreaded infection, which her grandmother believed to be *simori poks.* Her mother had sounded the battle cry in her household to quarantine her brood of three. She got a stick and gathered her children together.

"This stick will inflict more pain on you than that whooping cough will ever do if you do not follow these simple rules," she said very sternly.

She then laid them down. "When visitors come to the house, you leave everything and run to sit under that mutamba tree – come rain or shine. You stay there until we call you back."

The use of the word 'we' made two things clear – first, that mother and father, though father was not there, were together on this, and two, breaking the rules would therefore constitute a doubly serious offence, with punishment to be meted out by both parties.

"Even when we're in the middle of eating?" Naijo asked, horrified.

"More so when you are eating," her mother replied, closing a pot of cooked meat for that day's lunch to reinforce the point. "No rushing off to meet the bus on the road. No playing with other children and that means no school until we say so." She finished, with that 'we' word again.

The following day a family of six – parents and four children – visited the Mukwesa household for some advice from Baba Eriza. It was a perfect opportunity for Mai Eriza to apply the 'whooping cough laws'. Without a word, she took hold of the stick and with that, Chido led the stampede to the mutamba tree. Mai Eriza positioned the stick where it was visibly intimidating to her three children, who sat forlorn, as if there was no hope of ever returning inside where their parents sat with the visiting family.

After what seemed like half a day under the tree, Eriza and her siblings watched the visitors leave. Naijo forgot about the call back signal and immediately charged towards the house. Chido had to wrestle him to the ground. It was essential that Mai Eriza sterilised all the utensils used by the visitors in boiling water. Only once the process was complete could they return. Within 20 minutes, Eriza and her siblings saw their mother appear at the door with a smile. They smiled back. The all-clear had been given.

❖❖❖

When she attended to patients during the cardiology rotation, she thought about the pioneering work of the South African doctor, Christiaan Barnard, who had successfully transplanted a human heart from one person to another. That moment in history had brought South Africa to the attention of the world, and for once in a positive light. At her school, there had been a white South African teacher who claimed to have known Dr Barnard at the University of Cape Town and reported that he had not been a remarkable scholar at all.

"Sir, did you know Dr Hendrik Verwoerd? He killed 69 people at Sharpeville because they refused to carry *pasos*," a boy had asked the same teacher when Barnard was under discussion in one social studies lesson. The boy paused in expectation of an answer but was given none.

"Did you know Sir, that Tsafendas plunged a big knife into Verwoerd's heart, right in parliament? The Zambian parliament celebrated when that happened."

The class collapsed in hysterics.

"Some people say that Barnard could have quickly saved him by stitching a baboon heart in him. Verwoerd was a baboon, Sir. My father said so." He stopped and looked at the teacher with a faint, mischievous smile.

"Tell your father that Verwoerd was a white man like me and not a baboon like...," the teacher caught himself just in time.

❖❖❖

Eriza always thought back fleetingly to this incident whenever she encountered patients who did not like black people. Some would refuse to be touched by any black staff, others spat at them, others refused to take any medication administered by them, and others did all three.

Fortunately, the majority of patients appreciated the care that was given to them, regardless of whether it was given by a black or white nurse. On many occasions, she was told in confidence by some patients that black nurses were more caring. One man asked her if she had heard of Mary Seacole. Eriza hadn't and the man recognised that she'd had no clue.

He then said, "I bet you know about Florence Nightingale though."

Eriza smiled knowingly. She had to move on to the next patient but quickly looked at the man's medical card to check his name – Gerald Jenkins. The stage was set for many more exchanges between them over the three months that he was in hospital. He was a former Welsh coal miner who had moved to Essex so that the warmer and drier weather could help his bronchitis; unfortunately, it was then discovered that he also had a kidney condition.

During one of their conversations, he told Eriza how sickened he was by the prejudice towards black people. That's why he had asked her about Mary Seacole. He did go on to tell Eriza all he knew about the British-Jamaican nurse who had nursed many soldiers during the Crimean War, but was overshadowed by Florence Nightingale. He also gave her some interesting facts about Cecil John Rhodes, the man who had taken over her country, carving a niche of it for himself which he called Rhodesville, otherwise known as Kuwadzana, Mbuya Mukwesa's homeland.

"Your Rhodes hailed from just around the corner in Bishop Stortford," he said, pointing out the window. "He went to your country because of a chest illness like mine. He was told that the sun would burn the germs. Well, the silly bugger helped himself to more than the African sun. Greedy and disrespectful. That's all I saw in his ways."

One day, Jenkins said that he knew the way he spoke to Eriza and other African nurses was wrong, but that's how he and all white people had been made 'to see you'.

"As far as we're concerned every black man is likely to be a serious criminal. You heard about that woman in the next ward who lost her ring. Didn't you? And how she only reported the loss after the morning round carried out by a black doctor was complete. She'd insisted, and I say this word-for-word, 'It was with me up to the time the negro doctor touched me.' The way she spat the words 'touched' and 'negro' out of her mouth! It insulted the educated and professional doctor and she was not even embarrassed when the police brought the ring in a few days later to confirm whether it was hers. They had found it among other items stolen by her nephew. Her nephew!"

"Whenever we see a black person, particularly a black man, we close ranks. Women rally to their handbags and we men think that we have to protect our women," he added, shaking his head in disgust. "I've now stopped calling black people negroes. To me, as a white man, the term conjures dreadful visions of lynchings committed by our brethren in America. Sadistic." Jenkins looked down. Eriza interpreted this as a display of the provenance of shame.

The colour bar was indeed the white man's burden, Eriza thought to herself, feeling sorry for Mr Jenkins, who seemed to be lumbered with this load for his race. She always referred to racism as 'colour bar', as she didn't know what else to call it. All her discussions about it had always been with other black people. But hearing it from one of the tormentors of the African race left her bemused. She thought about her white friends, some of whom seemed genuinely friendly. But, after Mr Jenkin's monologue, she wondered how many of them bore the same burden and how many of them hid hatred underneath. *There is nothing I know about us which revolts them. Instead, they revolt us because of their racism*, Eriza thought to herself.

Eriza's pay as a trainee nurse was £61.46 per month after the necessary deductions for tax and national insurance. She'd received the first pay cheque on the 27th of September. Money per se did not excite her. It was what she could do with it, especially for her family in Chena that did. Even though the English autumn weather was beginning to challenge her, she felt warm sitting on her bed in her room on this, her first payday. Her mind was in Chena, where the September sun would be blazing and bathing the cicadas in its warmth as they chirped merrily. *Msasa* trees would be blooming. Grazing and water for livestock would be almost non-existent. Animals would wander everywhere, chewing cuds of dry grass and drinking muddy water wherever they could find it. Birds would have started to return to nest, but the pickings of food would be meagre.

She pictured the two village wells surrounded by girls collecting water in the early morning. The young novice water carriers were always enthusiastic about carrying buckets of water on their heads. Some teenagers organised romantic rendezvous behind some green bushes near the wells. These bushes were always green, whether it was a dry winter or a hot spring. Sekuru Fani had explained to her that this was because the water table was close to the ground and so would keep the bushes essentially evergreen. Eriza laughed when she remembered that the stolen moments, in most cases, were just early morning greetings and brief holding of hands between the couples. The encounters were nearly always an anti-climax, especially in those cases where the girls involved had younger siblings who were encouraged by their mothers to accompany their big sisters. Nevertheless, the couples would be the talk of the village for the rest of the day, among the teens that is. The boys spoke as if they had experienced the full consummation of love. September, for teenagers, was a time of bliss during a time of dust.

And dust was everywhere – rising behind goats and cattle like mini-tornadoes into which the boys would charge to be rained upon and blinded by dust. They found it exhilarating. The dry grass was perfect, raw material for wildfires, fires that would flush out hares and rabbits the boys would then hunt down with dogs. They were an easy catch when scrambling to escape. Unfortunately, this season, with its searing heat, devastated the livestock and any livelihood that came with it. It was miserable to see cattle so thin and frail criss-crossing the blackened landscape looking for pasture.

It was also a time when the movement of the sun was a hot topic. The primary school teachers explained that it wasn't the sun that moved, but the earth – which they called the world – that travelled around the sun. Only a few children and adults understood this concept but they too would often doubt this because they couldn't actually see or feel the world moving. Eriza was only convinced about the orbiting Earth after a history lesson on Christopher Columbus who sailed to the New World without his ship falling off at the horizon.

"Now I know how Columbus felt when he proved to everyone that the world was round," she had said to Naijo when it all made sense to her.

However, all the village could do was wait for the summer rains that would bring the landscape back to life. And that September, for the Mukwesa family and of course young Comfort, getting gifts from Eriza in the hot and dusty spring would energise them.

She looked at her pay slip now on the desk in front of her. Through it, she saw a picture of her grandmother wearing a new headscarf, black of course, and brown canvas shoes. Her mother sat to her right in a black and white polka dot blouse with a white shawl draped over her shoulders. Her father and Sekuru Fani stood behind them in blue long-sleeved shirts and gold ties. Prudence was all smiles as she held every colour of knickers and bras in both hands. Naijo was holding Che Guevara and Jimmy Hendrix t-shirts, beaming with pride. There was still room for Comfort. It would be unforgivable to send a package home without a gift for him. She nearly shed a tear just thinking about him. Such a kind boy. Eriza jumped off the bed, pulled out a list from her bedside table and was pleased to see that, give or take, she could part with about £19 to cheer her family back home, as well as buy all that Comfort had requested.

"Give or take," she said to herself loudly and laughed as Tomas' shop came to mind.

She recalled when the shop sign that read 'Tomas's' had created a literacy crisis which challenged the grammatical abilities of both teachers and pupils at Chena Primary. It could have been resolved very easily and quickly if people had listened to the new primary school teacher who had counselled that the last 's' was redundant and Tomas, though white, was an illiterate to allow a sign that so brazenly defied the rules of English grammar. But the senior teachers, all four of them, ganged up against the poor woman and argued for the sign to remain as was, thus perpetuating the misinformed grammatical goings-on to the rest of the school. The gang of four remained victorious until Reverend Hugh Pugh, the newly appointed school superintendent for Chena and the surrounding villages, visited the primary school on inspection duty one day. He examined five exercise books of standard six pupils and was struck by the proliferation of the apostrophe and the extra possessive 's' on nouns already ending with an 's'. When he raised the issue, Kumbirai challenged him, evidencing Tomas' shop sign. He confirmed he had seen the sign but added that Mr Tomas was from Portugal, where English was not even heard of in some parts of the country. In those same parts of Portugal, donkeys were the preferred means of transportation — but what that fact had to do with anything was anyone's guess.

"Tomas should actually be 'Tomaz'," Reverend Pugh added. "Obviously, he was trying to squeeze into what was left of the British empire by badly anglicising his name, given that the Portuguese-African colonies of Mozambique and Angola were orbiting out of Portugal's control."

It was very uncharacteristic of Reverend Pugh to speak so unkindly about another white person. What his sentiments made clear however, was that he was not at all enthralled by the idea of decolonisation in southern Africa, for which the Portuguese were seen as a weak partner in holding back African aspirations.

This episode of the misplaced apostrophe occurred a few months before Eriza had left the school so she too was a victim of the double-possessive problem. Unfortunately, she carried the practice with her to secondary school. It was her admiration of Julius Caesar that freed her. In one of her form one essays, she wrote: *Julius's conquest of Britain.* Her history teacher struck out the last 's' and said it could have worked perfectly if she had written *Caesar's conquest of Britain,* making it clear that the possessive 's' was never added to a noun which ended with an 's'. When she returned to Chena that April for her first holiday from secondary school, Reverend Pugh had already eradicated the problem. Within nine months, a new headteacher, Mr Philemon Kanyemba, was installed.

Anyway, 'give and take' was the way in which Tomas' carried out his business dealings. Transactions were a combination of barter and hard cash. There was never a precise price for any item. In the local parlance, 'give and take' was *buya tiyapangana,* and both Mr and Mrs Tomas had mastered this phrase as if it was their creation, coating it with a mystic smile. The Tomas' rural clientele was far from awash with cash, but had plenty of agricultural products such as maize and peanuts. Mr and Mrs Tomas accepted these products in exchange for sugar, tea, salt, dripping and clothing. Women like Mai Eriza trekked the nine-mile journey to Mawiro with loads of raw and dry products on their heads and returned home in the late afternoon with bags of refined and manufactured goods. The Tomas' put them through a tough bargaining process which displayed the ruthless business acumen of this Portuguese couple. Mrs Tomas was a calculating and benevolently mean co-shopkeeper. For five pounds in weight of sugar, which in cash was worth one shilling and six pence, she demanded 12 pounds in weight of peanuts worth three pounds ten shillings. If unacceptable, she would throw in a packet of tea leaves worth six pence, all the time watching and stalking the customer with that smile which preceded her saying *"Buya tiyapangana"*, and adding about ten or so lollipops worth three pence, saying *"pikanini"* – for the children. With that, the deal was closed. Year after year, Mr Tomas would sell bags and bags of peanuts and maize to the Grain Marketing Board as if he ran a farm and not a shop.

Still admiring her first pay cheque, Eriza wondered what her first day of serious shopping in England would be like. During the first few weeks, she'd only used the local corner shop for simple items but had noticed that the things she wanted for her family were not sold there. At Tomas', everything was stocked. She could see why the words 'General Dealer' came after 'Tomas's'. For this shopping trip, she would have to go into Colchester town.

Although all 23 of the girls in her intake were friendly with each other, Eriza had become close friends with Mary O'Driscoll, an Irish girl. Mary was Catholic and on one of Eriza's first Sundays, they bumped into each other at the local Catholic church. They immediately started chatting and walked back together to the flats via the corner shop. At the shop, Mary bought two lollipops and gave one to Eriza, just like her mother used to when she had returned from Tomas'. But the lollipop also brought back a bit of a nasty childhood memory, of Ndondo, a white farmer near Chena. But nevertheless, sharing lollipops was the first step towards a deep affection between these two girls, cemented by a Catholic bond which negated their racial difference. Both had identical goals with their first pay cheque too – to give to their families. Within five weeks into their training, they had become inseparable as they accompanied each other to evening prayers and Bible studies.

"*Nouvelle riche*," Eriza announced as Mary burst into her room a day after payday. The girls were so free with each other, so this was not unusual.

"I didn't know you spoke French in your country," Mary said, surprised.

"No, I don't, but I recall some French and Latin phrases I learnt at school. Didn't you do any languages at your school?"

"Oh ya, Latin. *Casus belli*." Mary was thrilled with her enduring knowledge of Latin. "But lots of Latin words are used in church, as you know," she added.

Eriza laughed too. She remembered her mother's prayers which now and then were gilded with Latin words. Eriza suspected that Mary's attachment to the Latin phrase which meant 'cause of war' reflected, as it did in her, the civil strife going on in their respective countries – denial of rights to Africans in Rhodesia and denial of rights to Catholics in Northern Ireland.

"We, the newly rich, must get into town," Eriza declared.

"In one hour," Mary said and ran out to her room.

Eriza knew that Mary would take that full hour to get ready, mostly dedicated to applying her elaborate make-up. This gave Eriza more time to reminisce over her shopping trips in Salisbury with David.

She, like the other rural girls, never had much money, but the other girls, the township girls, seemed to have endless amounts of it. Some students referred to them as *nouvelle riche*, but mockingly so. They would talk excitedly about their shopping sprees in the big stores, not just Barbour's, but also Greatermans, Edgars, Truworths, Woolworths and Meikles, reeling off the names like a roll call of honour. They'd go there during the school holidays in city buses, or were driven by their mothers, who they called 'mum', not *mhai* as the village girls did. They'd trawl the shops for the latest fashions – tight jeans, mini-skirts and Italian shoes. However, back at school, they couldn't show off their prized purchases because uniforms were mandatory, seven days a week.

But, just as they recognised and condemned her strong, simple but intellectually focused rural background, she loathed their supposed sophistication, which sustained one side of the argument of the perennial but utterly dull topic of school debates, 'Town Life is Better than Country Life'. They laughed and joked about their visits to their family villages that apparently always smelt of cow dung and goats. They shivered when they talked about swarms of flies, pit toilets, no electricity and all manner of unpardonable things. Then they would turn to any rural girl in their vicinity and ask, mouths curled in disgust, "How do you live there?"

If there was more time to tease, they would turn to the wonders of town life, prattling on about the pleasures of eating ice-cream sold by vendors riding special ice-cream cycles. They were regular cinema goers and had become avid followers of the Tarzan films they had first seen as youngsters. Now they had graduated to watching James Bond and Wild West films starring the likes of Sean Connery, John Wayne and James Stewart in the Odeon Cinema, where they sat apart from whites. Their favourite singers were the Simanje Manje girls who performed in the entertainment halls of the 'locations'. These Simanje Manje girls were from South Africa and regularly toured the towns and cities of Rhodesia. Occasionally, some of the local girls would try to imitate the group and usually got away with it. However, most disbanded as quickly as they had mushroomed because their supposed manager, usually a boyfriend to one of the girls, invariably fleeced the takings from the gate at the biggest show and ran off with another girl from the same group.

The township girls were also obsessed with The Beatles. At the school's Saturday evening socials, they danced to the band's music, shaking their heads like the hippie entourage that followed the world-famous band everywhere. They didn't like their natural hair so they straightened it with hot combs to make it move like the white girls' hair. However, that all changed at the start of form three. That January, they all nearly came back to school with semi-bald heads. The story was that during the school holidays, some nationalist youths had roamed about the locations armed with scissors and 'offered' to cut the hair of any young female who had straight hair. It was an offer that could not be refused. As they sheared, because that is what they did, not cut, they 'encouraged' their 'customers' to remain truly African. None of her immediate schoolmates had suffered this fate because once the first two heads had been shaved, word got around and the rest of the girls just walked into barber shops for a proper, even cut. Others exiled themselves to *kumusha* – the rural homestead – where they stayed with their grandparents to 'lie low', despite the fact that *kumusha* was dusty and smoky and no good for their hair. This cultural revolution even spread to those mostly young women who used face-lightening creams. It was tricky though because to stop using the creams suddenly led to unsightly blotches, and in some cases, permanent disfiguration. To continue using them was to incite the wrath of the nationalist youth. Nevertheless, as brutal as all this was, Eriza was pleased with this African awakening. Her heart and mind told her that it was needed, and Naijo confirmed it.

There were some behavioural traits that the revolution could not fix, however, as there was still much that the township girls could denigrate about African life. Take breakfast. They used the word to distance their morning meal from the rural one of tea with porridge, left-over sadza or occasionally, bread, the latter being a luxury. Instead they ate Kellogg's cornflakes, followed by fried or boiled eggs with bacon and buttered bread or toast. It was washed down with a cup of coffee or juice, not tea. Tea was common. Eriza was horrified when some of these girls said that they went for days without eating sadza, instead eating rice, potatoes, macaroni or spaghetti. For Eriza, it was natural to have sadza twice a day, for lunch and supper. While her vegetables were relished with peanut butter, these girls' vegetables were cooked in oil. Every meal had meat enriched with gravy cubes.

Then there was television. The location girls bragged about watching it till ten at night, when the one and only channel went off air. It wasn't as if they were deprived of electronic entertainment in Chena. Baba Eriza had bought a small portable, battery-operated radio for his children and granddaughter and, of course, for him to listen to the 8 o'clock evening news. In fact, on Saturday mornings, African radio channels lit up many a rural household. The DJs gave dazzling presentations, bringing all the Simanje Manje hits and the music of The Beatles right into the home. Eriza was particularly fond of the 9:30 slot on African Radio Station sponsored by Zimbabwe Furnitures. The advertisement, which came at the very beginning of the programme, was bold when blasted out by the DJ.

"Nyore Nyore Zimbabwe Furnitures!" It was quite ironic that the word Zimbabwe, which was banned from everyday use by Rhodesians as it was deemed politically subversive, was of no concern when it was referring to a furniture store.

The DJ always played the same songs, depending on where on the charts they had fallen that week. Baba Eriza's favourite was 'Turn! Turn! Turn!' by The Byrds but because he liked The Seekers, he thought the song was theirs, especially after learning that a man by the name of Pete Seeger had something to do with it. The rural logic of her parents always amused Eriza. Her father was often heard humming the song while in the fields attending to his maize crop, even after it had fallen off the top ten list. The only line of the lyrics he could sing was *There is a season, turn, turn*. It probably spoke to his livelihood, the one he carried out on the lush green landscape with animals grazing the green grass, that would change into a barren land in winter.

Then there was Bob Marley's song 'No Woman No Cry'. Naijo loved that song. The DJ used to announce it in a loud, dramatic manner and with a flourish.

"Aaaand! From Kingstonnnnn, Jamaica! Iiiiiiit's Bob Marley and the Wailerrrrrs."

Naijo would stand perfectly still to savour the wailing before he heard Bob Marley's voice, after which he'd bow his head and sway as if paying reverence to royalty. He admired Marley's Rastafarian movement but struggled to understand why they involved Haile Selassie, the Ethiopian emperor. Various other programmes would play on during the day, but nothing was like that first morning programme. At night-time, Sekuru Fani would take the radio with him to his hut. Naijo knew that he was listening to Radio Dar, which was broadcast from the Tanzanian capital, Dar es Salaam. Sekuru Fani disregarded the rumour the police had devices that pinpointed any household that tuned in to Radio Dar. The broadcasts were denunciations and admonitions of the white settlers in Rhodesia. They inspired Naijo immensely and he admitted that he was never the same again after listening to them. As far as he was concerned, Radio Dar presented a manual to take up arms against European rule in southern Africa.

❖ ❖ ❖

Eriza heard Mary finally coming up in the corridor of her flat, signalling that it was time for her to get ready. As she turned the handle to the bathroom door, she noticed a small pamphlet neatly posted up on the door. It was an advertisement for a music festival in Norwich in mid-October. She couldn't think of where Norwich was in relation to Colchester but remembered that the royal family made some sort of pilgrimage to Sandringham in Norfolk. The pamphlet also triggered memories of Lorenco Marques. Eriza, Naijo and Prudence would listen to Radio Lorenco Marques, broadcast from present day Maputo in Mozambique, well into the night. One show they all liked was sponsored by Lucky Strike and Peter Stuyvesant cigarettes. The music featured had brought Eriza's musical tastes on a par with that of the location girls, even though she lamented that such beautiful music was mixed up with cigarette smoking. Then she remembered something she had heard that dismayed her even more. At Glastonbury, the biggest music festival, she had heard the hippies indulged ferociously in drugs too. She wrinkled her nose in disapproval as she refocused on the pamphlet, with any further thoughts on the matter interrupted by Mary.

"Liz", Mary called out. Eriza had given Mary the go ahead to call her Liz about two weeks after they'd met. There was an English girl who had suggested that 'Betsy' would be a suitable replacement for Elizabeth. She flatly refused because this was the same girl who had said loudly, in the canteen a few weeks before, "I'm tired today. I worked like the blacks." As far as was Eriza was concerned, the nickname Betsy was tainted and so she calmly told the English girl to call her Elizabeth, and Elizabeth only.

"I think I want to buy a record player as well today," Mary continued. "And then we can buy some records," she added with excitement.

Eriza looked at Mary and could see why they had become friends. It was as if she'd sensed that Eriza had music on her mind.

"That would be fantastic," responded Eriza, as she thought about buying The Beatles' new album *Abbey Road*. She smiled at Mary, who was already redoing her make- up.

The shopping trip turned out to be memorable. Every possible moment was captured on camera, with complete strangers acting as photographers. They both had to feature in all photos with their shopping bags prominently displayed. Eriza could not believe that she, as an African, could walk freely in and out of any store, with a white girl, and be graciously served by whites too. The other few blacks and even Indians she saw were shopping freely too, so it must have been real.

The happy occasion was however marred by one white man who objected, with venom, to a black and a white girl going about their business led by the spirit of their hearts rather than the colour of their skins.

Mary shouted back at him with equal measure, "You vermin! Go back to the sewer!"

With that, Mary invited those around them to pile on more verbal abuse than she could if she wanted to maintain her modesty. Ironically, the man turned into a dirty alleyway that was a dead end. Groups of young men surrounded him, calling him a pervert even though they didn't know what the cause of the altercation between him and the two girls was about.

Eriza, who always remained calm in such situations, was taken aback by Mary's fire. However, she was pleased because Mary's reaction to the racial abuse also somehow released an anger in her, though she could not let it out in the way Mary had. She then spotted a middle-aged man with a collar, a priest, walking towards them; she was sure she'd seen him on a television show when she managed to watch some TV in the hospital common room.

"Well done girls," he said, before nonchalantly walking away.

She looked at Mary, the redness on her face now gone. Unknown to them, a young white man, who had agreed to snap them, had continued to do so during this nasty episode. He handed Eriza the camera with a very warm smile, and the girls resumed their shopping. The following week, when they had developed the pictures, the two girls doubled up in hysterics over their warrior-like poses.

There was no shop that was spared of their enthusiasm. Despite the temptation to overspend, both girls ensured that they had bought gifts for their beloved relatives first before splashing out on themselves, buying music, jewellery, knick-knacks and, for Mary, make-up. Six hours later they were finally done, after which they made their way to the station to take a bus back to Colchester Infirmary.

Back in the flats, each went straight to their respective rooms to organise their purchases. But Eriza was compelled to write Naijo a letter, especially after the confrontation that had interrupted their day full of adventure. She now had enough material to keep him amused.

SEVEN

Dear Brother,

I'm sure that you heard the news of my safe arrival. We can both imagine the relief and happiness it must have brought to Baba naMhai and Mbuya. Mbuya especially, because she had confided to me, just a few days before my departure, that she thought she had seen a bird falling from the sky. She was still not convinced when I told her that it was Comfort and the other boys who were catapulting doves as they flew over the back field in large numbers and downed several at a time. You know the same thing you used to do.

Anyway, I'm beginning to settle already. The hospital is very big and Harare Hospital is miniscule in comparison. I have seen a few African nurses but I think they are from the West Indies. They are very friendly but when they talk amongst themselves, I am lost. But then again, I've only been here for a few weeks and there is much to learn.

I don't know how soon you will be back in Chena but when you do go home, take those GCE revision books to Prudence before she returns to school. Her mid-year school report was not as we expected.

Look after yourself. There will be more news in my next letter.

Your loving sister,

Eriza

PS: By the way, the dressing gown set is beautiful. Tell your girlfriend that she has acceptable taste.

When Naijo read the letter, he had indeed already heard from Mr Kanyemba about the telegram from Eriza to their parents. Mr Kanyemba had been making regular visits to the university campus as he was studying part-time for a sociology degree. When he had news from Naijo's family he would drop in to see him or, if he could not see him in person, he would leave a note in his pigeonhole in his hall of residence.

With the letter on his desk, Naijo reflected on the life of his baby sister. He laughed when he read the *PS*. She was very clever so she could easily have done medicine, with those three Bs at 'A' Level, but she hadn't done chemistry. However, Eriza's priority was getting a salary as soon as possible so that she could provide for her family, and nursing was the one discipline that enabled her to use her intelligence and get paid at the same time. She was quite happy to do the training at Harare Hospital, but she had still applied to study in England, mostly at the insistence of Baba Eriza, who had dreams of his daughter becoming a doctor. But Naijo knew that his sister had an adventurous spirit, so it was not at all a surprise that when the opportunity to train in England came, she took it without hesitation. Her father ignored that she was going to train as a nurse because as far as he was concerned, she was coming back home as a doctor.

The letter in front of Naijo revealed a grown woman, one far removed from the teenage girl he had escorted, together with their father, to boarding school for the first time when she was 13 years and 11 months old. That was on a January day. It had rained and they were saved from being drenched and muddied because the bus stop was just about ten yards from their doorstep. That was the only time living so close to a dusty road was an advantage because in the dry winter months the house would be clouded with dust each time the bus drove past. Eriza and Naijo knew the bus driver as VaMusiyamwa – Musiyamwa being his totem name. To their parents and grandmother, he was also known by his real name – Karengera. Although Mbuya Mukwesa's totem name was Gushungo, her grandmother's mother totem name was Musiyamwa. That made VaMusiyamwa as close a relative to Mbuya Mukwesa as Sekuru Fani was to Mai Eriza, and that meant for all of them bus rides to any destination on the route to Salisbury were free. The light-brown bus was also known as 'Musiyamwa' and the name was written in black on both sides of the bus.

For the momentous two-hour-and-forty-five-minute journey to Salisbury, with VaMusiyamwa at the helm, Eriza was dressed in her primary school uniform and a new pair of black shoes with white socks bought from Tomas' General Store on those same *buya tinapangana* terms. There were multiple stops along the route but the first main stop was at Mawiro Railway Siding where some of the passengers alighted for Tomas' or for the slow afternoon train to Bulawayo.

Naijo could tell that it was all very exciting for Eriza, especially as she'd never been to Salisbury before. She'd heard a lot about the glamour and glitter of city life though, mostly through hearsay that had trickled down from those that worked in menial jobs among the sleek and polished city workers. As the bus approached the outskirts of Salisbury, traffic began to build up.

"So many different cars," she whispered to her brother.

"There are many more in town," Naijo said very casually. He was, after all, a one-year veteran of the journey into the city and not a novice like Eriza was. At one of the many minor stops, a couple known to Baba Eriza got off the bus saying that they were going to Mufakose, a township outside Salisbury. The only township Eriza had heard about was Highfields – *KuHaifiridzi* – which apparently was the centre of urban excitement. Quite a few of the location girls she would go on to meet at her new school lived there. These girls displayed the true character of *Haifiridzi*: an air of invincibility. Suddenly, a truck loaded with new cars overtook their bus and blocked Eriza's and Naijo's view. He knew she'd never seen such a truck before and smiled to himself as he caught the look of awe on her face.

"Eriza, when you finish school, you will be able to buy yourself one of those," a Chena woman whom she knew as Tete Mugodi said, pointing to one of the cars. She was jovial, short and plump, but pretty. She moved to one of the seats vacated by the Mufakose couple, something Baba Eriza was praying she wouldn't do.

"We didn't get a chance to say hello earlier," Tete Mugodi said to Baba Eriza, violently settling into her seat.

"I didn't see you at the back," he lied.

She was well known for blabbering and exaggerating gossip. When she got going, she often crossed the line that separated what was appropriate for a woman to say to a man. Fortunately for Baba Eriza, Tete Mugodi settled on talking to Eriza and Naijo. She told them that she'd been to their schools, and when Eriza showed surprise, she quickly clarified.

"Not as a student but as a janitor." However, her job description could be summarised as a cleaner. "When you are all *gradutes* I won't need to travel on this bus again. I can get a lift in your cars," she laughed loudly.

Tete Mugodi soon realised that Eriza's attention was taken by traffic and pedestrians. She also looked through the bus window and saw, for the umpteenth time, what Eriza was seeing for the first time: white men dressed in suits coming out of cars and going into tall buildings and white women scornfully referred to as *mamisisi*, knocking the pavements in their high heels. The African pedestrians were very friendly to each other in contrast to the whites, who looked so unhappy. Eriza wondered why. They were rich and had everything that she knew to be nice. She then spotted five burly and sun-burnt white men in safari suits. Their demeanour was aggressive. She had a good look at the fourth one at a traffic light. The rain had slowed down and those who were already wet crossed the streets.

"That's a *mubhunu* – an extremely racist white farmer," Baba Eriza said. However, he realised that the look of disdain on Eriza's face was probably because the white man's muddy boots were messing up a clean pavement. He knew his daughter, but he continued anyway.

"They've taken all the good farming land. Don't be fooled by his raggedness. His type represents some of the richest white men in this country, while their farm workers are the poorest," he added forlornly.

As Naijo listened to his father, he thought of his grandmother's ancestral home and wondered whether by coincidence, the ragged white man now 'owned' Kuwadzana. He also recalled, as told by Sekuru Fani, that Africans were once not permitted to walk on the pavements but in the streets, but he didn't know when that changed. His father had confirmed it. They all remained quiet for the remaining 16 minutes it took for the bus to stop at Mbare Market.

As they got off the bus, their father asked Eriza to hold on to Naijo's hand while he carried her new suitcase. She felt humiliated because it made Naijo feel pompous but she dared not disobey her father. They eyed each other, with Eriza making faces at her brother as their father bade farewell to VaMusiyamwa, thanking him for the free ride. They made their way to a United Bus to take them to the City Magistrate Courts, more popularly known as the Charge Office, simply because a visit there led to a...charge. From there, they took another bus to the railway station before getting a fourth, the school bus, to Chikabwe High School. They could have walked from the Charge Office to the railway station, but it was still raining in Salisbury.

❈ ❈ ❈

Naijo suddenly jumped out of the reverie that had taken him back five years and stared at Eriza's letter in his hands. He looked through his window and remembered that he needed to get to Mbare to buy some mesh wire for his mother, who wanted to use it to build a fowl run. Over the years, VaMusiyamwa carried goods back to his parents on his bus, dropping them right at their doorstep. Mbuya Mukwesa always gave him a bowl of her sour milk and hot sadza when he did. His passengers understood and allowed him time to eat while talking to Baba Eriza if he was at home.

Baba Eriza looked forward to seeing VaMusiyamwa because he updated him on the political goings-on in the city and the rest of the country. On top of that he would always leave him the daily *Rhodesia Herald* newspaper, allowing Baba Eriza to corroborate what he had just been told. On one of these sour-milk-and-sadza stops, Baba Eriza was told about a crucial political development. Apparently, the white Rhodesian government was setting up concentration camps in some parts of the country to stop freedom fighters from mingling with the masses. After VaMusiyamwa's departure, he went on to read about the progress made by Frelimo in Mozambique to rid the country of Portuguese rule. Given that the *Herald* was a mouthpiece of whites in Rhodesia and all colonials in southern Africa, its admission of the retreat of the Portuguese was no piece of propaganda. He was satisfied.

When Naijo made it to Mbare, he saw VaMusiyamwa and told him about the consignment of wire mesh. Mbare, as usual, was buzzing with people engaged in the same kind of market activity which had mesmerised him and Eriza during their school journeys – market women in makeshift stalls diligently and earnestly selling anything from sewing needles to hammers, sweets to cakes, handkerchiefs to yards and yards of cloth, and small perfumed face soap bars to huge bars of Matilda – *matirida* – laundry soap. Then there were the ice-cream hawkers and women with all sorts of wares, plying them illegally through any path they could make through the market. It only took one of the official stallholders to report them and the market police would be all over them.

Amid all this were young men who fell into two groups. The first group sold 'miscellaneous' items which Eriza would come to know during her time in England as goods that had 'fallen off the back of a lorry'. The second were those who were not gainfully engaged in any market activity but kept a very close eye on the proceedings. These were perhaps some of the most skilled pickpockets in the world. However, mingling with and blending in the market crowd were plain-clothes market police who could spot the likely victims of pick-pocketing as well as the pick-pockets themselves with ease. The market police generally ignored the illegal hawkers because most of them pretended to be working for some of the stallholders. When challenged they would often say they were taking goods as orders to the other side of the market and would even name a stallholder as the supplier. For the police to ask them to walk back to verify this was useless because the illegal traders led them all over the place until either something urgent came up or the police just gave up. On top of that, some of the stallholders were in cahoots with these illegal traders to maximise their sales.

Confidently, Naijo waded through the field of market merchandise and people until he got the best deal for mesh wire. In no time it was on the top of VaMusiyamwa's bus and, by three that afternoon, his mother would receive it.

EIGHT

Eriza's first year of nursing flew by. She had had her fair share of bouts of homesickness but the friendships she had forged, and the hectic schedule, all kept her suitably distracted. Her sense of adventure and practical approach to life had also blossomed and so as the British would say, she just had to 'get on with it.'

Naijo graduated during her second year. Before the ceremony, she had reserved herself a picture of Naijo wearing his graduation gown. Eriza was excited and had sent him a brand- new, Romanian-made black three-piece suit for the occasion. Just to be on the safe side, she also bought him a white shirt, a blue tie and a pair of black Italian shoes. To record the event, she wanted to be sure that her brother was suitably dressed for the day. She also sent Naijo some money to hire a photographer. Naijo was against the idea at first because he saw it as an unnecessary expense. Eriza got wind of it and simply subverted him by enlisting the services of his girlfriend, Nomsa. Nomsa knew that to be in league with the sisters of one's boyfriend would yield enormous dividends as one headed down the road to the altar. So, she happily obliged. The whole family attended the ceremony. Mbuya Mukwesa apparently wondered what all the fuss was about. But she loved Nigel's suit.

"It's like he's getting married," she'd said.

The graduation photo of the now Nigel Sibidi Mukwesa, LLB joined the array of Eriza's photos in the lounge in Chena.

Eriza had learnt so much in her first year. One was the danger of asbestos and she had not hesitated to warn her family. Despite this, they all continued to clamour for asbestos roofing on the new house Eriza was planning to build. But she stood her ground. Sekuru Fani, with whom she corresponded on the building projects, only became convinced when Eriza, in one of her letters, reminded him of his two boyhood friends who had been asbestos miners in Shabani and had died from severe coughs three years before her departure. They were not bewitched because of their money but had contracted asbestosis. She knew that once he had read 'asbestosis' he would acquiesce. In the same breath, she asked about Sekuru Mhizha's health; he'd been an asbestos miner too and when she'd left Chena, he was already coughing hard. So, in that very same letter she'd enclosed a postal order remitting the funds for corrugated tin sheeting.

From the moment he'd read that letter, Sekuru Fani practised the proper pronunciation of asbestosis to make a convincing case for zinc roofing to counter the village critics. And with him at the helm of the anti-asbestos movement, Chena became the 'Tin Village' it is to this day.

Eriza had made progress in rebuilding her parents' homestead. In letters to Eriza, Naijo confirmed and detailed the progress. The two huts were now a four-bedroom brick house with corrugated roofing. There was a master bedroom for her parents, a bedroom for her grandmother and Prudence, another for Naijo and yet another for Sekuru Fani which he never occupied. No one encouraged him to move in because it would not have been appropriate for him to have his companions, like Ceciria, join him, especially with Mbuya Mukwesa next door. Heaven forbid! However, Eriza was never told that Sekuru Fani continued to dwell in his hut.

Mai Eriza had objected to the inclusion of a kitchen as a room in the new house. She wanted to keep the old one. This suited Mbuya Mukwesa because her beautiful earthen pots remained undisturbed in the hut of a kitchen that Naijo was quick to call a museum once the house was finished. Naijo had written to Eriza that the old kitchen would remain.

"It seems to me that Mbuya believes that her earthen pots would lose their mystique in a foreign environment,' he joked in one of his letters to Eriza.

The one thing that Eriza did insist on was a fireplace in the sitting room so that her grandmother could warm herself in the house rather than in the outdoor kitchen. The lounge was now adorned with two large windows, one facing the east and the other the west, allowing abundant sunlight in for most of the day. Fencing around the house was successfully resisted by both her grandmother and father. They felt that it would isolate them from the other villagers where everybody saw themselves as part of one big family. Mbuya Mukwesa was frank about it.

"*Ndiye Eriza* – it was she Eriza – who had problems with the goats, not us," she said laughing, remembering the incident with Eriza's knickers. "But there are some people one wouldn't mind keeping out," she'd added, taking a swipe at Ceciria.

Eriza also sent money to furnish the house along with a list of items to buy. Mai Eriza was in her element when the time came to start buying them, starting off with sofas and a glass display cabinet. Once the cabinet was in place, filling every square inch of its interior was the next step. First were water glasses, china plates and cups and two medium-sized china teapots. Forks, knives, tablespoons and numerous salt and pepper cellars then filled every gap between the larger items. Mbuya Mukwesa wondered why these items were necessary. No one except Baba Eriza ate their food with a knife and fork, and for that he needed just one of each and could then alternate them with his old set. The grey three-seater sofa was placed along the wall under the east window to the left of the front door. This was strategic positioning – only visitors could sit there, giving them full view of the photographs which hung on the walls. Mbuya Mukwesa suggested though that the village visitors were ideally suited to be entertained under the trees during the day and in the kitchen or around the outside fire in the evening.

The bottom half of the wall of photos was taken over by a massive radiogram, on top of which were more framed pictures. A wall calendar, over which the months and dates of the year were obscured by the inscription *Nyore Nyore Zimbabwe Furnitures*, hung on one side of the radiogram. On either side of the words were images of two people, a man and a woman who looked as if they were pleased with the easy – *nyore* – credit terms of the furniture store. On Saturdays, as always, in the morning, this very radiogram instead of Sekuru Fani's small radio, now roared out the Nyore Nyore advert with the DJ narrating the virtues of the furniture giant. The small radio was now a dedicated Radio Dar mouthpiece. With the DJ's shouts from the radiogram, the images of this man and woman on the calendar came alive, especially when the DJ was joined by a sweet female voice describing various items such as a grey sofa set, a glass cabinet and a mahogany dining table and matching coffee table. It was as if they were broadcasting live from 'The Mukwesa Lounge and Dining Rooms' because, by then, they did indeed also have a four-seater mahogany table and a matching coffee table.

The only slight difference was that the chairs and table weren't from Nyore Nyore; well, not directly, anyway. Sekuru Fani, who was also a carpenter, had ignored the furniture store's advert and instead commissioned hand-made chairs and tables from an African carpenter he knew in *Haifiridzi*. His reasoning was that the furniture sold by Nyore Nyore was made by these Highfield carpenters anyway, so why not cut out the middle man. The tables were Mai Eriza's pride and joy. At one point, Mbuya Mukwesa and Prudence were worried that Mai Eriza was projecting her daughter on the tables, judging by the way she feverishly polished them every day even though they were rarely used. Anyway with the daily dust showers from the bus, she had to clean them every day.

But it was the photographs, all 53 of them, that gave a visual representation of Eriza's new life to all in Chena. Prudence had observed that each time visitors were entertained in the house, her grandfather always proclaimed at some point, with a grand circular movement of his right hand over the photos that "This is all Eriza." Mai Eriza, who was embarrassed whenever her husband did this, would comment, "They are just photographs." Prudence, with her incisive humour, nicknamed the wall of pictures 'The Memory of The Holiest Conception', especially after her grandmother placed a Catholic calendar with an image of 'Christ the Redeemer' among the pictures.

When Prudence described the scene to Naijo, he laughed 'till tears rolled down his cheeks. He in turn named the pictures of Eriza and her friend Mary, and there were many of these, 'Ebony and Ivory'. He was chuffed, when many years later, Stevie Wonder and Paul McCartney released a song with the same title. The pictures did indeed go on and on: Eriza in front of Buckingham Palace; Eriza in front of Big Ben and the Houses of Parliament; Eriza accompanied by Mary striding past Harrods struggling with shopping bags from John Lewis, House of Fraser and C&A. She looked quite young and carefree in all of them.

Baba Eriza's pride in his daughter meant that he even had a picture of his daughter in his bedroom. It was unusual for parents to do this but he wanted to see his daughter first thing in the morning. Mbuya Mukwesa, now proudly in her own bedroom in the 'big house' with a bed, tucked her special picture of Eriza under her pillow. In this photo, Eriza wore a red woollen hat and gloves, a white scarf and a black jacket. She was somewhere outdoors in the snow. From time to time, Mbuya Mukwesa held the picture in her left hand and caressed it with her right murmuring, "*Ishe* – God – let me see my grandchild again."

Even though she had her favourite photo, Mbuya Mukwesa loved all the pictures. She was especially captivated by those of Eriza and Mary. She had never imagined a scene in which a white person could be so close to an African, especially with the things that Rhodesians were doing to her people. What confused her was that they both looked so happy in each other's company, especially the white girl. Why then couldn't they be like that in her country, where they were technically visitors, and leave her people in peace? This question became increasingly urgent as the War of Liberation intensified. It was now clear that even if the Europeans decided to be jolly with the Africans, it was far too late to reconcile. Chena, like every corner of the country, was caught between nationalist political activists and guerrilla fighters on one side and the Rhodesian army and police on the other.

A few months into Eriza's second year, one of the first significant events for the people of Chena during those tumultuous times occurred. Dick's wife and her lover were shot dead while Dick was on military duty along the Zambia-Rhodesia border. The incident also marked the discovery of his wife's affair. The Rhodesian army blamed Chena for the killing and Dick reacted as if Chena had connived with his wife over the whole affair.

Dick's full name was Simon Dickson but over time the locals and his workers simply called him Dick. He didn't mind. He very much minded Rhodesia being in the hands of Africans though and was one of the founder members of the all-white Rhodesia Front. Even though it was the leader of his party, Ian Smith, who told the world that majority rule would never 'in a million years' manifest in Rhodesia, it was Simon Dickson who first muted the idea at the inauguration of that political party a few years earlier. Smith liked the saying and made it his own. Dickson backed it up by joining the army reserves.

To get to Mawiro Railway Siding on foot, the people of Chena had to walk along a road that passed between Dick's farm and that of another white farmer nicknamed Ndondo. He was given that name, which meant 'mean', because he was a thug to any African that crossed his path. The morning after Marilyn – as the newspapers revealed her name to be – was murdered, Mr Kanyemba drove to Mawiro, totally unaware of the incident. Unbeknown to him, a roadblock had been mounted at the blind spot at the juncture of the two farms and the village. Soldiers and police had spread out on both sides of the road cordoning Chena.

Mr Kanyemba was stopped. Some of the local police knew him well but the army commander in charge of the operation demanded that his car be thoroughly searched. They did so, and when they opened the boot it turned out that the little humans that the people of Chena joked that he kept in there, were in fact AK47 rifles, grenades and landmines, all made in Russia and China. Mr Kanyemba and his car were never seen again. Chena was branded a 'hotbed of terror' and searched with a fine-toothed military comb. Many young men were abducted and some, like Mr Kanyemba, were never to be seen again.

No one in Chena would have known what had happened had it not been for Sekuru Soromon. He'd spent the night of the killing at Dick's farm and so was not allowed to return home in the morning, when every worker had been accounted for and questioned. His host for the night was his friend and Dick's foreman, known by the workers as 'Foromani'. Foromani's hut was situated close to the road, and from this vantage point and with his temporarily acquired status of being one of Dick's workers, Sekuru Soromon had seen Mr Kanyemba's car on top of an army breakdown vehicle. It was then towed towards Mawiro. Sekuru Soromon had thought this very unusual but it would be a few hours more before it all made sense to him.

Foromani had been asked to escort a few soldiers and police officers into every farmworker's hut to identify them as genuine farmhands. Some of the policemen were themselves African and Foromani had heard them say that the headteacher had refused to say anything about the weapons found in his boot. He was subsequently beaten so badly, and as they spoke then and there, they didn't think he was still alive.

When Foromani returned to his hut and told Sekuru Soromon of what he had heard, both men sat in silence. They barely looked at each other, lest they frightened each other with the looks of shock and horror etched on their faces. Sekuru Soromon wondered whether Mr Kanyemba's body was stuffed in the car as it was towed away. By now Dick's farm had been transformed into a military garrison with army sorties despatched in groups into Chena. Both Foromani and Sekuru Soromon were shaken, because they knew the brutality and unbridled savagery of the Rhodesian army against villagers wherever they suspected the presence of guerrillas. When Sekuru Soromon finally dared to speak, all he could say was, "To think we all thought that Mr Kanyemba kept little humans in his car boot…"

By mid-morning, Dick had arrived at his farm by military helicopter. It landed right in front of his farmhouse. A civilian helicopter, which Dick thought he recognised as belonging to Colonel Wall, occupied the heliport. A close friend of Dick's and a rising star in the Rhodesian army, Colonel Patrick Wall oversaw the operations at Dickson's farm.

"Simon, I'm very sorry for your loss," Colonel Wall began to console his friend.

They were both tall men and in their military uniform were a formidable sight. They looked each other in the eye and Dick nodded as he was led into his massive farmhouse. He didn't notice the pile of men's clothes on the deckchair at the edge of the swimming pool.

"By the way, Simon, we removed an unexploded grenade from under your helicopter," said Colonel Wall, trying to be gentle with his friend.

"What helicopter? I don't own one." Dick looked over at the aircraft with venom. "That?" he exclaimed, pointing at the civilian helicopter. "I thought it was yours."

The two men then looked at each other and read each other's thoughts.

"We checked the identity of the dead man," said the police chief, who joined the two men just as the penny about the helicopter dropped. "His name is Frederic de Kock."

He looked at Dick to see if the name rang a bell with him. It didn't seem to and the three men walked towards the house, past police officers who stood to attention and saluted them. The police chief whispered to the Colonel, "It's registered in de Kock's name."

"Simon," Colonel Wall said as they entered the house, "I'll put it to you straight. There are two catastrophic happenings here and you must separate and prioritise them quickly in your mind. The work of insurgents and Marilyn's behaviour." He stopped as Simon turned to look at him.

"Patrick, since when have we started calling these killers 'insurgents'?" Dickson spoke in his harsh Boer accent, with his eyes darting all over the large entrance hall. His eyes zeroed on a man's jacket hanging near Marilyn's. The sight ignited such anger and hatred in him that he was momentarily relieved Marilyn's killers had done him a favour. "Betrayal," he muttered.

Colonel Wall was not sure whether Dick was referring to his use of the word insurgents, Marilyn's infidelity or to this fellow Rhodesian white man who was sleeping with his wife. In Dick's mind, the dead man was probably avoiding fighting for white rule which was making him so rich that he could afford a helicopter. The chopper was obviously used for these trysts with his wife in his home, when he knew that, he, Simon Dickson was risking his life to protect this brute's opulent lifestyle.

"It's situations like this that fracture and weaken the laager," said Colonel Wall. He could feel the weight of the turmoil engulfing his friend.

The bodies had been removed but the evidence of their evening together was still there. It seemed Marilyn and her lover, Frederic, had enjoyed a hearty meal washed down with an expensive wine. Their two plates flanked dishes of left-over prime veal, Kariba bream, potato salad, mixed vegetables and a jug of water.

The account given by the two housemaids and the cook was that the *baas*, as any white man was called, had landed in the afternoon. As usual, when he came, the *missis* gave them the afternoon off. They would normally only come back to the house when the helicopter or car – de Kock sometimes drove – had left. But tonight, the helicopter stayed all night, so they thought it was either Baas Dick who had come back, or a relative of hers. The cook also said that he had not prepared any food that day. It was Marilyn who had cooked and Dickson, who couldn't recall when last his wife had prepared a meal for him, began to comprehend the depth of his wife's affair. He felt heat rising in him.

Eriza read a short article in one of the British papers headed, 'Another White Farmer Killed in Rhodesia'. The story also said that the war in Rhodesia was no longer confined to just border skirmishes but had reached the gates of Salisbury. The article went on to say that the Portuguese were also losing their grip on Mozambique on the eastern border of Rhodesia and tied this to the revolt of the Tangwena people in Rhodesia.

To enforce the Land Apportionment Act, the Rhodesian government had ordered the eviction, as it had done with the people of Chena years before, of the Tangwena people, whose homes were along the border with Mozambique and which had been there for time immemorial. Chief Rekai

Tangwena had led one of the most noble resistant movements against the act deep within his mountainous chiefdom. Eriza could not believe that this story of the Tangwena people had made it into a British newspaper. She wondered whether her grandmother knew about what was going on there, as it was exactly what she'd recommended, in hindsight, should have happened in 1938 when her own people were driven from Kuwadzana. They should have refused as vigorously as the Tangwena people were now doing.

She re-read the story of the farmer who was killed, paying closer attention to the details. The couple, Mr and Mrs Dickson, were shot in their home near the farming town of Martley. The name Dickson didn't ring any bells, but Martley did. That was where the District Commissioner's offices which served Chena were located and this was where the personal details of Chena villagers were processed. She'd collected her birth certificate from Martley.

Any civil disputes, if not resolved by the chief, were taken before the District Commissioner. Baba Eriza was always asked by the villagers to accompany them when they had to attend the offices to resolve their disputes before the District Commissioner. That was one reason why people referred to him as 'Mr' Mukwesa – a sign of respect for the 'legal' advice he gave so freely. The other reason was that the District Commissioner himself called him Mr Mukwesa, rather than John or Jim or Boy, as other white men freely 'assailed' the dignity of any black man in their path. This was what had inspired Naijo to study law and in the first year of his degree, his father would consult him especially on the interpretation of African customary law. Eriza suspected that she would be hearing more about Chena and the surrounding area because of the killing.

Eriza was however more taken by the story of the Tangwena people. It seems that they defeated the Rhodesians without having to bear arms. They simply retreated into the misty summit strongholds of the mountains whenever the armed trucks of Rhodesian soldiers came to evict them. The siege to starve them out was not effective because their kith and kin in Mozambique gave them supplies. The Portuguese army had by now been cut down by Frelimo fighters, so much so that its soldiers were no longer even sure they were still safe on the beaches of Beira, let alone in the mountains. Eriza made cuttings of these two articles – the killing of the Dicksons and the struggle of the Tangwena people. She put them in the top drawer of her bedside table and resolved to collect more newspaper cuttings on the situation back home.

❖❖❖

Correspondence between Eriza and Naijo was regular. He usually wrote about the family. In one letter, Naijo confirmed that Prudence had made good progress at school and was now predicted to get first-class grades in form three. Prudence had told her already, but it was good to hear it from a more reliable and objective source. Naijo also told her of the passing of Sekuru Mizha. That cough had finally got him. Eriza remembered how violently he had coughed, right in front of her, on the morning of her departure. That bout had been put down to the cold weather but it had persisted, and not long after her departure, Prudence had mentioned his deteriorating health in one of her letters. He had even missed the Easter 'Road to Damascus' walk he so dearly loved. When Eriza was growing up, she'd listened to Sekuru Mizha telling her, with gusto, over and over, of the time he worked in an asbestos mine in Shabani – *Zvishavane*. His illness and painful death were another nail in the coffin of asbestos roofing. After reading this letter, Eriza had spent the rest of the day in despair.

Then both Naijo and Prudence became suspiciously quiet. They hadn't responded to two of her letters which Prudence should have received during the school holidays. Eriza then decided to write to her through school. However, what she liked about Prudence writing from home was that Mbuya Mukwesa dictated to her and Prudence would write it verbatim. In one of Prudence's earlier letters, after receiving photographs of Eriza and Mary with two white males, Prudence had written what only Mbuya Mukwesa could have said.

"*Usawanikwe ne murungu,*" Eriza could hear her grandmother say – You better not think of getting married to a white man.

Prudence did reply to the letter Eriza had sent to her school and in that letter were the grim details of what was thought to have happened to Mr Kanyemba.

Sekuru Soromon had told them all after he was eventually allowed back to Chena from Dick's farm, where he had been held for three days. He'd told them that Mr Kanyemba had been killed by white soldiers and his body buried on Dick's farm. One sure thing he'd seen with his own eyes was that his car was towed away but no one knew where to. Prudence also revealed that the police had visited their home several times, questioning them all about Naijo and Mr Kanyemba. They also searched their houses and after finding nothing of interest, they informed them even though by that time they knew, that Mr Kanyemba had weapons in his car with ammunition like that used in the killing of Dick's wife. They'd said that Mr Kanyemba was in and out of the university campus and always met with Naijo. Then they'd shown them photographs taken in Salisbury of Mr Kanyemba with Naijo and other men they called 'troublemakers'.

The article she'd read a few weeks before now made sense but sadly Dick, and more so Ndondo, was still very much alive. Eriza did not care much for any Rhodesian, but she would rather that Ndondo or Dick had been the ones to die instead of Dick's wife. Rhodesians, and indeed all Europeans, including their priests, treated Africans like animals. Eriza had learnt of this at a young age through the tirades Sekuru Fani unleashed from time to time about them. When she'd later told some of her West

Indian colleagues at the hospital about the mischief between De Kock and Marilyn and their murder, they all replied that it was a classic case of 'dog eat dog'. She'd chuckled.

❖❖❖

The Mukwesa family questioned Sekuru Soromon over and over about the demise of Mr Kanyemba.

"Did you see him being buried in the field?" asked Mr Mukwesa.

"No, but Foromani said he heard from one farm worker who was hanging around that his body was definitely buried on the farm, just behind the barn," Sekuru Soromon answered. "The only thing I saw with my own eyes was his car on top of an army truck," he reiterated for what felt like the hundredth time.

"We heard that he was arrested," interjected Mbuya Mukwesa.

"That could be so because there were two police jeeps driving both in front of and behind the army truck," Sekuru Soromon replied.

"Aha! I heard that when the soldiers opened the boot of his car, there was screaming followed by a puff of thick smoke. The police couldn't see anything and when the smoke cleared, Mr Kanyemba was nowhere to be found," Sekuru Fani exclaimed. His eyes darted from Mbuya Mukwesa to Baba and Mai Eriza. "We'll find him. Mark my words." He spoke in an accusatory tone directed at Sekuru Soromon for not sharing this, which he considered a crucial piece of information.

"Mai Kanyemba doesn't know what's happened to her husband. The police have told her nothing," said Mai Eriza. She wanted to be sure that her brother did not propagate news of a miracle that only Jesus could have performed. "Shouldn't a wife be told the truth about her husband?" she asked, soliciting Mbuya Mukwesa's approval.

However, Mbuya Mukwesa considered herself first among equals if anything serious were to happen to her son. She strongly believed, and on this occasion made it clear to her daughter-in-law, that "Women are the ones who bear children. If his mother is alive, she needs to know, even before his wife, what happened to her son."

"He comes from KwaMtoko, remember?" Baba Eriza reminded them. "It would take a whole day to get there from here, even with the fastest bus and no stops."

"Mai Kanyemba already told me that she is waiting for her sister and brother-in-law to come and help her to move back there. At times like this, she needs to be with her family," continued Mai Eriza.

"She can't stay in the headteacher's house. It's government housing. It comes with the job and she is not a teacher in her own right." Baba Eriza was quick to explain the legal ramifications of the situation.

"What happens if Mr Kanyemba returns?" Sekuru Fani asked.

"*Ko* – Oh – you said he disappeared in smoke," Baba Eriza replied and sighed in exasperation. "Anyway, if he did, he won't necessarily be a headteacher again."

"Do you think the police will welcome him back with open arms?" Sekuru Soromon chimed in sarcastically.

"Those little boys of his will grow up without their father," Mai Mukwesa lamented.

The discussion was not going well for Sekuru Fani at all. No one was buying his version of events. He excused himself, saying that he had to go and set up for a roofing job arranged for the following morning at the Catholic Centre. In the end, it was Sekuru Soromon's version of the demise and burial of the much-loved Mr Kanyemba that was widely accepted. That didn't stop other versions and rumours cropping up over the years until the truth finally came out some 15 years later. It turned out that Mr

Kanyemba was one of thousands of Africans killed during the unrest and fed to crocodiles bred on white-owned commercial farms.

Sekuru Fani's mind was on the Mau Mau freedom fighters of Kenya who were said to have used magic to crush the British. One story was that Jomo Kenyatta himself had simply walked out of prison to the colonial governor's house. He strode straight through the front door and sat on the governor's armchair in their grand living room. The governor's wife and children immediately ran out of the room, screaming. The governor, who had been in the garden with the Commissioner of Police, raced into the house and met his wife in the expansive hallway.

"He's on your chair," the governor's wife panted.

"Who?" asked the governor.

"Jomo Kenyatta," his six-year-old son, who was partially buried in his mother's skirts, replied.

The governor marched into the living room but Kenyatta was nowhere to be seen. The commissioner raced to the maximum-security prison, where he found Kenyatta sitting in his cell. It was said that Kenyatta nonchalantly asked him if he had come to release him to take part in elections, making the commissioner red in the face and squirm in his size-twelve shoes. Sekuru Fani wondered if some magic would ever make its way to Chena, and the rest of their beloved country.

However, there were more immediate matters to attend to. It was time to prepare for cropping. The first showers of the season had already fallen, green grass had sprouted, and the animals could finally graze. However, the scorching heat of the sun literally sucked out what little moisture the rains brought to the earth; this was why no one ever rushed to plant with the first rains, but preparations had to be made. Sekuru Fani was relieved to see a promising cloud rising from the east. He could smell the fresh dung from cattle and goats which were chewing cud under a large muhacha tree. They did so, periodically sniffing the air, sensing the coming rains. That raised Sekuru Fani's spirits because he understood and trusted the animals' instincts. He gathered pace as he saw the wooden spire of the church. The roofing job was now a pressing matter. He looked at the cloud again and, as much as he wanted the rain to come, he hoped it would hold on until he was done. From the church grounds, he surveyed the building and turned his nose up at the plastering. It would not flatter his handiwork on the roof much, more so because he didn't like the man who'd done it. Just then, a gentle breeze blew in from the west, cooling the air and dissipating the cloud. The roofing job had been given a reprieve.

"I have to finish it tomorrow," he said to himself as he examined the timber and corrugated tin roofing sheets strewn across the grounds. He felt just a little bit guilty looking at them, as he'd ingeniously made the church order twice the amount of material needed.

"It's not as if I'm going to get it for free. I'll pay them a quarter of the price," he mumbled, trying to ease his conscience. "It'll save Eriza some money but that she doesn't need to know."

Suddenly, he heard a dog yelping, startling him out of his guilty mutterings. It ran past him and as it did so, looked him in the eye and yelped again. Clearly, the dog suspected that Sekuru Fani was in league with whatever it was running away from. He thought of Hezvu, his family dog. Her offspring and grand offspring were to be found in almost every household in Chena, so this scared dog could easily have been her progeny.

Eriza had always counselled the boys who clamoured for Hezvu's puppies. "Feed them every day," she'd commanded them. Sekuru Fani recalled this with a slight tilt of his head, thinking about how much his niece cared for Hezvu and her puppies. He knew then that he hadn't cheated the church after all, as it had all been done in the name of his niece, an angel.

With the threat of showers gone, Sekuru Fani headed to the primary school to get the latest on Mai Kanyemba. As he walked, he surveyed his surroundings. There was some greenery among the trees growing in defiance of the scorching sun. Dung beetles were rolling balls of cow dung. He smiled as he remembered his cousin Abero arguing that everything humans claim to have invented was copied from the behaviour of animals and nature. He had singled out the dung beetle as the 'inventors' of the wheel. It could fashion clumps of fresh cow dung into a ball up to twice its size and roll it like a wheel to its nest. Sekuru Fani peered closely at the army of beetles and indeed saw the little creatures rolling their loads from what definitely smelt like cow dung.

Further along, he came across a noisy swarm of schoolchildren on their way home. He was showered with all manner of good afternoons.

"Maswera here Sekuru?"

"Maswera here babamunini?"

"Maswera here babamukuru?"

He recognised the last greeting as coming from Ceciria's sister. She'd no doubt told the others that he was her sister's boyfriend. No wonder they were being so respectful.

He continued on his way but, within a few minutes, he had to break up a bloody fight between some boys. He took the bully with him with the intention of delivering him to his home, where his father would give him a thorough whipping. Ahead of him, he saw Ceciria talking with Mai Kanyemba and realised that the bully was now a burden.

"Iwe – You – go home! Straight! I'll talk to your father tonight. Aren't you ashamed to fight such a young boy?" Sekuru Fani wagged his finger in the bully's face

"Aasi Seekuru ndiye anditanga," – He started it uncle – he stammered, sobbing.

"Just shut up and go before I give you something to cry about!"

At that, the bully sprinted down the path behind the rest of the pack who had been wise enough to stay clear of Sekuru Fani.

"Fani! Fani!" A male voice shouted out loudly. It was his friend, Josefa, a teacher at the school, emerging from a path to Sekuru Fani's left.

"I collected a letter from the post office today. It's from *Ingirandi*. Eeh, from Eriza." He smiled at Sekuru Fani. "How are you?"

"I'm fine. Did you see that Chirunda boy? He was beating up this small boy. Very badly too. Do you have the letter with you now?"

Josefa pulled the letter out of his jacket pocket and handed it to Sekuru Fani, as he started on the Chirundu boy.

"*Chimupengo!*" – Mad boy! He laughed and Sekuru Fani joined in the laughter, but his mind was on the letter.

"I've come to check on the Kanyemba family. Any new developments?"

"Oh ya. Kanyemba's brother arrived this morning and the wife's sister is expected this evening," replied Josefa.

"Ah, but the Musiyamwa bus has already come and gone!" Sekuru Fani exclaimed. "Is she coming by car?"

"Mai Kanyemba told me that they hired a small truck so that they can carry everything one time. She's finding it hard. I think she knows her husband is dead.

"Not me. I don't believe it. Without a body or a grave, a person is not dead." Sekuru Fani said this looking at Josefa sternly, as if to chastise him for believing that Mr Kanyemba was dead.

Josefa evaded the glare because he certainly did not buy into Sekuru Fani's miracle story that Kanyemba had been saved by his little humans. Sekuru Fani decided that Josefa had told him all he wanted to know. With Eriza's letter in his hand, he turned back towards home; Ceciria had to wait for another time.

The path was now clear of school children but the emptiness evoked memories of his two nieces and nephew. Even though Chido had disappointed the family by getting pregnant out of the blue, they were broken when she became sick and died unexpectedly. It can only be a blessing that she left Prudence, who was now thriving, especially as she was no longer overshadowed by Eriza. Of course Sekuru Fani had badly thrashed the teacher who had impregnated his niece. The young teacher then left the area, as per Sekuru Fani's order and promise of further beatings if he ever showed his face again. From that time, anyone who crossed Sekuru Fani was reminded that *Sekuru vanopura* – this uncle can give a beating.

The road also reminded him of how sweet it was to go home after a day at school for Chido, Naijo and Eriza, in that order, as they trekked home with dry lips. When they got home, Mbuya Mukwesa always livened up their spirits with drinks of *mahewu*, a refreshing drink made of maize and *zviyo* – grain flour. Mbuya Mukwesa had failed to teach Eriza the art of preparing this drink, but Prudence became, from an early age, a master at it.

"Prudence is a natural," she'd say to anyone who was refreshed by the drink.

Prudence revelled in the compliment and now that she was in boarding school, she knew everyone lamented over her absence. Meanwhile back at home, Mbuya Mukwesa extolled the *mahewu*-making skills of her granddaughter.

"Today you will have to make do with water; the mother of *mahewu* is at boarding school." She would repeat this to every visitor with a broad smile.

"*Mahewu*," Sekuru Fani muttered to himself as he suddenly found himself just outside his hut; he'd really lost himself in the warm memories of his *wazukuru*. He missed them all badly.

For Sekuru Fani, a letter from Eriza was like a holy offering. It had to first be savoured in the same way his sister did with enlivened bread at holy communion. This reverence was warranted as a letter was the harbinger of gifts from England and an emissary of remittance by postal order. However, what stirred his soul was the elegance of Eriza's English on that sheet of paper. It fascinated him that this little girl had grown into someone who could write *chirungu chakaoma kudaro* – such captivating English. In a letter for Naijo sent via Prudence at boarding school, to avoid it being opened by the police in the aftermath of Mr Kanyemba's demise, she had included the phrase 'unbridled greed and savagery of the Ndondos'. Naijo had explained the phrase to him and he found it befitting of the Rhodesians and their culture. Listening to Radio Dar, he'd heard the likes of Ndondo being referred to as vermin. Together, Eriza and Radio Dar provided him with an ample and appropriate armamentarium of terminology that he would one day spit into European faces and they would not be able to do a thing about it.

He also liked the phrase 'tantamount to'. It was not just because Ceciria liked it too – she used it often – but it was so easily vernacularised.

"Kutizira munaZambezi kwakanga kuri tantamount to kuzviuraya," he'd heard someone say – speaking of a man who jumped into the crocodile-infested Zambezi to escape the fury of a murderous husband as being tantamount to suicide.

The letter that day was full of details of her exciting life and the odd habits of the English. For one, they didn't wash regularly.

"Once a week. That's it. Imagine! Washing your body just once a week," she wrote.

Dog owners happily left their dogs' faeces on the pavement where others added to the nastiness by spitting their phlegm. Birds then made a meal out of it. Sekuru Fani had screwed his face in disgust as he read this. With the last paragraph, however, he was all smiles when he read that Eriza was missing home and could not wait to complete her course and fly back. The smile spread even wider across his face when he read that she was to wire a hefty amount for additional furnishing to the new house.

NINE

For nearly two years, Naijo sat in the same lectures as one of Ndondo's five daughters. Her name was Helga. Neither of them knew that they were neighbours because they never spoke to each other. That was the social set-up at university; whites did not speak to blacks and blacks did not care.

Ndondo's real name was Willem de Villiers. He owned Laagersdorp, the farm next to Dick's. No African, apart from his workers, whom he terrorised, were allowed on his farm. The only time that the residents of Chena could even be near Laagersdorp was when they travelled to and from Mawiro Railway Siding, usually to Tomas'. Even then, they walked on the side of the road that was closest to Dick's farm. Ndondo sent many a villager to hospital with his beatings, but was never charged. No one in Chena spoke to his workers about him. Most of his workers were migrants from Malawi and very few of them ventured into the surrounding villages, and it was thought that de Villiers specifically chose foreigners to minimise mingling with the locals. However, some of his workers would venture to Mawiro for a drink and once drunk, would vent their anger and frustration with him. It was then that the people of Chena would gather some insights into the monster that was Ndondo.

Ndondo often rode his horse around the farm. It was on one of these farm patrols that Eriza had her only clear sighting of him. She was eight years old and was walking back home with her mother from Tomas', sucking on a lollipop. It was her first time seeing such 'a big donkey', she'd reported to Naijo later. The animal had frightened her with its grunts and she felt threatened even though it was inside the farm's fence and she and her mother were walking on Dick's side of the road. Unfortunately, as the horse grunted, and she jumped in fright, the lollipop popped out of her mouth. Her lollipop – the one thing she looked forward to after a trip to Tomas. It was at that moment that Ndondo became her number one enemy.

Ndondo's blood line of racial hatred had also bedevilled his daughter. It came to light one day when Naijo accompanied his father to Martley, about seven months before Eriza left for England. Baba Eriza had been asked to assist a neighbour who had not paid his cattle tax. The neighbour was summoned to appear before the District Commissioner, Mr Bennett. The ancillary staff at Martley and DC Bennett knew both Naijo and his father well. That day, as the three men were talking in the office, DC Bennett revealed that he had Helga de Villiers working in his office during university breaks, expecting Naijo to know her. Then Helga appeared. Naijo recognised her as the white girl who sat in the front row of the lecture theatre. He didn't know her name, until that day, which was almost a year after they had started at the university.

"Oh Helga! Come in. Your classmate Nigel is here," said DC Bennett, beckoning Helga over enthusiastically.

"I've never seen this *kaffir* before in my life," she responded venomously.

In her white world, she knew that no one would accept an African's version of the truth over hers. DC Bennett was nevertheless embarrassed by her callousness and probably more so because he knew the truth but had to side with Helga. The cornerstone of the rules that governed his line of work was that he should not believe the word of an African. Not being Rhodesian yet himself, he found it difficult to accept the white supremacist attitudes of people like the de Villiers. He detested having to wade through their quagmire of racial hatred. What a mess the whole business was, inherited from their forefathers with myths conjured with each passing generation to denigrate the African. It took time to be converted to this type and though he had no intention of being converted, he nevertheless maintained the paternalistic view that saw Africans as a people who could only be redeemed by the presence of Europeans like himself. Unsurprisingly, these same Europeans could not tell you exactly what Africans needed to be redeemed from.

On the other hand, Naijo and his father saw nothing unusual in Helga's behaviour. To them, it was exactly this attitude that distinguished mere bad mortals from children of God. All they were interested in was the welfare of their neighbour. As it turned out, their neighbour's testimony that some of his cattle had died was upheld. In fact, his herd had decreased by three that year. DC Bennett accepted the man's plea, probably out of guilt after Helga's behaviour towards two men he respected, even though they were African. Baba Eriza, Naijo and their neighbour thanked them profusely before leaving his office. They walked past Helga without saying a word; she in turn looked at the three men with utter contempt.

Naijo was somewhat excited that he was at last able to put a name to one white woman among many at university. When they arrived home, he rushed to tell Eriza about all that had transpired at the District Commissioner's.

"How did you know that she was Ndondo's daughter?" Eriza had asked. Naijo could tell that she was thinking of her ill-fated lollipop of 11 years ago.

"Because she was eating a lollipop," Naijo replied, roaring with laughter.

Eriza laughed too.

❁ ❁ ❁

It was 1965 and Eriza was still too young to understand the affairs of the country unless they had a direct bearing on Chena. However, she had now figured out that Ndondo was not the only evil white man there was. In fact, they were all *ndondo*. Her father described the Rhodesian Unilateral Declaration of Independence of November of that year as 'a vehicle driven by Ian Smith, carrying all the *ndondos* to crush African people.'

Naijo was about to complete his second year in secondary school as a boarder. Sekuru Fani had repeatedly counselled Naijo about the responsibility that came with being educated.

"It's for us, your family, and all African people in this country. It's an education to free your people. That's what Kwame Nkrumah and Julius Nyerere did," Sekuru Fani would say expectantly.

"*Ko iye Kwame Nyerere waunongotaura mazuva ose, ndiyani?*" – Who is this Kwame Nyerere you keep going on about every day? – Mbuya Mukwesa had asked.

Laughter rang through the kitchen that evening. Mbuya Mukwesa did not understand that Sekuru Fani was speaking of two different people. Eriza was both envious of and inspired by her brother, who was being likened to legendary African leaders. Envious because Naijo had become somewhat arrogant ever since he'd started boarding school and being lauded as the next African revolutionary by Sekuru Fani. Inspired because she had, as a result, resolved to work as hard as she possibly could to guarantee her place at boarding school too. A few days later, Baba Eriza and Mbuya Mukwesa bore witness to an altercation between Naijo and Eriza which revealed the changing dynamics between brother and sister.

"Just because you're going to secondary school doesn't mean that you get to kick me around," Eriza lashed out, storming through the kitchen, leaving Naijo at the mercy of their grandmother's glare. "In two years, I will go to an even better secondary school than your ugly one…"

Her tirade was cut short by the sudden appearance of their father. Baba Eriza liked the ambition he had heard in the venom of his daughter's words. He didn't say anything on the matter but sent a powerful message to Naijo by ordering him to go to the well to fetch water, a task which tradition assigned to Eriza. Mbuya Mukwesa chuckled and Eriza's red, teary eyes were soon overshadowed by a wide grin. Naijo and her were even.

❖❖❖

When he had started secondary school in January of 1963, Naijo was given a textbook which had been used by Henry Masauko Chipembere, a Malawian who had become one of Dr Hastings Banda's most able lieutenants in the battle to end the Federation of Rhodesia and Nyasaland and create the independent country of Malawi after ditching the name Nyasaland. Chipembere became Minister of Education. Within a few years there was a dramatic fallout between Banda and six or seven of his senior ministers, including Chipembere. This turn of events, just like the betrayal of Patrice Lumumba in The Congo a few years earlier, did not escape the nationalistically charged young minds of Naijo's generation, who were then in their last year of primary school.

Banda had started making overtures to apartheid South Africa. With his big mouth, he had made it clear that he would prefer to get aid from an apartheid regime rather than from Communist China, which Chipembere's group was leaning towards. Apparently, Banda had worked in the gold mines in Wits as a young man. It was said that he was after some of that gold, at any cost, now that he was leader of Malawi. The Rhodesian government seized the opportunity to create some propaganda surrounding him, especially as they were still smarting at the redundancy of 'Southern' in Rhodesia after Northern Rhodesia had become Zambia at the dissolution of the Federation of Rhodesia and Nyasaland. Rhodesia touted Banda as a role model for African leadership. Malawi was dubbed the new frontier against communism and promoted to a pivotal position in the cold war battles in Africa. It did not work. The more the Rhodesian and

161

South African governments supported Banda, the more he was reviled by Africans in Rhodesia – even schoolchildren disliked him.

As he called himself *The Ngwazi* – The Lion of Malawi, the people of Chena referred to him as *The Bere* – The Hyena of Malawi. The evolving political drama inspired Naijo to become a playwright. He wrote a play for the standard six production that was based on how he imagined the last cabinet meeting between Banda and his 'communist' ministers to have transpired. The production received a standing ovation at the final Saturday variety show of that year. It had not proceeded without a little drama of its own, as no one wanted to play the 'sell-out' that was Banda; eventually someone accepted the part though and, of course, Naijo played Chipembere. So, to have then been given an English textbook, once used by Chipembere more than a decade earlier and within days of starting secondary school, left Naijo in awe. He had no idea that Chipembere had attended the same school until that moment.

Needless to say, he couldn't wait to tell Eriza about the play and she couldn't wait to tell him about her star performance at the school debate. Before she could say more, Naijo shouted, "Country life is better than town life!' That interjection did not go down well with Eriza, who glared at him with a look that said, "Who do you think you are? Just because you are going to secondary school." That had been the trigger for the row that ended with Naijo drawing water from the well.

When she started standard five the school was ablaze with the news of Naijo's genius stage play. Some of her teachers had attended the variety show and were enamoured by the way in which real-life political events were so deftly dramatised by the youngsters. In Naijo's absence, Eriza received all the glory. This is the moment she began to understand, cautiously, the force of the nationalist movement in her country. She also started to appreciate her grandmother's earnest desire to see Kuwadzana reclaimed by its rightful owners.

These childhood memories came flooding back each time she sat at her desk reading newspaper articles about the goings-on in Rhodesia. Her scissors were always at the ready, on her bedside table. The folder she had created for her cuttings labelled 'Home', was now bulging.

❖❖❖

Meanwhile, unbeknown to her in England and her family in Chena, Naijo had been taken to the Central Police Station in Salisbury for questioning in the aftermath of Marilyn Dick's killing. This had happened about a month after the murders. The special branch team wanted to investigate all of Mr Kanyemba's connections and Naijo was, in their minds, a key one. Naijo made it clear to the special branch that his association with Mr Kanyemba was inescapable – same hometown and same institution of learning. He then disarmed them completely by referring the same inescapability between him and Helga de Villiers. They left him alone after that. Naijo laughed all the way back from the police station to his room at the university.

Around the time that Eriza was preparing to leave for England, Britain was still busy trying to legitimatise UDI in Rhodesia. The last initiative that Eriza remembered was the Lord Pearce Constitutional Proposal on granting independence to Rhodesia. Her knowledge of and insight into that constitutional undertaking had now widened beyond the propaganda meted out by Ian Smith to coerce Africans into accepting the proposal. Smith promised enormous wealth if only they voted 'Yes' in the referendum. As she looked back to this time, Eriza was so proud of the unyielding resistance put up by her people and their rejection of the proposal even when offered such tantalising goodies. Naijo had been in the thick of the 'No Campaign', and Chena had a 'No' poster plastered on every tree. As a result, Mbuya Mhizha had wondered whether the trees would grow 'no' leaves that year. When Eriza told her that the very paper on which the 'No' was written was made from trees, she exclaimed *"Eh hezvo!* – Oh really! – God works in mysterious ways." That had put the case to rest as her conviction in the infallibility of God had once again been affirmed.

After the resounding 'No' vote against the Pearce proposal, the excitement among Africans was such that people in the cities would say 'no' to just about anything. They sensed that victory was around the corner. However, the vote had resulted in a fallout within the white community. Nearer home, DC Bennett was summarily removed from office. He, like a few other commissioners, were accused of a dismal failure to convince Africans in their areas to vote 'Yes'. This wave of sackings was carried out by the newly appointed Minister of Internal Affairs. Bill Sharper, the then incumbent to the post, was also a casualty of the 'No' vote. His dismissal was a surprise as he was known to be on the extreme right of the Rhodesia Front. It was believed that Bill had opposed the referendum in the first place because he knew the outcome would be a 'No' vote. In so doing, he had automatically put himself as a strong challenger to Ian Smith. The referendum results signalled danger to Ian Smith, and Bill was accused of sabotaging the 'Yes' vote for political expedience. The accusation alone was not enough to force him out though. Smith needed more, so he pulled out the gloves. He'd known for some time that Bill was consorting with a *mukuradi* – mixed-race – woman who then went on to bear him a child during the middle of the referendum campaign. After the results, Bill had put up a fight in the cabinet and walked out, threatening to mount a public challenge. Smith shouted, "I will tell the world!" thus silencing Bill forever.

Race laws criminalising mixed marriages or sexual intimacies between the races were taking hold in apartheid South Africa. Though they hadn't been glaringly enshrined in legislation in Rhodesia, they were implied in laws such as the Land Apportionment Act. Under these laws, whites were breaking the law if they were found in African areas or tribal lands. African people were summarily arrested if they were in the suburbs outside of their capacity of a house boy or house girl. So, the liaison between Bill and his coloured girlfriend would have broken the law wherever the rendezvous had taken place. Naijo, being the keen law student that he was, had picked up on the legal analysis of events from his white law professor, as well as these goings-on in the white establishment. He had to explain all this to his father, with young Eriza listening, considering DC Bennett's sudden demise as District Commissioner.

❀❀❀

Eriza's second winter in England was unforgiving. It curtailed her urge to travel outside Colchester, only doing so when absolutely necessary; that meant two return journeys to the immigration offices at the Home Office in Croydon and one shopping trip with Mary. The day of their shopping trip was exceptionally cold, but this one was necessary – it was Christmas. The two girls wrapped themselves up in multiple layers of clothing, bracing themselves for the wait at the bus stop. As soon as they stepped out of the flat, Mary screamed. Loudly.

"It's freezin' and my make-up will be ruined!" With that she rushed back into the building to check her face.

"*Yuwi*," Eriza said out loudly, and incredulously, to the chilly air and then turned to follow Mary back inside. She continued speaking in Shona, muttering about how someone can be so obsessed with make-up, forgetting that Mary had no clue about what she was saying. Not that it would have mattered anyway, as Mary was dealing with a major crisis on herself. Eriza could not figure out how cold air, even as piercing as this was, could dent make-up on somebody's face.

"I'm calling a taxi," Mary declared.

"What?! To go to London?!" Eriza exclaimed. "And don't look so fretful. Your face is fine." She could tell Mary needed reassurance.

"No!" she sighed out loudly. "To go to the train station. It's just too cold to walk and wait for the bus and there's no way we're missing the Christmas sales." With that she walked to the communal phone in the main entrance and called for a taxi.

The taxi arrived within five minutes and before it could even get halfway up the drive leading up to the main door of residence, the two girls ran like rats being chased by a cat, violently jerked the rear doors open and dived into the sanctuary of the burrow of the back seat. They laughed hysterically as the driver stared at them in disbelief and drove off without a word. They looked out of the window, still laughing, as their warm breath clouded the windows, daring the cold air to follow them into the warm vehicle.

The ride was very short, so short that Mary had no time to check her make-up, though it didn't stop her from taking a glance in the rear view mirror before the taxi drove off. They ran into the station, were lucky to find their train just pulling in and with their ticket money ready, jumped straight on. They sat in silence, like everyone else, facing each other. Silence was particularly difficult for Mary but on their last train ride to London, she had announced that she didn't want 'all these weird-looking men in the train to know her business.' Today, Eriza took the opportunity to survey these weird-looking men. On the face of it, they seemed absorbed in their newspapers and books. One such weird man in spectacles, sitting next to Mary, kept eyeing Eriza each time he raised his head from his book. She glanced at it. It was Chinua Achebe's, *Things Fall Apart*.

It was one of the set books for 'O' Level English Literature at her school. Everyone loved it. Each time they walked the corridors to their literature lesson, the boys expressed joy at the impending relief from the boredom that came with English novels.

"*Umuofia kwenu*," they'd shout in unison, referring to the chant of the *egwugwu* in Achebe's novel.

That would set the tone for the lesson. Of course, boys being boys, they had nicknamed one particular girl 'Things Fall Apart', because in one lesson she'd fallen off her chair, landed flat on her back with her school skirt up over her face, baring everything; the boys had seen the unimaginable – her knickers. The way they'd behaved, one would have thought that they'd seen much more.

As Eriza recalled the incident, and as she looked at the man again, she realised that he resembled one of her teachers, a Mr Tyler, who disliked African girls. Brushing memories of him aside, she noticed that the weird bespectacled man was almost at the end of the book. She wondered whether he had understood that western civilisation was trying to destroy African culture under the guise of religious conversion. She remembered what she'd read about the Benin bronze that was looted by the British from West Africa and now installed in the British Museum.

"They not only destroyed but also stole,' she muttered, looking at the man with a cold hard stare. "Sekuru Fani was right," she concluded emphatically.

She shifted her attention to the women in the compartment. Some of them offered friendly smiles which she returned but no words were ever exchanged. The silence was in sharp contrast to the travel experience back home where Africans engaged in friendly conversations with total strangers. Indeed, it was clear that in England, for most people, the train ride was a time for introspection.

The train arrived at its final destination, Liverpool Street Station. Everyone surged off the train. Eriza was now accustomed to the rush and the noise of footsteps amplified by the silence. Immediately Mary opened up, like a dam bursting forth.

"Let's get to Oxford Street first," she said, pointing towards the steps which would take them down to the tube for Oxford Street. She was excited, telling Eriza, yet again, about the festive mood of Christmas in Ireland and how much she missed it. It was clear she was going to make up for that loss with a shopping spree. Eriza just smiled, recalling the routine of Christmas mass at the Catholic Centre in Chena.

There was always mass on Christmas Day. Most children would be dressed in new clothes purchased from Tomas' but a few of them, like her and Naijo, wore outfits bought at Amato's. She remembered how they would brag about their city attire much to the chagrin of those who were dressed by Tomas'. After mass there was the festival of food with a banquet spread on tables set under the shady trees of the churchyard. There were biscuits and buns to be washed down with Coca-Cola, Fanta and Cherry Plum. Lollipops were everywhere, compliments of Mr and Mrs Tomas via Father Patricio, who had replaced the disgraced Father Patrick. Being Portuguese, the Tomases discovered his value as a promoter of their business among his congregation. He was reasonably fluent in Shona and enjoyed the local cuisine which meant he got on very well with his parishioners, especially when visiting them at home. His popularity was fully exploited by the Tomases. No African customer ever left their shop without being asked about Father Patricio. This guaranteed at least five to ten minutes of excited conversation during which time another one or two purchases would be made.

Christmas Day was truly joyous as everyone left church laden with left-over biscuits and lollipops. Next was Christmas lunch. For the Mukwesa family, lunch was chicken, vegetables and rice. For many years, Naijo had chased, caught and joyously handed the Christmas chicken over to Sekuru Fani's knife. When he'd left for university, Prudence had taken over, drafting in Comfort as an able assistant. However, Sekuru Fani retained the rights to the guillotine. *Sadza*, the cornerstone of every meal, was rested on this day for everyone except Mbuya Mukwesa. She insisted that *sadza* and chicken could not be separated, more so at Christmas if it was such a luminously ordained day as Christians billed it to be.

"What a waste of delicious meat to eat chicken with rice," she'd say.

Eriza heard the now-familiar sound of the tube and soon she saw the one-eyed giant, hungry snake emerging from its hole. She was a little more comfortable with the maze that was the underground though. Everyone in Chena had by now heard about this maze as she'd written detailed descriptions after her first ride, accompanied by many pictures. Nevertheless, she still worried about the roof of the tunnel collapsing on them, though she had told herself that with the short hops between stations, if that were to happen, rescue would not be too far away.

Next to them on the platform, waiting to board the train too, was a group of about eight white, young males. They started harassing two young, black males, stopping them from boarding. In a flash, one of the white males was thrown heavily to the ground. Mary and Eriza rushed to board and watched the rest of the fight from the train. The two black males jumped in just before the doors closed, while the white boys remained on the platform unable to abandon their mate. As the train disappeared into the darkness of the tunnel, Eriza and Mary were appalled by the sudden appearance of British Rail police, who proceeded to pounce on the two African men.

"Did they expect them to take that nonsense lying down?" Mary said calmly.

The other white passengers looked at her as if asking, "Whose side are you on?" Eriza could feel her blood boiling, but it would be a different kettle of fish if she were to vocalise her thoughts. Mary spoke for them both.

The policemen held on to the black men until the next station where they hauled them out of the train and across the platform to God knows where. Both girls remained silently angry.

Finally, they arrived at Oxford Street. They emerged above ground and were greeted with the dazzling lights of the Christmas decorations which were everywhere – high on the lamp posts, low on every street corner and across every square inch of every shop window. Eriza was so dazzled that the bitter cold did not register this time round. The unasked question in their minds was, "Where shall we start?" Soon, they were sucked into the crowd of excited and animated shoppers.

"Eriza! Look at those platform shoes!" Mary had at last come alive again. "I need to have them. I hope they have my size."

Eriza followed Mary's finger pointing at some very high, green and white platforms, but before she could comment, Mary had already made a beeline for the door. Eriza was about to follow her when she heard the sound of female voices speaking in Shona coming from behind her. She stopped in her tracks. Mary beckoned frantically, urging Eriza to join her.

"Wait," Eriza said in her gentle but firm voice, one which Mary had come to recognise as an indication of an irreversible command that she should not question.

"Iwe, ndakutaurira kuti handeyi kuFinsbury Park kwatinobhagena. Zvemuno munana Oxford Street, izita chete," – I told you that we should go to Finsbury Park where we can bargain. Here in Oxford Street we are just buying the name, – said one of the girls.

"Ah, shamwari rega timbozvitengerao mbatya dzekupoza nadzo paChristmas pano," – Ah, my friend let's spoil ourselves and show off during this Christmas season, – replied the other.

"Ibvapo! Unoda kushainira chikomana Jesu?" – Get out of here! Do you want to show off to baby boy Jesus? – the first girl responded in a jocular manner, triggering hearty laughter from them both. They talked and laughed with much gesticulation of the hands. When joking about Baby Jesus, they'd touched each other's shoulders which to Eriza signified a close friendship. One had an Afro hairdo and the other wore a woollen hat. They both moved with the grace of African beauties even though they were swathed in fur coats.

For a moment, Eriza was transported back to the streets of Salisbury. The sun was shining brightly and laughing men and women were everywhere. Girls gawped at the window displays and darted in and out of the stores in packs of six, hands full of shopping bags. She suddenly snapped out of her reverie.

"Kwedu kwaRuya…," – At my home in Ruya – said the one in the hat.

That was enough for Eriza to realise that they could have been neighbours. Chena and Ruya were very close to each other. She gave them one last look before they were engulfed by the Christmas crowd. They in turn had hardly noticed her. As regular Londoners, they were used to lone African faces, and so didn't pay her much mind. A few years previously, they would have gawped just as Eriza had done. Spot an African face, listen to them speak and try work out where they were from. As Eriza had not uttered a word, to them she was just another black face from anywhere in Africa or the Caribbean.

"Had I heard her name, I'm sure I would've known her family," Eriza said to herself as she followed Mary into the store. A wave of homesickness suddenly washed over her. Fortunately, Mary was so completely absorbed by the shoes that she didn't notice the change in her friend's demeanour.

Eriza thought about Finsbury Park and what it would be like to shop there if one could bargain. The thought helped her to re-engage with Mary and get on with the Christmas shopping.

After just four hours, Eriza and Mary were finished so they decided on some lunch before heading back to Colchester. They ate a comforting winter's meal of bangers and mash with peas, surrounded by their many bags. Of course, they had to document the day and begged a young man sitting next to them to take pictures of them eating, surrounded by their bags of shopping. In their chattering and excitement, they nearly forgot to ask for the camera but fortunately the man remembered to hand it over. Mary always said that she preferred to ask young men rather than girls, because girls got jealous and would happily walk away with the camera only to throw it in a nearby bin. Eriza remained forever baffled by the workings of white women.

Eriza's load was much lighter than the one six months ago in the summer – one that had cost her dearly at the post office. She should not have bought her family anything else really but this was Christmas and they would be expecting something, especially Mbuya Mukwesa. Even though she had doubts about the authenticity of Jesus' birth, she nevertheless welcomed the spirit of Christmas with open arms.

Mary, who now knew a lot about Eriza's grandmother, had bought her a delicate silk shawl and that left Eriza to pick up some small items for the rest of her family including Comfort. Mary on the other hand did not hold back. She had gone way overboard. The good thing with her though was that she made quick choices. Eriza was careful about what she bought. She checked the seam, the way the buttons were sewn on and quality-tested the material by rubbing it between her fingers. Today, she'd bought her second pair of trousers. She'd been disappointed by the first as they were too tight at the hips. Mary had pointed out that the cut was not made for African hips. So, this time they were both on a mission to find a flattering pair. It was an arduous undertaking as they marched in and out of the changing rooms with trouser after trouser until one of the sales ladies finally stopped them.

"Girls. Select as many as you want and take them all into the changing room."

The whole process was made more painful by Eriza's quality control inspections. At last, one of the final five pairs satisfied them both.

"It keeps your hips firm. Look! Look! It's fabulous," Mary was urging Eriza to look at her rear end.

"Yes Mary, I can feel the soft landing." Eriza was so moved by Mary's determination and patience to help her find the right fit, especially as she spent so little time on her choices.

They both laughed because the term 'soft landing', popularised by the successful landing of spacecraft on the moon, had become a euphemism in the nurses' residence for anything that had succeeded against all odds. Indeed, they'd achieved the impossible.

❀ ❀ ❀

The journey back to Colchester was uneventful, partly because they were too exhausted to notice anything but mostly because they were eager to just get home and comb through their shopping bags. They dispensed with a taxi this time, knowing how much they had spent but as soon as they got off the bus at the hospital, they made a mad dash for the warmth of the flats, straight to Mary's room for the obligatory post-shopping catwalk featuring Mary as the main and only model and Eriza as the audience of one. Each change of outfit was accompanied by fresh make-up and a different hairstyle. She invited Eriza, as usual, to try her purchases, but she declined.

"I did my bit in the shop, remember," Eriza said, lying on Mary's bed, on her side, with her head resting in the palm of her left hand. She spotted some faults in the finishing of some of Mary's new clothes but nothing worth getting Mary upset about. When the show was done, Eriza got up. "I've got to go and wrap up my gifts and post them tomorrow," she said heading to the door. "I want them to get their parcels before Christmas," she added, imagining Comfort serenely beaming at the Christmas service in his new brown shirt – not from Tomas' or Amato's, but from *Ingirandi.*

"Bye, and thanks Eriza," Mary said, face in the mirror, combing her hair again.

"I hope it won't rain in Chena this Christmas," Eriza thought out loud as she closed Mary's door. "People here wish for a white Christmas while back home we wish for a dry, sunny one." In her room, she peeked out at the late English winter afternoon through the window in the hallway between the two blocks of flats. It was already dark at 4:30 in the afternoon and the cold air hit her once more. She rushed into the silence and warmth of her room.

TEN

Eriza flourished as the course progressed and was inspired to work hard, given all the learning opportunities available to her. The experience was made more enjoyable with Mary as a study partner. She was quite clever and diligent and for Eriza, to be able to work with someone of equivalent academic calibre was a joy. Mary had a weakness though. She was squeamish, becoming near-hysterical at any bodily fluid that was not her own – blood, urine, even saliva. However, one of her many great attributes was her tenacity. Over the course of the first year, she had worked hard to get over this weakness but she remained intolerant of vomit. In fact, she herself would vomit at the sight of anyone else's vomit. Mary had confessed that her sisters had not allowed her to look after their infant children because of the drama that ensued when the babies vomited.

"That really hurt me because I love children. It wasn't as if my vomit would harm the babies," she'd said to Eriza one day, as they admired the new-born of a colleague in the maternity unit of the hospital.

Eriza understood to some degree because she was occasionally nauseated by some of the hospital smells, like the disinfectant that was used to clean the floor for one. With time though, she got used to it.

Both girls did well in all their rotations, receiving quite high marks in their written papers at each assessment in both the first and second years. But of course, there were always learning revelations. On one of their assignments, Mary had a run-in with the words 'prostate' and 'prostrate'.

"Sister Spencer was not at all present today," she had reported to Eriza. "She scribbled across my essay that males had 'prostate glands that could lead to prostate cancer,' when everyone damn well knows that they were known as prostrate glands."

"Well Sister Spencer was right," replied Eriza.

Normally, Mary deferred to Eriza on such things, but on this occasion, she had to disagree with her friend and together they decided that the only course of action to take was to consult the English dictionary. Of course, Eriza and Sister Spencer were both right, leaving Mary a little red in the face with embarrassment. To save face on behalf of her friend, Eriza quickly changed the subject. As they'd leafed through the dictionary, she'd spotted the word 'Qantas'. It was the word emblazoned across one of the airplanes at Nairobi Airport and she had wondered how on earth such a spelling error could have been made for such a magnificent machine.

"Mary, look at this word!" Eriza exclaimed. She had not bothered to read the meaning.

Mary glanced casually at the dictionary and said, "It's not a word. It's the abbreviation for Queensland and Northern Territories Aerial Services." She triumphantly turned to re-organising her file.

"I used to think there was a 'u' missing too," she added, looking at Eriza from the corner of her right eye with a wily smile.

"Oh really?" Eriza exclaimed with a light laugh. She was relieved that Mary's intellect had been salvaged.

"Do you remember me telling you about my eldest sister and her family emigrating to Australia?" Mary asked.

"Yes, to Tasmania. I remember," Eriza responded eagerly. She noticed Mary eyeing her suspiciously but wasn't sure why.

"Tasmania is part of Australia," Mary uttered quickly. "They flew Qantas from Dublin Airport. That is when I found out about the airline's full name."

Eriza smiled.

The two girls remained full of confidence throughout their second year. For Eriza, this was despite the racial abuse that she endured. The 'n' word was banded about freely by patients and some nurses whenever the African nurses attended to them. One patient did not hesitate to tell Eriza that in her part of the world, she was a *kaffir*. Some patients even refused to be touched by them. On one drug round, Eriza had held the hand of a white man to calm him for an injection. When Sister had finished with him, he had the audacity to ask Eriza to hand him a tissue so that he could wipe off the very spot where she had touched him. Sister remained silent, so Eriza did the same though she was seething inside.

The African nurses from the West Indies, especially those from Jamaica, always had the last laugh...literally. They would retaliate in their native patois followed by raucous laughter which left the patients confused. They just couldn't understand how the people they insulted could still laugh. Little did they know that the nurses were dishing it back to them twice over. When Eriza learnt the meanings of some of the patois words and phrases, she herself collapsed in fits of laughter. In time, Eriza could articulate them herself and those same words and phrases became a sort of body armour against the sickly and pathetic racial abuse. She didn't tell Mary about her new-found defence mechanism against racial abuse though, as there was a code of silence among the African nurses about the patois rebuttals.

It was Petrona who had taught her the key phrases. They too had become quite close as they had spent some rotations together. Petrona regaled Eriza with stories from her native Jamaica, all in patois, making no exemptions for Eriza. So, it was easy for Eriza to learn what she soon started to see as her fourth language after Shona, English and 'Latin'. Petrona had no idea how fluent Eriza had become until one day when the two of them were among a group of nurses attending to a new white female patient. The patient abused them each time she opened her mouth.

Smiling, Eriza quietly said, "You b....c....."

Petrona could not believe her ears. She burst out laughing, to the dismay of the group and the patient, who all of course had no idea what was so funny. Petrona on the other hand was just bursting to give the other African girls a blow-by-blow account of the drama.

"Elizabeth, you turn bad ii! You a bad bad gal now!" said Roxana, the senior member of the group to an embarrassed Eriza. "Look! Look! Yuh fren' comin'. Don' tell ar nuttin!' You can' trust dem, but you, bad bad bad maan," she whispered to Eriza. "Hello Mary," Roxanna greeted Mary with the broadest smile. "Yuh come fi yuh fren? She tired. She had a very busy day today." Roxanna stood up amid the laughter of the other girls. She then said she was going but sensing that something interesting might be said, she hung around. Then out of the blue she said she was a 'Windrush baby'. Eriza had no idea what this Windrush business was about.

"Hello everyone," Mary said. She didn't know and would never know about the day's proceedings. April, a Grenadian nurse, then chimed in.

"I think myself so fortunate to be with Elizabeth. She is straight from the homeland. She is not diluted like us from the West Indies." April was always open about her admiration for Eriza. "I want to go and work in Africa and live there."

"Yeah, yeah, yeah," the others agreed.

"Yeah April. Grenada too too small. You need a bigger yard," joked Roxanna. "Af'ica big big yuh know," she added, amid raucous laughter.

Eriza blushed before bidding her West Indian friends goodbye and walking with Mary back to their flats.

"And she is so full of dignity. Even when she called the witch b....c..... she did it with such class," Petrona said, out of Mary's and Eriza's earshot.

She laughed out loud again but was quick to remind everyone that Mary should never know about Eriza's mischief in the ward.

"No Petrona. The word you want is finesse," Jackie, also from Jamaica corrected her.

"That too," Petrona said quickly. "Of course, Jackie would know the difference. She come from one a dem posh schools ina Kingston." She spoke as if Jackie was not even there.

"Not like we Maroons from Westmoreland," Roxanna added, quick as a flash. "We fight anytin'. We mash up the British dem ina country with stone, wood, stick and spear." She then spoke directly to Petrona, "Come na, we need to go."

"Oh yeah, mi figet we suppose to do da ting. Sorry ladies. We 'ave fi love uno and leave uno." With that, Petrona and Roxanna walked away, leaving April and Jackie to continue giggling over Eriza's induction into the Hall of Patois.

Eriza continued to keep abreast of the political goings-on in Rhodesia. In her first year, she would read all the papers, but had now more or less settled on *The Guardian*. It was relentless in its reporting of injustices across the globe. The other papers didn't, in her mind, give straightforward information. She read a lot about the anti-apartheid movement which, to her surprise, was very active and vocal in Britain. It spearheaded boycotts and protested against South African cricket and rugby teams playing in the country. At one point, a cricket pitch was even dug up to prevent a match between England and South Africa. The movement didn't see any difference between the racism in South Africa and that in Rhodesia. They were right. The British establishment however wanted to pretend that there was a difference because they wanted to concede to Ian Smith. To equate Rhodesia with South Africa would not allow for negotiations with Smith to legalise his UDI. For the British activists this would have been unacceptable, and so majority rule in Rhodesia became part of the anti-apartheid movement's clarion call.

Eriza's political views also broadened beyond those of her homeland. The Mozambican-Portuguese stand-off was one that intrigued her, least of all because Mozambique and Rhodesia were neighbours. The deadly hits of Frelimo against Portuguese rule were beginning to shake the Portuguese army. One newspaper article reported that, "once the Portuguese are kicked out of Mozambique, Ian Smith's wild dream of no majority rule in Rhodesia will be blown to smithereens.' That article had also made her think back to the Magaya family, her neighbours in Chena; when she was preparing to leave for England, Baba Magaya was preparing to return to a free Mozambique. She thought about how excited the white Rhodesians had been about the Portuguese using Mozambique to break the oil embargo imposed on Rhodesia. Stickers emblazoned with *Obrigado Mozambique* were plastered all over their car windscreens. It was a wonder they could see through both front and rear screens. In one of his letters, Naijo had written that "in our hearts is a sticker that says *Obrigado Frelimo* as the *Obrigado Mozambique* stickers of Rhodesians are getting worn out". He'd added, "*mabhunu* are so stupid".

Then Frelimo had triumphed. Portuguese soldiers deposed their leaders in Portugal and the whole edifice of Portuguese colonial control in Africa had collapsed. Eriza read in the papers that before fleeing the country, Portuguese settlers looted. Their flights were paid out of the government's account and the Frelimo government was saddled with a huge bill. Eriza tried to follow the story but couldn't understand how this could happen. All she could understand was what the papers said: *ZIMBABWE NEXT.*

Meanwhile, Mary educated Eriza on the history of Ireland, starting with the Easter Rising of 1916 in Dublin. At secondary school, Eriza had read Pearse's poems in English Literature. She would be the first to admit that they made no sense to her whatsoever. The literature teacher was a Miss Pearce, who was so passionate about her students appreciating the call to freedom in these poems. So fervent were her recitals that one of Eriza's classmates one day asked Miss Pearce if she was related to the poet. Miss Pearce had just smiled wistfully, and Eriza's classmate was none the wiser.

One thing that Mary's historical monologues showed Eriza was that the ways of colonialists were universal. The plight of the Irish from the time of the massacres perpetrated by Oliver Cromwell, through to the potato blight for which the British establishment's behaviour could be described as no less inhumane than the attitude of Cromwell, to the division of Ireland in 1921, Eriza could see the parallels with the Rhodesians.

Then there were the marches of the Orange Order in Northern Ireland. Catholics deemed these marches to be provocative and they irritated Mary immensely. She particularly disliked Reverend Ian Paisley, leader of one of the unionist parties in Northern Ireland.

"I'm Sinn Fein, but that horrible man Ian Paisley is going to make me join the IRA," she'd confided to Eriza one day. They'd laughed when it dawned upon them that Ian Smith was terrorising Eriza's people and Ian Paisley had no kind words to say about Catholics. They took to calling them 'The Ians", said in a mocking tone with a curl of the lip.

It was now June, nearly the end of their second year. Eriza was in her room at the end of a day on the geriatric ward, lying on her bed with her face buried in a newspaper. Mary saw the headline as soon as she opened the door.

"It's those marches again," Mary moaned.

Even the newspaper seemed to headline Protestant marches with annoyance and impatience. Much to Mary's dismay, there was a picture of Reverend Paisley leading the march.

Eriza was however absorbed in a story about Brazil because she had heard that some of those Portuguese colonials who left Mozambique were welcomed in Brazil. She stared at the accompanying picture of the statue of Christ the Redeemer on top of Mount Corcovado. The statue that she had seen on every calendar in every Catholic's sitting room back in Chena at last had an origin. The article detailed the spectacular scenes, regal costumes and joviality of Afro-Brazilians during carnival. She was mesmerised until the article credited slavery for 'inventing' carnival; in fact, the underlying tone was that were it not for the Africans being enslaved, there would never have been a carnival. Eriza was furious. She looked at the statue again, looking down on the revellers and she realised just how brazen the European exploitation of African people all over the world was, using Christianity to subjugate whole continents.

"They are making money out of the talent of Africans just as they did and are still doing with their blood and sweat." She muttered as she briefly thought back to her social studies and geography lessons on tourism in Brazil with the Rio Carnival as a case study. Mary heard her murmurings and assumed that she was on some story on Rhodesia.

"You know something Liz? The Protestants in Northern Ireland are no different from the Rhodesian whites." Mary spoke earnestly. "Think about it. In Rhodesia, you have separate schools for Africans and whites. Your schools are poorly run. White schools, like that Mount Pleasant where your brother and his friend were passing through and were insulted by some white boys who told them to go back to Zambia, are first class. It's the same in Northern Ireland except that the discrimination is based on religion and not race. We Catholics get the leftovers in everything. It stinks." Mary spoke with an anguish that Eriza had never heard before. "And you know what," she added, "the Protestants in Northern Ireland are descendants of English and Scottish settlers." She paused for effect and looked at Eriza.

Eriza held on to her paper but was now giving Mary her full attention.

"Didn't you tell me that Ian Smith is Scottish?" Mary asked.

"Yeah. His father got a free farm at a place called Selukwe. It's Shurugwi actually, but those Rhodesians are good at debasing our African names. I didn't know you also have this 'settler' problem in Ireland as well? Look, I'm reading about Portuguese slavery and colonialism in Brazil and the stupid writer thinks that without them, there would be no Rio carnival! And on top of that, he writes such rubbish under a picture of a statue of Jesus, then implies that the African revellers are thankful to God for the carnival. Can you believe the audacity?!"

"For centuries," Mary was now encouraged to continue, 'the Protestants' argument has been that a united Ireland will make them a minority and the majority Catholics will discriminate against them, but they don't see anything wrong with their bigotry in Northern Ireland now, as we speak."

Eriza wanted to hear more about the politics of Northern Ireland but Mary suddenly decided to go to her room. However, the discussion had adequately set the stage for their journey to Trafalgar Square, to an anti-apartheid rally the following day.

❀ ❀ ❀

They set out early that Saturday morning. Both had heard about Speakers' Corner in Hyde Park where a person could say anything they wished with impunity. They wanted to see and hear the characters there, some of whom were said to be quite entertaining, before attending the rally. Roxanna had once done a hilarious impersonation of one such character when the African Queens, as they now called themselves, were lounging in Roxanna's room for one of their get-togethers. It was of an African man who took to the stage and harangued the British to go back where they came from. After her raucous display, the consensus from the group made up of two Trinidadians, five Jamaicans and Eriza, was that Roxanna would be a hit on Speakers' Corner. So Eriza eagerly anticipated the detour before the rally.

The weather was ideal – sunny and warm. The two girls were dressed for it but had jumpers with them just in case the English weather did as the English weather was always guaranteed to do.

"Shall we go by train or coach?" Eriza asked.

"I think we should go by coach. We'll really get to witness the true beauty of the countryside at this time of year." Mary spoke longingly as she visualised the Irish countryside. For a moment, she wished she was back home in the green lands of County Tyrone where, as a young girl, she'd spend the summer holidays with her grandmother, aunts and cousins.

"I agree. I remember when I first came here, the fields were brown from scorching sun. Yes, let's go by coach and I can see the countryside in all its glory!"

With that, they set off on foot towards the coach station. As they walked, Eriza, once again, took in the sights of the Roman garrison that was now Colchester town. Where once stood the Roman soldiers' quarters was now a shopping mall; as they took a shortcut through a narrow side road, she was sure they were walking on the original cobblestones laid down by Roman soldiers.

"I generally don't approve of invaders and oppressors but I'm not at all unhappy that the Romans conquered Britain," Eriza casually said to Mary.

Mary looked at Eriza. "Your relationship with the Romans and the British can be unhealthy at times. Be careful. Soon you'll be walking around chanting 'Herr Hitler, Herr Hitler'."

Both girls collapsed in a fit of giggles.

"Do you know I grew up thinking that Hitler's first name was 'Herr'? Eriza said in between snorts of laughter.

"Blimey!" Mary exclaimed, after which they burst into another round of hysterical laughter.

Suddenly, a siren sounded. A police car was pursuing a speeding vehicle. The vehicle under pursuit made a sudden left turn into a road that the two girls were just about to cross. Eriza gasped as Mary screamed. At the same time each girl stretched out an arm to stop the other from stepping into the road and straight into the path of the maniacal driver. Soon after, the police car also sped past. It was all over within seconds and they hurriedly stepped back and sat down on a low wall to catch their breath while gesticulating the sign of the cross.

Another police car came and stopped in front of them. A young officer came out of the car and walked up to the girls, or rather, walked up to Mary. His demeanour made it clear that he was not interested in Eriza's well-being or anything she might have wanted to say. His gaze was firmly focused on Mary.

"I'm all right, thank you," Mary responded.

On cue, he got back into his squad car, certain that his job was done. The girls looked at each other. Eriza's countenance indicated that she didn't expect anything less from the young officer. How could a *mujoni* – white police officer – in England be different from one in Rhodesia? She'd never thought there could be any difference between them.

"If there was a theft or robbery, I'm sure he would have been very much interested in you." Mary spoke with an annoyance that betrayed her knowledge of the Ulster Constabulary towards Catholics in Northern Ireland.

"Believe you me when I say it would have been very much the same back home. Even an act of kindness from an African to a Rhodesian can lead to death," Eriza said solemnly, not for dramatic effect but because it was true.

The pair finally stood up, gathered themselves and straightened up. For Mary, that included touching up her lipstick. As they continued walking to the bus terminus, Eriza elaborated on her dramatic declaration.

"Back in Chena, there was a young man, Gideon, who had landed a job as a house boy with a Rhodesian couple with two young daughters. All indications were that Gideon was a hard worker who was rewarded with gifts to take home to his family whenever he was off. He lived in the boys' *kaya* – male servants' quarters – at the back of the big house belonging to his employers. One day he came back from his day off with a treat for the two little girls. He'd seen them enjoying lollipops before on several occasions and so he thought he'd surprise them with one each.

"Gideon entered the house from the kitchen door. That was the rule. House boys and house girls never entered the house through the front door. He exchanged pleasantries with Molly the house girl who was well known in Chena as a spirited woman. The little girls heard him and as usual were delighted to see him. They were even more excited when he gave them a lollipop each. The pair ran to the living room where the parents were relaxing, no doubt happy that their workhorse was back. They waved their gifts in their parents' faces.

"What? That *bobojani* – baboon! The father exploded. He ordered his wife to confiscate the lollipops as he rose from his seat to the bedroom, returning with a revolver. Both his wife and Molly screamed. He shoved his wife out of his way and headed straight to the kitchen where 'Johnie' was getting ready to start his duties – they'd totally disregarded that his name was Gideon ever since he'd started working for them. Anyway, it didn't matter, he was now a *bobojani* who had no idea that his short life was about to come to an abrupt end."

"Bloody hell Eriza! You're not going to tell me that...," Mary gasped, her eyes wide open.

"Well, Molly and the wife were rushing behind the murderous Rhodesian, but thankfully the little girls had remained in the living room, lollipops in hand, baffled by all the commotion. Remember how I told you that Molly was no wallflower? Anyway, she managed to shout out a warning to Gideon, otherwise known as Johnie the *bobojani*.

"*Tizai!*" – Run! – she'd shouted.

"Without looking up, because he understood the urgency in her tone, Gideon threw the back door open. But he didn't manage to set one foot in front of the other. The bullet caught him in the back and he fell dead across the doorstep."

Mary stopped in her tracks, horrified, and for once, speechless. Eriza was about to continue the story but spotted their bus and heard its engine start to roar.

"C'mon Mary. Quickly! Let's get on the bus. My father told us the story because he attended the court case to help Molly who was state witness. The court didn't believe her and the white man walked free." Eriza stopped as she held the door rail of the bus. Her eyes searched the bus as if she was looking for the murderous Rhodesian.

Nearly two-and-a-half hours later, they arrived at Trafalgar Square. It was packed. Eriza counted numerous organisations, coalitions and factions announcing their presence with name banners, and all opponents of apartheid. There was what looked like a trade unionist with a megaphone calling upon British businesses to withdraw from South Africa. Another was shouting out that Barclays Bank was a major 'money vault' for white South Africans and was therefore a partner of apartheid.

"Your money has blood with Barclays," he shouted.

Eriza and Mary eyed each other as they'd both opened bank accounts with Barclays.

"I think we should close our accounts, don't you?" Mary said.

They then saw another banner warning one establishment church to divest from South Africa.

Eriza wondered whether it was worth the trouble, as the most she ever had in her account was £65. They gravitated towards a group of white people holding a banner which read, *NUS is against Apartheid and Barclays Bank*. A young white man came out of nowhere and eagerly explained to them how Barclays Bank was financing racial discrimination, killings of anti-apartheid figures and the incarceration of Nelson Mandela at Robben Island. He held a placard that read 'John Harris, Sharpeville'.

Dropping by Speakers' Corner was no longer necessary. The rally was captivating enough. Eriza decided that it was more than worth the trouble to switch banks.

She'd never heard of John Harris but she remembered Sharpeville. It was spoken of in hushed but chilling tones back home by all Africans as they feared that such a slaughter would be visited upon them too in Rhodesia. After the massacre, some of the residents of Chena who had migrated to South Africa for work had returned. They told of the mayhem and carnage. One of the prodigal villagers had 'married' a white woman with whom he had eleven children, one a new-born. The laws in South Africa mandated that they had three homes: one for their mixed-race children, one for the mother and another for the father, with all three homes in different locations. The Sharpeville massacre and the brutal and immoral division of his family forced him to return to Chena. Overnight, Chena Primary inherited ten mixed-race pupils who could speak neither Shona nor English. They spoke Afrikaans which everyone found far too crude to be considered a language. How anyone could declare love, harmony or peace in that tongue was a mystery to all in Chena. The family certainly added a new shade of black to the region for miles around, legitimately outnumbering the progeny of the Catholic priests.

"I don't know about this John Harris but I know about Nelson Mandela. They want him to die in prison," Eriza said to the young white man.

"I'm Tony," he replied. "And you are from..." He looked at Eriza awaiting her response.

"...Rhodesia."

"Oh. Those white Rhodesians are just as much of a menace as the Boers. All your leaders are in prison or detention. Tell you what eh, eh...," he stuttered, his eyes pleading for her name.

"Eri...Elizabeth," Eriza replied a little embarrassed and surprised at herself for overlooking the fact that Tony was a white man who couldn't possibly grasp 'Eriza', no matter how impassioned he was about the plight of Africans.

"Tell you what Elizabeth," Tony continued, "there are guys from Rhodesia I know quite well. They might be here somewhere in the crowd. I will tell them about you. You may know them already."

"No, I don't know anyone from Rhodesia but I'd really like to meet them."

"I'll let them know," Tony added as he rushed off to catch up with his group. "And bye. Nice meeting you! By the way, John Harris is the only white man killed by his fellow whites for violent opposition to apartheid," he shouted in his stride.

Eriza looked at Mary who had stood by quietly as Tony and Eriza were in dialogue.

"Mary, this is the first time I've heard a white man saying anything unkind about Rhodesians."

"You haven't heard us Irish laying into the English. But they give as good as they get though. "Bastards" is one word we freely trade against each other. Not in each other's faces but in our separate ethnic enclaves," she said laughing.

"Well back home we insult white people right in their faces because most of them don't understand what we're saying anyway. It's so liberating though," she chuckled. "The only thing is that their children understand us. Naijo told me how once he was in Salisbury with his friends happily insulting each white person that walked past them in Shona, quite confident that none of them would understand. One of the 'victims' was a man in his early twenties; as he walked past them, one of Naijo's friends shouted at him.

"*Ndizvo zvimabhunu izvi, fanika ichi, zvinoda kuurawa.*" That means 'these are the Boers we need to kill'. The white boy replied, "*Mhoroi machinda. Mutauro wenyu ndewe hondo. Musawhikwe nemapurisa*". Translated that means 'Hello gentlemen. This is war talk. Don't let the police hear you.' My brother and his friends were stunned. The white boy laughed and carried on his merry way."

"I better be careful when you speak in your language around me then just in case you are insulting me too," Mary joked and they both laughed.

"*Kaka ngwarisa aka,*" Eriza said in between giggles.

"What does that mean?" Mary asked. "You're being naughty Elizabeth, I know." Mary pouted jokingly.

"Oh Mary, it means you're a very clever girl."

"I knew that."

"You mean you understand Shona already," Eriza responded with a hint of sarcasm.

"No, silly. I meant I know I'm clever. Hey, look at the Irish green over there!" She pointed at a group of men and women all clad in green and white. "I wonder which organisation they belong to."

"Maybe it's a belated St Patrick's Day celebration," Eriza murmured, remembering how Father Patrick had almost turned the Diocese of Chena into an Irish parish one St Patrick's Day. She thought twice about telling Mary as she didn't want to go into the details of the disgraced Irish priest.

They walked slowly through the crowd heading towards the Irish green group. The sun was shining, it was pleasantly warm and the whole rally was taking on a carnival mood. They passed three young African men and Mary whispered to Eriza that one of them was ogling them. Eriza resisted the urge to look back just in case they got ahead of themselves and misinterpreted things. There was no way they could be interested in Mary, nor Mary in them, just as she had never been interested in any white man.

As they walked deeper into the crowd, they saw more and more Africans. Eriza listened out for Shona but all she heard was a variety of other African languages and English. Then she heard this: '*Apartheid ichangofa somufiro wemuridzi wayo, Verwoerd. Banga pamoyo*' – apartheid will die a violent death like its founder, Verwoerd. A butcher's knife to the heart. It was pure Shona coming from a bald-headed man about two bodies away from them. He was with a younger-looking man and three women, all about Eriza's age. Eriza drifted towards them. She wasn't going to miss this opportunity, especially after not having spoken Shona to anyone apart from herself for so long.

"*Moroi*" – Hello. She waved at them, but reverently for the benefit of the bald-headed older man. As she got closer, her greeting was followed by a curtsy and gently clap of her hands as per the customary manner of greeting elders. They all looked at her and that bemused Mary, especially as they had abruptly stopped walking, leading Mary to think that *moroi* meant 'halt'.

"*Moro mwana'ngu*" – Hello my child. The man responded with a broad smile but with searching eyes as if he was trying to figure out if he had met her before. He looked at his group to see if any of them recognised this well-mannered girl. They were of no help – their faces were blank.

"Wauyawo kuzondzwa zvekwedu pano?" – Have you come to hear some home politics? he asked, as his eyes continued to search out her identity.

"Hongu Baba" – Yes father. Eriza was being even more respectful by referring to him as father. He switched to English.

"Where do you come from?"

"Chena, Baba."

"Ah, ah!" His eyes lit up. "I used to teach a few miles south of Chena, at Kuweza. You must know Philemon Kanyemba. He was the headteacher at Chena Primary." He looked at Eriza earnestly as he had been fond of his colleague Philemon. Perhaps he'd met Eriza at Chena District's Annual Primary Schools' Athletic Meet.

"Ooh Mr Kanyemba. We knew him quite well. He's the one who took me to the airport to fly here." Eriza hadn't known Mr Kanyemba's first name until now and that made her feel sad.

"You must have come here recently then. Do you know what happened to him? Those Boers want to kill us all." He shook his head with anger and kissed his teeth.

"It's hard Baba," Eriza whispered, looking down at her feet. The emotion she'd contained for so long after hearing about Mr Kanyemba's murder was beginning to overwhelm her. Meeting this man with his confirmation of Mr Kanyemba's death made her realise that she was never going to see Mr Kanyemba again, him or his grave. She thought about his very beautiful and very reserved wife and how her mother had liked Mrs Kanyemba because she never bragged about being the headteacher's wife. Their two boys were always washed and smartly dressed. That went down well with her mother's motto of 'cleanliness is nearer to godliness', though Naijo never failed to correct her that it was 'cleanliness is next to godliness'.

The man instinctively realised that Eriza was in pain. He wondered whether she was related to Philemon. "I'm Claudius Musevanhu," he introduced himself gently. "What's your name?"

"Eriza. Elizabeth Mukwesa."

"It's painful Eriza, my child. I know."

Eriza's head rang with her name. At last someone knew her 'real' name. That made her even more emotional and at that point she wanted nothing more than to be back in Chena to mourn Mr Kanyemba properly and pay her respects to his family. Somehow, she managed to pull herself together. They then exchanged information about events in Chena but none of them had any additional information about the circumstances surrounding Mr Kanyemba's death or where his body could be.

As Eriza and Mr Musevanhu continued to talk, Mary had introduced herself to the other four members of the group, who turned out to be the nieces and nephew of Mr Musevanhu. Mary could get blood out of a stone if required, so it was not surprising that she had already established who they were, and more. It turned out that two of the girls, Kudzai and Phyllis, were trainee nurses in Ipswich. The young man, Jemias, was Kudzai's brother, and was a medical student in London. The third and youngest of the group introduced herself as Millicent, who had just started a degree course in veterinary science. She was Phyllis' younger sister. The four of them were from the brood of Mr Musevanhu's two sisters in Rhodesia. Mary had also established that their uncle had lived in London with his wife and two of his four sons. The other two were studying at Leeds University. The two at home were still in secondary school and had opted to stay home to watch football that afternoon.

"You lot are Irish really!" Mary exclaimed, followed by laughter from her new acquaintances.

"Why?" Jemias asked.

"We Irish love family and stay together wherever we are."

There was a spark between them which had taken Jemias by surprise – in all the three years he'd been surrounded by white women, none had given him the warm feeling that Mary had. He found himself thinking about how long the journey from London to Colchester would be.

"Yes, we're like that, but Irish we're not…yet," he joked. He was laying the groundwork. Everyone laughed while Mary purred with delight.

Mr Musevanhu turned towards the laughter and so did Eriza. "Let me introduce you to my nephew and nieces," he said eagerly.

They all exchanged pleasantries.

"I see you are already well acquainted with…who might this lady be?" Mr Musevanhu asked courteously, looking at Mary.

"I'm sorry," Eriza said embarrassed. "This is Mary O'Driscoll, my friend from Ireland. We're training together in Colchester."

"We already know," Jemias said cheekily, but with a hint of affection. Everyone laughed and Eriza knew just why. Mary, her dear Mary, never held back.

"Glad to meet you Mary," Mr Musevanhu said.

"You too…Sir," Mary responded hesitantly. Everyone realised the challenge Mary faced with 'Musevanhu", and at that they all laughed.

"*Vanhu*, let's go," Mr Musevanhu then suddenly said to his family.

They all said their goodbyes and then carved their separate ways through the crowd. That wasn't to say that Eriza and Mary hadn't wanted to follow them, for their own reasons of course. However, they decided to walk towards the steps of the pavilion where they could find a spot to sit and listen to the speakers. They were lucky to find a space, but the gala-like atmosphere didn't make it easy to hear what the different speakers had to say. It dawned on Eriza that maybe it wasn't the content of the speeches that mattered, but the atmosphere and size of the crowd. Indeed, as later reported in the news, this was a record crowd, which was a measure of the revulsion the British held against apartheid in particular and colonialism in general. By the end of their adventure, foremost in her mind was what role she should play in the struggle against white rule in Rhodesia.

❀ ❀ ❀

When Eriza was undergoing her political awakening, things were not going so well for Naijo. Even though he now had an LLB degree, he couldn't land a job. There was no legal firm or government department that was willing to take him on to do his articles to become a professional lawyer. A few days after the rally, Eriza received a letter from Naijo:

❀ ❀ ❀

When I visit these law offices all I see are the white faces of people who graduated with me or before. They don't recognise me, or rather, they pretend not to recognise me. Just the other day, a white receptionist at yet another firm handed me an application form whilst telling me not to bother as I wouldn't be hired anyway. She said it right to my face. Warungu ava are the children of Lucifer, as mother would say about any mean person. I wanted to ask her why not. Then I asked myself, "Why ask to be given an answer I already know?" Anyway, I told her I would be back.

The few African lawyers that are practising in Salisbury would like to take me on but they are already inundated with applications from other African graduates. It looks like I will just have to do my articles privately and write the exams without any practical experience. Anyway, I'm certain that Zimbabwe is just around the corner and we can do whatever we want.

❀ ❀ ❀

Eriza was heartbroken not just for herself but for the entire family. Naijo's income as a lawyer would have transformed the family's fortunes, whereby her nurse's pay just bought temporary relief. The whole saga strengthened her resolve to not just do well with her studies but also step

195

up her political activism. She thought back to how Naijo would urge himself on when faced with a challenging task with a quote from the Chinese leader Mao Tse-tung, 'A journey of a thousand miles starts with one step'. She considered her trip to the anti-apartheid rally to be her first step.

❖ ❖ ❖

She wasn't the only one undergoing a political transformation. Her high school sweetheart, David, was too. Their communication had continued over the past two years and had become predictable. She would receive a letter from him every other Wednesday. That same night, she would write a lengthy reply and post it the following day, on the Thursday. The letters always ended with, *I love you and I miss you.* Sometimes they'd exchange romantic lyrics from the most popular songs in the music charts. Just as Eriza was becoming thoughtful about her involvement in the liberation of her country, David's letters had also morphed to part love manuals and part political manifestos. This delighted her but also made her fear for his life.

Naijo was a seasoned operator but David, not at all. He was a total novice in this game of politics. When they were in secondary school, students like Wilfred and Willard were considered politically rebellious as they spoke passionately about using AK47s to shoot Rhodesians. David on the other hand always spoke of the rise of an unnamed African messiah who would negotiate and strategise a way out of oppression. In their final year, Wilfred was expelled for insulting one of the white teachers. The story was that on the evening after arriving home, he crossed into Zambia to be trained in the use of an AK47. David had never spoken to her about Wilfred's gallantry, but here he was, in his latest letter, talking about joining the armed struggle in Mozambique. His last sentence was:

196

My allegiance is to Zimbabwe where we will meet again.

❖❖❖

Little did Eriza know that that would be the last word she would hear from either David or Naijo for some time.

❖❖❖

Having failed to land a job as a lawyer, Naijo took up a post as a teacher at a boarding school in Matebeleland. He thought the move fortuitous but in fact it was by design. His work with Mr Kanyemba was well known by the liberation movement in the southern part of the country. He didn't know that he had been classified as a reliable cadre and behind the scenes, strings had been pulled to ensure he landed the job. He soon realised that his real job came at night and weekends when he was required to guide people across the border and received weapons for safe keeping. Naijo being Naijo asked no questions and merely saw it as a continuation of the work he had done with Mr Kanyemba. In fact, in his mind, he was in a way, honouring his mentor's memory.

It was during this time that Naijo met David. David knew him when he was a final year student and of course as the brother of his girlfriend. Naijo just remembered the face – the face of the first university student he'd helped to cross the border. As he was never to write down the names of people who crossed under him, he learnt to remember faces. David's was imprinted in his memory. They talked a lot about the state of politics at the university before David jumped the border in broad daylight.

"Don't worry guys, the settler army sleeps during the day," Naijo told David's group of five men that Sunday afternoon. Within an hour the five were mingling with men and women in the fields of Botswana. They blended in well even though they couldn't speak the local language. There was one man who spoke Kalanga and Tswana though and it was him that took them onto the second leg of their journey the following day. That night, Naijo returned with a cache of arms back to the school just as Mr Kanyemba had found the university campus in Salisbury to be a safe arms depot. The perfect place to hide them.

Monday morning, Naijo was back in front of his geography class, quoting Abraham Lincoln. "We do not know what the future holds but the best way to predict the future is to create it." As he spoke, he recalled his grandmother's words at the wake of a young prominent nationalist. She'd said, "The future is the greatest gift to mankind. It is heavily pregnant with beautiful possibilities that promise to wipe away the horrors of today and yesterday".

"How do you do that, Sir?" asked one of his brighter students, Vukile. "How do we create our future?"

"What I'm doing now is preparing you to change our country," Naijo answered.

"You mean to remove *amabhunu* – white Rhodesians – from ruling us!" Vukile was excited. "I like that, Sir. It's politics."

"That's the easy bit. The most challenging part is how we run the country afterwards. That is what I want you to be ready for *mufana*. OK, so we are going to go through the human geography of Canada first and then finish the lesson with our country's geography." He then turned to Vukile and said, "Politics and the beautiful future."

ELEVEN

It was now her third year and Eriza was two weeks in. How things had changed. First, she hadn't heard from David for months. Her family was facing the spectre of a civil war between Africans and Rhodesians. As much as her family missed her, they urged her to stay put in England for a while. Mai Eriza was the only one with reservations about the family decision though.

"What's the point of her coming back now when she hasn't finished anything?" Sekuru Fani posed the question to Mbuya Mukwesa. "Besides, it's better she just goes straight into studying medicine rather than take a risk and return here and end up not being able to go back."

"That's all she's ever wanted. To be a doctor," Baba Eriza added. Everyone looked at him, silently saying in unison, "That's all you've ever wanted." The country had produced its first African female doctor a few years previously and having missed that opportunity, Baba Eriza was certain that he was destined to be the father of the second African female doctor.

"But she should at least visit. Mbuya is old and misses her so much," Mai Eriza pleaded. Sekuru Fani looked at his sister who he knew spoke more for herself than for Mbuya Mukwesa.

"Are you forgetting how the Rhodesian security forces massacred that whole village up north not long ago?" Sekuru Fani reminded his sister. With that, Mai Eriza capitulated.

Mbuya Mukwesa remained quiet. Her worry was that if Eriza stayed too long in England, she would end up with a white husband. The thought of her granddaughter literally sleeping with the enemy appalled her. Her sacred home had been stolen by a white man and she could not bear the thought of her granddaughter being given away as a bride to such a being. Eventually she couldn't help but weigh in on the conversation.

"She can stay there as long as she wants once she does not end up with a white husband. What would we do about *roora* – bride money? And *mombe dzacho* – bride cows. Are they going to be flown over here? She spoke as if Eriza had announced her engagement there and then.

Prudence and Sekuru Fani looked at each other, desperate not to laugh.

"You see VaMusiyamwa told me his niece had married an English man. He even showed me a picture of the couple. I told him I didn't like it one bit. Then he told me that she is very happy even though some of her husband's relatives don't like her. How can that work? A marriage is a community effort. If the community does not like your wife, who is she going to ask for salt when she's run out in the middle of her cooking?" Mbuya Mukwesa always distilled things down to domestics when it came to matters of human relations.

"On top of that, VaMusiyamwa's niece is also my relative and that taints my bloodline. If Eriza went that way too, eeh I don't know." With that she squeezed the hem of her dress where a red ant was lurking. The poor creature bore the brunt of her anger as she squashed it with her forefinger. She sucked her teeth as she thought of the photo being seen by the other members of the family, leading to them softening on the issue of mixed marriages.

"I saw the photo too," said Baba Eriza, "and VaMusiyamwa's niece does look happy. In fact, they both look happy."

"But you do know that side of the family can be stupid at times, don't you?" she retorted. And with that, the conversation ended.

VaMusiyamwa was however far from being stupid. Not long after news had filtered through about that village up north being decimated by Rhodesians, a sole survivor, a girl, had made her way to Chena on the Musiyamwa bus. For a few days before that, VaMusiyamwa had seen her hanging around his bus at the market in Mbare. What was unusual was that her hands were empty; unlike all the other girls her age milling about, she carried no merchandise and wore the same clothes every day. In fact, she looked lost, as if she was looking for someone. He saw her eventually sneak on his bus but did not fuss at all, telling the young man who helped to load the bus to just leave her alone. He drove with her to Chena and beyond.

When the journey ended later that evening, she refused to leave the bus. After much coaxing, she eventually told him her name – Rosie Muchururu – and where she was from – Mazumba. VaMusiyamwa knew immediately that her surname was a typical one of that area. Then it all came out – how *mabhunu* had come out of nowhere like a pack of hyenas, shooting and slashing everyone in sight before setting the village on fire. She had been out in the fields and for some reason, that day, had taken a different route home through the bushes to the west of the village. This was the only opening *mabhunu* had left. But no matter how he tried, he could not convince her to get off the bus. After her harrowing tale, he understood exactly why. So he handed her a blanket and let her sleep at the back.

The following morning, when dawn broke, VaMusiyamwa went to check on her. She jumped up as soon as she heard the door creak open. He slowly walked towards her with a bowl of porridge and tea, being careful not to make sudden or fast movements in case he frightened her. Before he could hand her the food, she clapped her hands as a way of thanking him. She ate slowly because she didn't want the food to finish. What horrors this child must have seen and how famished she was, he thought to himself. He knew then that he could not abandon her.

"Do you want to help me run this bus?" he asked her as she slurped the hot tea. "Which title do you prefer, bus conductor or bus assistant?" She stopped slurping and slowly looked around the bus. Then she put the cup down and folded the small blanket, resting it across her lap, before gazing outside. She had no idea where she was but it reminded her of what her home once was and was certainly more peaceful than that market.

"*Zvose zvinoita, Baba,*" – Either title will do Father, she responded meekly. "Thank you very much, Baba." Tears now rolled down her cheeks.

"Call me Sekuru. You are my sister's daughter. That's what we'll tell people. The mother of that house, pointing at a house where he had slept, has some water for you to wash if you want." They smiled at each other because both of them knew that she needed a proper bath. With that, VaMusiyamwa set the stage for what became an enduring and loving relationship between a *sekuru* and his *muzukuru*, one that even saw Rhodesia become Zimbabwe. Of course, he'd told the Mukwesa family the truth about Rosie, as he knew that they would protect her identity.

No doubt marriage was the furthest thing from Eriza's mind, even as Mbuya Mukwesa fretted over the prospect. However, that hadn't stopped Eriza from worrying herself silly over David's sudden break in communication. It had been nearly five months since she'd heard from him. Little did she know that David, her beloved David, was now settling into university in Scotland.

❋ ❋ ❋

When David had crossed the border into Botswana, he'd walked for days with a group of other young male refugees. Botswana was very sympathetic to their plight and had made arrangements for these young men and women to continue their education in Europe. David accepted an offer to resume his degree in agriculture at a Scottish university. He'd never heard of it before but it was an offer he couldn't refuse. Maybe, he'd accepted, he wasn't made for the rebel life.

What this whole repatriation of sorts signified was that the British government was at last becoming sensitised to a situation it had allowed to develop into an armed conflict. It was now time to ease the situation somehow, especially as many countries continued to remind them that Rhodesia remained its problem. Documented, clothed and plane-ticketed, in the middle of September, David flew into London and then continued on by train to Edinburgh.

❋ ❋ ❋

With Naijo deep in clandestine liberation activities, Sekuru Fani had ended up taking over Mr Kanyemba's job. He grew to admire the former headteacher's courage and becoming his successor was both an honour for him and a tribute to Mr Kanyemba's bravery. Even though Sekuru Fani and all of Chena now knew that Mr Kanyemba had kept an arsenal of weapons in the boot of his car, he still believed that the little humans that nestled among the grenades and AK47s had helped him to escape the clutches of the Rhodesian army.

Sekuru Fani didn't have a car so he hid smuggled arms in a tunnel under Chena's main road. He had put a lot of thought into preparing this tunnel and in fact he thought the idea was ingenious. The road itself had been built years before, when Naijo was in standard six, using labour from the nearby prison – petty criminals who were not considered dangerous. Sekuru Fani would spend a lot of time watching these *mabhantiti* – prisoners – working. In the end, their security guard had offered him a prison uniform, teasing him that he might as well join the convicts.

Two things about the construction process had struck him. The first was the drainage tunnel that was built from one side of the road to the other. The second was the medium-sized hole that remained on the side of the road where *mabhantiti* had dug out the gravel. So now, years later, when the honour to secure an arms cache was bestowed upon him, the drainage tunnel came to mind. Under the pretext of collecting gravel for church repairs, he redug the gravel hole into the tunnel and concealed the entrance with a fallen log. He referred to his tunnel as a 'fannel', and the tunnel a dam. So, the words combined became 'Fannel Dam', the codeword for weapons that was known only to him and the fighters.

He'd nearly spilt the beans on his pivotal role in the liberation movement to Ceciria, partly to show off, especially because he was also the local procurement officer for freedom fighters in the surrounding district; at last his turn to be like the Mau Mau had arrived and he relished it. The other part of him wanted to get her involved.

Fortuitously, Mbuya Mukwesa, during an unrelated conversation between the two of them, had hinted at the dangers of a loose tongue in the current climate. They had been sharing the shade of her *msasa* tree, both wanting to talk about Eriza, but neither initiating the subject. Mbuya Mukwesa was not sure whether Sekuru Fani would see her point of view. Meanwhile, Sekuru Fani, confident the war would be won, was sure that within two years, Eriza would land at Harare and not Salisbury Airport. He would be there to meet her and at the same time, see off the settlers, shouting "You settlers go back and don't ever, ever come back!"

❖❖❖

"Us women can be destructive," Mbuya Mukwesa said in a casual manner. "Especially when we have too many friends," she added with a knowing smile.

Sekuru Fani was bemused. He knew she was referring to Ceciria, especially as she had always been suspicious of her. He had no idea why. What could Ceciria do that would be so destructive? Before he could probe, she surprised him.

"VaMusiyamwa told me yesterday that Ceciria was in his bus talking to a detective, who gave her money." She stopped, but her eyes were fixed on the road, as if she was looking out for the bus to catch Ceciria in action. "All sorts of people travel on the bus these days," she reminded Sekuru Fani.

He was speechless – shocked in fact – because some of the weapons were on that same bus en route to distribution among the freedom fighters.

"Were you not going to the school this afternoon?" Mbuya asked calmly. She wanted him to go and think about what she'd just told him.

"Ah yes. I'd almost forgotten." Sekuru Fani was relieved that he'd stayed calm in front of Mbuya Mukwesa.

He walked in a hurry but not sure where to. He had no intention of going to the school, that he knew. Once on the main road, he looked to his left, then his right, not expecting to see anyone, because all he could see in his mind was Ceciria and the detective.

"They were talking", he muttered to himself.

The arms cache was under the road about five hundred yards away to his left. In a flash, he turned to look. There was now a lone figure walking towards him. He resisted the urge to run and examine the 'depot', even though all he could think about was that Ceciria had opened her mouth to the detective, even though he was sure he'd told her nothing.

The lone figure, a young man, continued walking in his direction, but Sekuru Fani couldn't identify him. He noticed that the man was carrying a leather bag in his left hand, big enough to carry a few items of clothing. It was very similar to Naijo's. Naijo carried shirts, a pair of trousers and a few groceries in his whenever he visited home. A tweed jacket was draped over his right shoulder, in a way typical of young men walking in the blistering heat on their last leg home from the train station. Sekuru Fani knew all the young men in Chena. As this one came closer, it was clear to Sekuru Fani that he was not local, especially as when he greeted him, 'Fannel Dam' was not the response. This man failed the test and that heightened Sekuru Fani's concerns. Surely, he had to be an agent of the government. Was this Ceciria's detective?

He looked and behaved quite innocently though as he told Sekuru Fani how he had far to go as he'd been told that there were no buses on this road. He'd got off the train at Mawiro at ten in the evening the day before and had slept at the station. In the morning, he'd set off on foot to Mariva. Feeling awkward under Sekuru Fani's scrutinising gaze, he cut his tale short, politely excused himself and resumed his journey.

"No, wait. There's a bus coming soon and it will take you as far as Mariva."

Sekuru Fani was warming up towards the man. He was now sure that he wasn't Ceciria's detective and after a quick glance at the 'arms depot', he smiled at the man. It was time to find out about this new arrival in the village.

"My grandparents live in Mariva and I didn't want to go back to England without seeing them. My name is James Chipanda," he volunteered, as if he'd read Sekuru Fani's mind. He had no idea what impact his revelation would have.

"From England!" Sekuru Fani shouted, as his eyes darted all over James. *"Ah shuwa*? Where in England?" His guard was now completely down. This was surely a sign that Eriza would be back soon.

"A small town called Ipswich in Essex. For seven years now, I've been working as a nurse there."

"Don't tell me! My niece is in Essex too. In a town called Colchester," he said with heightened excitement. In Chena, a male nurse was known as an 'orderly', a title that was incorrectly interpreted as cleaner or porter. Fortunately, Sekuru Fani knew better because one of Eriza's many photos featured her alongside white male nurses.

"Ah yes. Colchester. It's only twenty miles from Ipswich. I've been there several times. What does she do there? What's her name?"

"It's Eriza. She's finishing nursing very soon and should be home in two years." Sekuru Fani said this with confidence, while discretely keeping an eye on the site of the arms cache. Then they walked over the very spot with Sekuru Fani stamping the ground to test all was intact. He smiled. It was. He then looked behind them and had a vision of Eriza being driven home in a car bought by Naijo.

"Ko imi mukoma munondzi ani?" – What is your name big brother? – James asked tentatively, not wishing to appear intrusive.

"Fani *muningina* – young brother. Oh, there's our home there with the big house." He pointed at the house with such pride that James knew instantly that Eriza had something to do with it. His sister, who was also doing nursing in England, had done the same with their grandparents' house in Mariva. He had chipped in now and then.

"Hey, the bus will be here soon. It will take an hour to get to Mariva and the driver, he's my relative you know, will stay overnight then leave at 7 o'clock the next morning. When are you returning to England? I would like to give you a letter to take to Eriza." He said it in a way that indicated to James that it would be a big favour.

"That means my grandparents can travel with me to Salisbury and stay with me until I fly back next week," James said. "I can take the letter for you. In fact I'm more than happy to but it will be a while before it gets to Eriza."

"As soon as you get on the bus...*ehe*...talking about the bus, here it comes. I will write the letter tonight and you'll see me waiting here with it. Actually, I will talk to the driver so that he can look after you all the way."

The bus stopped and a cloud of dust engulfed them. Rosie, the bus conductor, liked to call it her 'rain of dust'.

"Where are you going today, Sekuru? Who is your friend, Sekuru? Get in before more dust lands on you," Rosie fired commands at the men in the fashion of a country bus conductor.

"You shut up *muzukuru*," Sekuru Fani hit back jokingly. "It's James here travelling, not me. Get on James. I'm going to talk to the driver." Sekuru Fani walked around the bus to speak with VaMusiyamwa, then explained the arrangement to James. VaMusiyamwa was very excited and gave James a welcoming smile.

"Muzukuru, I got you a boyfriend in there. Be nice to him and you will travel places," Sekuru Fani teased Rosie. "And not by bus either!" He, like the rest of the family, had grown fond of Rosie as she blossomed through the aftermath of the massacre of her people.

Rosie looked at James from the back. He had a corner haircut. She'd always wanted a boyfriend with a corner haircut. Not only that, but James also had broad shoulders, big and tender hands and seemed to lack the crudeness of a country man. She caught sight of his profile, which was arresting. As he settled into his seat and looked ahead, their eyes met in the profusion of diesel, sweat and food smells. She liked his big eyes and his smile. Within minutes, James began to sweat from his brow and drops of sweat formed between his nose and upper lip because of the heat in the bus. She liked the way the sweat made his black skin glow. When he offered to sit a little girl on his lap, to help a young mother with three other children, Rosie's heart softened, but she was also decidedly jealous. The bumpy movements of the bus seemed not to shake his serenity. Rosie had no idea that James had barely 'noticed' her. He was already planning to pick up the letter for Eriza the following day on his way back to Salisbury then hand-deliver the letter to Eriza in a week's time, once back in England.

"Hey, Queen Rosie, come here," VaMusiyamwa called out to her.

Rosie was startled out of her reverie. VaMusiyamwa was very protective of her and had instantly noticed the dreamy way she'd been looking at the new arrival.

"That man lives in England," he said, and laughed when Rosie opened her mouth in surprise. "He's visiting relatives in Mariva. We shall probably drive back with him tomorrow on his way back to England."

"Ya Sekuru. I could see that he was different," Rosie responded without betraying her amorous feelings for James. Before VaMusiyamwa had finished, she'd already come to terms with her 'loss'. She was very familiar with loss.

❋ ❋ ❋

Sekuru Fani rushed home. He didn't have far to run as the bus had caught them about 300 yards from the house. VaMusiyamwa had given him *The Rhodesia Herald* for Baba Eriza before he'd tooted and driven off with his new passenger from England. Baba Eriza came out of the house as he always did when he heard the toot and saw Sekuru Fani emerging from Rosie's rain of dust with a spring in his step. That step told him that there was going to be more news than that which was to be found in the newspaper that Sekuru Fani was waving at him.

"It had better be good news," he whispered to himself, because he liked to read his *Herald* in peace.

"Good afternoon Baba Eriza," Sekuru Fani saluted his brother-in-law, handing him the paper. "You wouldn't believe this!" Baba Eriza was already scanning the headlines, but he put the paper down on a stool and looked at Sekuru Fani with a mixture of impatience and anticipation.

"I met a man from England today and he just went on that bus. He lives near Eriza and I'm going to write to her today so he can take a fresh letter to her on his return."

He then gave a blow-by-blow account of his chance meeting with James Chipanda. The manner in which he did this elevated this chance meeting to one that had been orchestrated by the spirits.

"*Midzimu!*" – Spirits! – he said.

"VaMusiyamwa should have stopped so that we could meet with this man," Baba Eriza said looking in the direction of the bus. This was worthy news indeed.

"You'll meet him tomorrow," Sekuru Fani assured him. "We have to give him the letter for Eriza."

Mai Eriza had heard her husband and brother talking from the kitchen at the back of the house. She was soon at the front of the house with the two men.

"Eriza! What about her?!" she exclaimed, both surprised and concerned.

The two men were quiet, not because they did not want her to know, but were waiting for the other to reply. Unfortunately, the silence tipped Mai Eriza over the edge, which was obvious to her husband and her brother. Baba Eriza nodded to Sekuru Fani to tell her. After Sekuru Fani's repeat blow-by-blow account, Mai Eriza gasped. She too asked why VaMusiyamwa had not stopped at their house. Baba Eriza smiled at her.

"We have to write the letter today. Mbuya will want to dictate her own letter too.' With that Mai Eriza turned to go and find Mbuya Mukwesa.

Sekuru Fani was to be the scribe. He went to his hut and came back with an old *kopa book* – exercise book – which once belonged to Prudence.

He held it in his left hand and a biro pen in his right hand. He was already composing his letter with lips moving as he tried to articulate his thoughts before putting pen to paper.

❁❁❁

Up in Scotland, David was battling with winter and the cold November days and nights. Eight in the morning was like midnight back home. It was exceptionally, bitterly cold and the rain was incessant. The sun, on the rare days it shone, brought little relief from the Arctic conditions. He knew all about weather, climate changes and differences from his agricultural studies but never had he imagined the cold to be like this. Scotland was surely in a meteorological league of its own. He suffered in silence because he dared not write home to his parents who he knew to be under surveillance, and he held back from contacting Eriza. It was essential that he settled down to his studies first before doing so. The university gave him all the assistance they could and David was grateful for this.

Ironically, his assigned tutor was a lecturer by the name of David Smith – Dr David Smith. He was very attentive and from what David could see, he gave him far more guidance than he probably needed to. David also sensed that he was, in an odd way, overcompensating for something? Had he fallen short as a tutor in the past perhaps? Or had a previous student of his complained about not getting enough support? David couldn't picture either of these scenarios. The man was genuinely diligent. As was customary for tutors, apparently, Dr Smith and his wife Margo Smith, also a lecturer but in the Department of Politics, invited him to dinner. David gladly accepted the chance to get to know this kindly man better and to have a complete, home-cooked meal.

At dinner, it had all become clear. Margo, it turned out, had been a prominent student activist and had now matured into a campaigner for

Scottish majority rule. Liberation movements anywhere in the world were her natural allies, and so, naturally she was excited to meet someone from Rhodesia. Not long into the pre-dinner chat, she mentioned that her husband, and David's ever-so-attentive tutor, was a distant cousin of Ian Smith. They all laughed and David, who Margo now called 'David from Rhodesia' to distinguish him from her husband, instantly understood the apologetic manners of Dr Smith.

In early December, he wrote a short letter to Eriza to tell her that he was now studying in Scotland. By this time Eriza, had given up on ever hearing from David. It had become a burden for her just to walk past the pigeonholes hoping, but knowing that there would be nothing from him. Even Prudence hardly wrote to her and when she did, she barely had any news to tell.

✪ ✪ ✪

On that 12th of December, Eriza had walked from the wards straight to Mary's room.

"Oh Elizabeth, I was just coming to call you. There is a maaaaan waiting for you!" Mary dragged out the word 'man' with a smile. She suspected that it could be David, apart from the fact that he had all but disappeared. "He's waiting in the common room. And oh yeah! There's a letter in your pigeonhole as well," she added, proud that she was the bearer of the good news that Eriza had been waiting for.

Eriza gazed at Mary with a half-smile. She wondered which one was more important, the letter or her visitor, even as she walked towards the pigeonholes. As soon as she spotted the letter, she snatched it up and was immediately confused – the postage stamp was of the queen's head but the handwriting was David's.

"David!" she exclaimed with a gasp. She could hardly open the letter as her hands were shaking. Her lips parted as she opened the envelope. Wide-eyed, she zeroed in on, *My Darling Eriza*, at the top and David at the bottom. She then read it from the bottom up.

❖ ❖ ❖

I miss you Eriza. We shall talk more when we meet, which will be very soon. Continuing to study agriculture. They put me into first year at a Scottish university.

❖ ❖ ❖

Her heart was pounding and she was so immersed that she didn't even hear her fellow colleagues saying 'Hi' to her as they picked up their mail. They didn't take it personally though, as the look of intense scrutiny on her face as she read her letter said it all for them. Eriza soaked in every word and then, at long last, when she'd finished, she looked at the address and immediately started formulating her reply in her mind. She walked dreamily through the common room and saw a man sitting comfortably on a sofa. Jolting out of her trance-like, loved-up state, she remembered that she'd had a visitor.

They looked at each other, smiling, though Eriza's smile was reserved. He stood up and walked towards her. Shaking hands, he signalled that the conversation was to be in Shona by saying, "*Moro Erizabeth*" – Hello Erizabeth.

She hadn't been addressed like that since she was a little girl. Since then, in Chena, it was just '*Moro* Eriza'.

"*Moroi*," Eriza responded. She looked suspiciously but expectantly at this man.

"*Ko, hanzvadzi* – So, little sister – how are you getting on?" he asked. "*Ndinondzi James* – My name is James," he introduced himself.

With that greeting, she immediately warmed to him. He reminded her of Naijo.

"*Zvirikuita hazvo mukoma* – Everything is going fine, brother," Eriza replied.

James decided to dispense with more customary greetings. "I was in Chena just a week ago." He looked at Eriza. Her eyes practically popped out of their sockets and her mouth was wide open in disbelief. She hadn't seen anyone from the only home she'd known all her life, for over three years. James however remained calm but inwardly, he was excited because he knew the emotions that engulfed Eriza. He remembered those emotions very well.

"The only person I didn't see was your brother, Naijo. He's teaching at a secondary school in the south, so Baba said."

"Ah!" was all Eriza managed to say. Her heart jumped as she looked into the eyes that had just seen her family. She was touched to hear James speaking of Naijo as if they were brothers. In their short exchange so far, he certainly felt like a big brother to her. Finally, she could speak.

"I'd heard Naijo was teaching." She paused and could hear her heart pounding and wondered whether James could hear it as well. "How are they? Mbuya especially?"

James laughed. "I wish I had more time with them. I only managed to see them when the bus stopped outside your house on the way back to Salisbury. Mbuya was waiting with a letter for you and Baba, Mai and Sekuru Fani were with her. There was much drama. As soon as the bus stopped, she told the passengers that they would have to wait while she talked to her grandson, me, who was in the bus. VaMusiyamwa asked me to get out of the bus quickly. The passengers, who had all been staring at this stranger in their midst all the way from Mariva, peered even closer as I stepped out. You could see their jaws fell straight to the ground at the sight of Mbuya hugging me, as soon as I got off the last step of the bus. As she laughed merrily, she introduced me to Mai and Baba, all the while ululating. Mai showed me a photo of you but Mbuya said it was no use showing me the picture because I knew you already."

"*Handiti varivese naEriza ikoko?*" – They are together over there, with Eriza, isn't it? – she'd said, laughing even louder.

"I took pictures of them and you will smile when you see the pose Mbuya said was especially for you. I'll get them from the chemist next week and post them to you. Oh, by the way, here is the letter."

He handed her the letter and urged her to ignore him and read it. She read a few lines and gave up. All she wanted to do was listen to James, someone that had seen her family, loved ones she hadn't seen in what felt like a lifetime. Feeling more relaxed with James, she started laughing.

"I thank you for photographing them. Yes, that does sound like Mbuya for sure!"

"It was hilarious." James was encouraged to continue as he saw Eriza's smile. She was comfortable with him now. "She even wanted to feed me with sour milk but Mai said she would put it in a container for me to take and that Rosie would bring the container back on the return journey later that afternoon. By now the other passengers were enjoying the show. They found it so funny. And it was."

"Who's Rosie?" Eriza asked with curiosity.

"She's the bus conductor." He looked at Eriza in anticipation but she didn't ask any more. "You know Mbuya nearly forgot to hand me the letter until Rosie reminded her. That started another round of laughter." James was enjoying reliving the events with Eriza now. "Mbuya launched forward to hand me the envelope."

"Put it in your suitcase. Don't forget," she'd commanded.

"Then she gave me further instructions. Her face was beaming as she showered me with all sorts of things to tell you."

"Like what, Mukoma?" Eriza asked in a way that was part-excited, part-terrified, because she knew what her grandmother was like.

James laughed because he hadn't planned on telling Eriza all this, but he now realised she would find it humorous too. "Tell Eriza not to marry a white man," she'd said. "This was followed by loud applause from the passengers who heard her loud and clear despite the revving of the bus engine."

Eriza laughed. "She says the same thing in every letter, but she doesn't have to worry about that." With that Eriza glanced at David's letter. Then she peered closely at the letter from home, as if searching for her grandmother's fingerprints. She then asked James about the house and was delighted to get a good review.

"It stands out because I heard one passenger say "The bus stops at the Mukwesa house. You can never miss it!"

"Oh! I nearly forgot! Mai gave me roasted peanuts for you," he suddenly said, rummaging in his bag.

"I would never have forgiven you if you had forgotten to give me Mukoma," Eriza said jokingly, already savouring roasted nuts salted with salt from Tomas'.

As they were laughing, Mary walked into the common room. She stared at them, trying to work out if this was 'The David'. Eriza knew exactly what her friend's eyes were asking and quickly introduced James.

"Mary. This is James. He saw my family when he was back home and came by to share the news as well as give me some letters."

As per Mary, she immediately and animatedly greeted James and asked about all of Eriza's family members as if she had known them all her life too. James was bemused and lost for words.

"Elizabeth, you don't seem to have offered James something to eat." She frowned at Eriza's oversight.

"I'm actually fine, Mary. Thanks," James interjected.

Mary ignored him and ran to her room, returning with a variety of soft drinks and biscuits. James, out of courtesy, drank a can of coke with some Rich Teas. They chatted some more about families and their work now that they had started working in the hospital as qualified nurses.

"There are a few girls from home training in Ipswich. We met one of them in London a while ago," Eriza said.

"Yes. I know them, but since I live on my own, I don't see them much. Besides, I work at a different hospital in Ipswich. Now, since you are both not working, let me take you all for an early dinner before I catch my bus," he said looking at his watch and then through the window.

"Ah, Mukoma! It's me who should be taking you out," Eriza protested.

"Never refuse an offer of dinner from your big brother. I must spoil you," James grinned as he shut Eriza's protests down.

"You better go Elizabeth. I will go without you. You know that, don't you?" Mary quipped. With that, Eriza complied.

"Let me just put these letters in my room and we will get our coats." The reply to David would have to wait.

As she walked to her room, she couldn't help but think that had she not received David's letter, she would have invited James to sit with her in their kitchen. That's what all her flatmates did with their male guests, but after that, they would always end up in the bedroom 'till morning. Eriza's Catholic upbringing frowned upon this behaviour until she realised that it was the norm for boyfriends to stay overnight. The hospital authorities didn't condone it however, but it was difficult to police. Her position was that she wouldn't have wanted James to be the subject of gossip among her colleagues, more so now that David was just around the corner in Scotland. What her Catholic upbringing couldn't stop her from doing was fantasising about entertaining David in her room, although in the end it had remained a fantasy when David had disappeared. But with the letter in her hand, the dream had been revived.

❖ ❖ ❖

The dinner was a simple one of cottage pie and green beans, washed down with more coke. The conversation was now focused on nursing, with James giving pointers to Eriza and Mary about career routes and good hospitals to work in. Eriza felt like a girl under a warm shower that went on and on. She thought back to her mother's mantra that 'people who brought good news were messengers of God who must return from whence they came and collect more good news. You then had to reflect upon the gifts they brought you'. She also felt guilty that in her heart, she wanted to be in her room at that very moment and attend to David's letter while closeted.

It was as if James had read her thoughts because he soon excused himself to go to ring for a taxi to take him to the bus station. Soon after he returned to the table, the taxi had arrived. He paid the bill, ignoring the protests from the two girls who walked with him out of the restaurant. They said their farewells, with promises to keep in touch.

As they walked back to their flat they chatted non-stop. Then Mary shared some news.

"Guess what Elizabeth! I forgot to tell you. I got a telephone call from Jemias. He's inviting me to a party in London," Mary said smiling.

"I knew it! You've been talking about him ever since the day we met him at the rally. Are you going? You must go," Eriza urged Mary.

"I'm thinking about it. It's next week."

Eriza knew her friend would most certainly be going. She thought about telling Mary about the letter from David but she felt that she needed to absorb it first. Getting a letter from him, finally, was one thing, but to know that he was so close was too precious to reveal, even to her best friend. They were now at the front door to their block.

"Mary, I will see you later, *shamwari*."

James' visit had clearly transported Eriza back home, as she was talking to Mary as if she were a Chena girl.

Mary looked at her. "I know what that means. Friend, ain't it?" Mary was honoured.

"To be honest, Mary, I didn't even realise that I was in Shona mode again."

"You're homesick my friend. James took you back to your village."

Eriza entered the main entrance and ran to her room. She hoped, and rightly so, that Mary would stay away from her that evening.

TWELVE

A lone at last with, in that moment, the two most valuable things she owned – her letters. She sat on the bed, clutching them, working out which one to start with, and finally settled on the letter from home. Family first, always. Sekuru Fani's handwriting was as beautiful as ever. He had prided himself, and in fact gloated over the fact that all throughout his seven years of primary schooling, he was hailed, year after year, as the best scribe in school.

"Wese munhu aitoda kuona copa book rangu," he'd declared with pride, *"including vashaniri vaiuya pachikoro"* – Everyone wanted to see my exercise book, including VIPs.

She opened it, started to read and the words took on a life of their own, especially after James' earlier and very vivid account. The pristine handwriting invoked the summer-green maize fields; the clusters of lush trees whose leaves shook from the playful flutters of birds; cattle, sheep and goats chewing cud under the trees' cool shade; dogs yelping and barking here and there; her grandmother, perhaps solitary or with her mother, sheltered from the unforgiving summer sun under her favourite *msasa* tree; and, then in the distance, a dark cloud threatening to blot out the scorching sun, promising a cool afternoon shower.

Next was David's letter. It was short, much shorter than she'd expected considering that he had disappeared so suddenly, without warning. However, it was long and tender enough for Eriza to forgive him for his absence. He didn't give much away and she presumed he wanted to fill in the missing information face to face. She read it over several times before laying on her bed to assimilate all that had happened that day.

When she'd first arrived in England, she often lay like this on her back, with her eyes closed and relived moments in Chena. As time passed, she did this less and less, but tonight, it felt as if it was her first night away from home with Chena and David competing incongruously for her attention. She now in a way understood what her grandmother felt about Kuwadzana. No sooner had she said to herself, *"Oh Chena woye"*, in the manner of her grandmother's, *"Oh Kuwadzana woye"*, she fall into a deep sleep, emotionally exhausted.

❁ ❁ ❁

The following morning, she woke with a start and was surprised to see that she was still fully clothed. Then she heard the faint rumblings of a new day outside her door. She saw the letters on her bed and that triggered her into action. In no time, the reply to David was done and sealed. Just as she was about to dash out of her room to the post box, she realised that it made sense to reply to the letter from Chena as well. Back at her desk, she laughed and cried as she wrote it; laughed because it was as if she was chatting with her grandmother, who was as cutting as ever, and cried because it had been such a long time since she had interacted with her family. In the quietness of the morning, what consoled her was that James had confirmed that they were safe. She finally finished then headed to the post box, telling herself that no one would see her at that time of day so she could go just as she was and then wash on her return.

After dropping the letters in the box, she looked around it to be sure she hadn't missed the slot. Not that she would have but she was so anxious for the precious letters to be delivered in a timely manner. Besides, with the efficiency of Royal Mail, there was no doubt that David would receive his letter the following day. Prudence would have the family letters in good time for Christmas. Reassured, she took in a deep breath of the cold winter air and walked the short track back to her room where, apart from a wash and some Saturday chores, she just had to wait. Even though the Christmas break for universities was just about two weeks away, it would be longer before David came to see her. He had to catch up with his studies and Eriza, though agonisingly so, understood.

David took the coach from Edinburgh for his first trip to Colchester. It was a long journey through the cold and gloomy countryside. He had one change, in Cambridge, which he made during a dark, wintry late afternoon. Despite the gruelling conditions, he remained with a warm feeling inside knowing that, at the end, he would be reunited with Eriza.

The eve of David's arrival in Colchester was a quarrelsome night for Eriza. She knew that David would not arrive until the following evening, but the wait was unbearable. Her mind raced everywhere as she went over and over the arrangements for his arrival. Even though he was going to stay in a bed and breakfast for the duration of his visit, she still fretted about the set-up in her room: where to put their photo as high school sweethearts and where to put the portrait of David she'd enlarged from a small picture he'd sent her when he was still at university back home. Each time she'd just about settled into bed, she'd change her mind and reposition them to what she thought to be a more prominent position.

At one point, Mary, who had now taken to referring to herself as 'The Bridesmaid', had popped in and suggested that she should put the high school sweethearts' picture on top of the Gideons Bible, thus seeking forgiveness in advance. Both girls had collapsed in a fit of giggles and Hail Marys.

❖ ❖ ❖

David's bus arrived at 8:30 the following evening, three days before Christmas Day. Eriza was at the bus terminus 30 minutes before the arrival time – she wasn't taking any chances. As the coach pulled into its designated bay, she strained her eyes to catch a glimpse of David. She then focused her gaze on the door, not wanting to miss him the minute he stepped off the bus.

"Eriza. I'm here," his voice came from behind her, as she felt his hand envelop hers. She swung sharply to her right.

"How did you come out?! I've been here even before your bus arrived. How could I have not seen you?! Oh David!" She let go of his hand and embraced him, or rather fell limply onto his chest, then wrapped both arms around his torso. He, of course, was ready to catch her.

He then had to drag her out of the other passengers' way. One of them, who clearly understood the workings of love, picked up David's holdall and waited patiently for the two lovebirds to disentangle themselves before handing it over to him.

"Do you recognise it as yours, young chap," the passenger said loudly but jokingly.

"Thank you," David answered sheepishly.

"I thought you might just forget all about it," the passenger added.

The three of them had a good laugh before the passenger headed towards his own reunion.

"Is that all you have?" Eriza enquired curiously.

"I'm only here for a week you know Eriza." He lifted his bag with both hands, as if to say it was weighty enough for his short stay.

Eriza stared at him. She feared that it was all a dream and grabbed his hand tightly to be sure that it was real. David freed it from its hold from his bag. They then walked together out of the terminus until David asked Eriza where they were headed.

"We're going to your B and B. It's halfway between here and the hospital."

"It could still be miles away from here though," David joked.

"You haven't changed have you?" Eriza said, feeling a warm glow inside her. "Anyway, I just want to walk with you, holding your very-cold-but-warm hand."

David smiled, impressed by the poetic sound of *very-cold-but-warm hand*. He hung his bag on his left shoulder to free his left hand, then touched Eriza's breast. He laughed and Eriza realised that he was teasing her about their first intimate encounter of over seven years ago.

"Ah haunyare iwe" – Behave yourself. *"Uchiri kuita zvekumombe,"* – That's how cow herders behave – she said with a gentle pat on David's naughty hand. "See, there's the B and B," she suddenly announced, pointing at a white building with a sign, *Moira's B&B*. "It wasn't too far now, was it?" She teased him again, hinting that all his cow herder ways would be upgraded in Moira's B and B.

As they walked up the drive, Moira herself opened the door for them. She was delighted to see Elizabeth with her boyfriend and ushered them straight upstairs.

"Here's your room and see you at breakfast." Moira then warmly wished them goodnight.

As soon as she was out of sight, Eriza said to David, "Moira was born in Chimanimani."

"*Hoo!*" David was surprised. He opened the door of their room and let Eriza walk in first.

"But she and her parents were deported after the failure of that sell-out Pearce Commission," Eriza continued.

David wanted to mention that there was talk of Ian Smith working on creating a Zimbabwe-Rhodesia, a halfway house led by a multi-racial government. He decided against it and continued with the Moira inquiry.

"What's her surname? I might remember their story," David asked. "Oh! Was it Reverend Stanley Richardson? That was the father and Moira Richardson was a schoolteacher, I think."

"That's them," Eriza said. "Reverend Richardson heads a Methodist Church here in Colchester now."

David interrupted excitedly. "Let me tell you a very interesting story about him." All Eriza really wanted was to find out what she had missed in David's life, and he in hers, but she let him. He absolutely had not changed.

"The father and daughter duo were a thorn in the side of Ian Smith's white establishment. The Reverend spoke fluent Chimanyika. He used to start sermons to his large congregation by saying "*Tandanisai mabhunu!*" – Chase out the whites – and the people would respond "*Pasi nemabhunu*" – Down with the whites. It was funny him saying that, being a white man himself. To the police who cautioned him, he used to say, 'I say these things in the presence of God and no man can decide for me what is right or wrong between me and God.' That is how his sermons concluded each time he was hauled to the police station, so it was rumoured. On the day they were officially deported, practically all of Chimanimani descended on Salisbury Airport to say goodbye.

David was getting carried away and Eriza had to stop him. "Just as I thought. You only have a toothbrush with your clothes in this bag," Eriza pointed out as she unpacked his things. With that, she triumphantly pointed at a small, neat pile on the bed which included a blue flannel, a bath towel, pyjamas, bedroom slippers and a toothbrush, all wrapped up in a blue dressing gown. Eriza's overnight bag was sitting beside the pile.

"Is that all for me?" David was pleasantly surprised. "Thank you, darling," he said meekly, hugging and kissing Eriza. They both willingly fell on the bed. Eriza just managed to utter, in submission, "*Unotendei...*" – Don't mention... – before the room was filled with the sounds of heavy breathing.

The following morning, all that Eriza had choreographed for that first night with David, her unopened overnight bag and the purchases for David, lay in ruins on the floor. Joining them on the floor were the clothes they'd been wearing. Neither of them cared and they continued to lay naked and tranquil between the sheets.

Back home, events were now progressing relentlessly. Sensing that the writing was on the wall, and in very bold letters at that, Ian Smith unleashed murderous attacks wherever he felt his regime was losing grip. People like Sekuru Fani were not cowed into curbing their activities and Naijo continued to direct more young people out of the country from his school base. He couldn't visit his parents during school holidays because he didn't want the underground trail to be infiltrated by the wrong people in his absence, nor his family put at risk. But like many people in and outside of the country, he could feel that the noose was tightening on every white family. He remembered how a few years earlier, the South African president and Ian Smith's mentor, John Vorster, had advised Ian Smith that the consequences of the strife in Rhodesia were 'too ghastly to contemplate'. The tip of the iceberg of these ghastly consequences was the stampede by white people fleeing Rhodesia as a Zimbabwe was clearly on the horizon. They could not envisage that the Africans would be forgiving, and so it was a requiem mass with a musical score of the sound of plane, car and train engines. Being white, they were welcomed with open arms in Australia, New Zealand and above all, apartheid South Africa. Some quietly invoked their British heritage and flew to Britain as returning citizens. Most got into council flats, a far cry from the mini mansions in the leafy suburbs of Rhodesia that they wished they had carried with them.

"We're resolutely buying the spacious bungalows abandoned by whites," Naijo said to his colleagues. "I wish I could get the house of those little white fellas who ordered me to go back to Zambia when I was walking in Mount Pleasant," he added.

"I put a deposit last week on one in Highlands," one of his colleagues interjected, surprising all of them.

"*Ko VaMashayamombe*, why didn't you advise us to do the same?" another colleague asked in disbelief.

"Zimbabwe is here and guess what, it's going to last a thousand years, so we can get all the houses we want. But to be honest, I want to get that farm in Kuwadzana. My grandparents were driven out of there by the Land Apportionment Act 40 years ago and my grandmother longs to go back." Naijo spoke with an intensity of emotion that surprised him and his colleagues. The three continued to share their dreams of life in a new Zimbabwe, which were becoming achievable with each reported wave of white emigrants. A few days after that conversation, Naijo was advised that he should no longer direct fighters into Botswana, so he resigned his teaching post and headed for Salisbury. On top of that, he'd heard about the coming 'Zimbabwe-Rhodesia plans' and was not at all impressed. For one, his grandmother would be loathful of the name. For now, though, it was mere speculation, so he rested his thoughts.

The week together was both a whirlwind and rollercoaster of emotions for Eriza and David. Much of their time was spent in the B and B, in bed, filling in the missing gaps during their time apart. Many of Eriza's co-workers had left to stay with relatives or friends over the Christmas period, but David did manage to meet Mary on the eve of Christmas Eve, before she left for Ireland. Mary was nearly as emotional as Eriza had been when she met him and, in typical Mary-style, she even managed to charm David into sharing some of his life story. In turn, Eriza told David about the love that had blossomed between Mary and Jemias and how Mary had even convinced him to accompany her to Ireland over Christmas. For Eriza, this was the first time in her years in England that she felt she'd had a true Christmas. When David returned to Scotland, it felt as if he had gone home to Bulawayo for the holidays, while she remained in Chena.

The day after David left, James paid another visit. Instead of posting the pictures of Eriza's family, he'd decided to deliver them in person. Eriza was delighted by the distraction and welcomed him happily into the kitchen. As they talked, Eriza was astounded to hear that he had started the process of buying a house in Salisbury.

"In reality it's Harare now," he'd corrected himself.

The first thing that came to Eriza's mind, just as it had to her brother thousands of miles away, was how wonderful it would be to buy back Kuwadzana, for the sake of her grandmother. In one of the pictures, Mbuya Mukwesa looked very alert, just as James had described her. Eriza wanted her grandmother to experience the joy of returning to her beloved Kuwadzana, in the same way that she was excited about going back to Harare, Zimbabwe and not Salisbury, Rhodesia.

"The word Zimbabwe is no longer limited to the confines of hushed conversations. It's now being shouted out openly and confidently. If you want any assistance to make a foothold in Zimbabwe let me know. I have property contacts there."

"That will be helpful but I need to contact Naijo first."

✿✿✿

Naijo was in Salisbury, where he initially had to live with old friends and acquaintances while looking for a job. Surprisingly, it wasn't long before he was hired as a solicitor by a firm called Clarence & Hayes. The husband and wife team who owned the firm had been deserted by five young, white lawyers who could not countenance African rule, leaving them with their daughter as the only young solicitor. When Naijo first walked into their offices in Second Street, he was taken aback by the welcome.

"Good morning. My name is Nigel Mukwesa and I am here for..."

"Oh! Mr Mukwesa. I remember you. We were at university together, remember?" said the woman at reception, who he later found out was Judith, the daughter of the owners.

Nigel was amused, because why would he remember someone who would not have even cared to look at him, much less speak to him back then? "I'm afraid I don't remember you. Can you help me?"

"We were in Professor Jameson's tutor group and you were very good at Criminal Law."

Nigel wanted to laugh at the incredulousness of the situation. Oh, how the tables had turned. Here was a *missis* who actually acknowledged not just the presence, but also the ability of an African. However, he bit his tongue and suppressed the urge to be sarcastic; after all, he needed a job just as much as they clearly needed to give someone the job.

"Yes, I do recall you now. Remind me of your name please, madam?" he responded.

"It's Judith. Judith Hayes."

"Oh yes, now I remember you. It's a pleasure to see you again Miss Hayes."

"Please come this way with me." Judith ushered him towards a desk to the right of the reception room.

The interview that followed was short and surprisingly pleasant. He could not believe that he was offered the job straight away and, based on the offer, he was to be paid handsomely while he did his articles. This was the moment that Naijo realised that indeed, Zimbabwe was reborn, forgetting the fact that had he been living in a 'normal society', with his legal acumen, he would have already been commanding his own firm by now.

When he turned up for work on his first day, there were more surprises in store for him. He was given a company car and a rent-free house in Mount Pleasant which had been left vacant by one of the deserters. Naijo knew that there had to be a catch in all this but he was determined to make the most of the unfolding situation while he figured out why Clarence & Hayes were so generous. They in turn had figured out that their future in Zimbabwe could be assured by connecting with people like young Naijo. Unbeknown to Naijo, Clarence & Hayes had become aware of his active role in the liberation struggle, as well as the fact that he had become a 'solicitor' for one very prominent nationalist. Naijo did learn with time that even though Africans were now ruling, some whites would always align themselves with those that would allow them to maintain their Rhodesian economic and social privilege.

The time had come for Naijo to visit Chena, as was customary for any young man who was becoming 'big'. However, he was not interested in showing off. He simply wanted to see his family and their joy now that the whites were finally on their way out. He had made this clear to his mother, especially the fact that he did not want an entourage when he arrived.

Needless to say, she was heartbroken by this, as the whole point was for the family to show Naijo and his achievements off to the entire village.

It was wonderful to see his family after nearly a year with no contact, and there was no time wasted as they exchanged news. He heard that Ndondo had vanished after little persuasion. In fact, the Rhodesian army told him that he had two choices: either to barricade himself and his family in his house and wait to die there, or go to Martley where other whites were in a safe house of sorts. It was a sad reversal of fortunes because, only a few months earlier, Ndondo and his neighbour Dick had commanded the 'Chena keep', where villagers were confined in a bid to contain guerrilla fighters. Dick had co-commanded from afar as he had moved to Salisbury after his wife's murder. Ironically, the 'keep' had enhanced the security of Sekuru Fani's cache of firearms, as Ndondo and Dick had not suspected that the 'simple' folk of Chena could be involved in such activities.

In addition to his many misdemeanours over the years, Ndondo had recently tortured one of his workers by roasting him in the tobacco barn. The worker was alleged to have fallen asleep while attending to the curing process. Ndondo then had the worker bound and placed close to the furnace and told him that he would feel how the tobacco leaves felt when they were left unattended. After he left, the whole of Chena and his workers retaliated. The fence around the farm was cut and his stock was roaming everywhere, but strategically directed into Chena. Naijo heard a lot about the changes in Chena, but the news of Ndondo's demise needed to get to Eriza as soon as possible.

❖ ❖ ❖

Eriza was over the moon when she received that first letter, the first in a long time, from Naijo. She was so proud that he was now the lawyer he'd always wanted to be. As their communications grew to a steady flow,

232

she was increasingly torn between David and her family, so she had to tell Naijo about her relationship with David.

"David and I want to get married,' she wrote. "He knew you from university and when he crossed into Botswana to fight for Zimbabwe, but he then came to Scotland to continue his studies."

Naijo was pleased that Eriza had not only met someone but that it was someone he knew. He was impressed that David hadn't told Eriza that her own brother was the conduit of his escape from Rhodesia. It would not matter in terms of Naijo's security vis-à-vis the Rhodesian army and police, because they were dissipating, but David had kept the code of secrecy that was sacrosanct in that one step from Rhodesia to Botswana.

As winter became spring, Eriza and David were in constant communication, either by phone, letter or after David's 12-hour sojourns from Scotland, which he did every few weeks. They were clearly heading to the altar, and the question was now whether they should get married in Britain or Zimbabwe. Eriza had set herself up to train as a midwife while waiting for David to finish his degree. So, they settled on a home wedding – in Zimbabwe.

All these plans were relayed to Naijo, who advised them two things: first, that the wedding be preceded by the traditional procedures in Zimbabwe and, second, that because it would mean a lot to their parents and grandmother, Eriza should return on holiday first, before the proceedings began. Both she and David had agreed, and soon, after hurried preparations, she was ready to fly home with two huge suitcases. She couldn't have picked a better time. The Lancaster negotiations, to formally end Rhodesian rule and establish an independent nation, were in their nascent stages, but the signs were that they were irreversible. The rumour of a Zimbabwe-Rhodesia was soon quashed, making way for just 'Zimbabwe'.

❖ ❖ ❖

She arrived at the British Airways checkout desk in Heathrow exactly three hours before the 9 o'clock departure time on a Thursday evening. The queue was full of her own people returning home, so there was no need to be embarrassed by her luggage as almost everyone else was gleefully laden with gargantuan cases. The queue was long and slow. Practically every suitcase was over the maximum weight and the owners were forced to remove items from their suitcases. Some simply opened them, shuffled things around without removing a single item, only to be told to reopen the cases and remove what should have been taken out the first time round. The women were the main culprits. Some took out a few items and forced them into their hand luggage. Some asked single men to put their excess items into their half-filled suitcases. With pen and paper, addresses were exchanged so that they could be reunited with their items at the homes of the willing carriers, if they didn't happen to meet at Salisbury Airport. Others simply went to the unaccompanied luggage section and paid extra for their over-weight items. Watching all this, Eriza was rightly concerned about the weight of her two cases.

"I did tell you that you were taking too many things," David reminded her.

He had of course accompanied her to the airport and, as they approached the front of the queue, suggested that he take any extra weight back to Colchester. That of coursed didn't go down well with Eriza as she was determined to lavish her family with every gift she had so carefully selected. Her turn finally came. The cases were just within the required weight. She triumphantly smiled at David who shook his head with amusement.

As they strolled towards the entrance of the departure lounge, they chatted comfortably in the certainty of seeing each other again in a few weeks' time. They then embraced each other tenderly before exchanging goodbyes.

On the plane, her fellow countrymen were excited. Going home for good at last! Finally, around midnight, after everyone had been fed and watered, the chattering diminished, and she fell asleep until 5 o'clock the next morning.

THIRTEEN

The bright morning sun over the Tropic of Cancer beamed through the plane's windows and woke her from her slumber. She had never imagined that the sun could be so beautiful; a sun she had known all her life, before leaving for England. As the plane gently descended, the lush greenery below burst into full view and she wished the buildings that appeared could just be swallowed up by the vegetation. Then the plane landed and the bodies came back to life.

Arrivals was a cacophony of Shona, Ndbele and English. Her people were excited and she just about managed to spot one or two very subdued whites in the dense crowd of new arrivals. Little did Eriza know that departures was just as crowded but with white people, most of them on a one-way ticket out, much in the same way that Africans were on a one-way ticket in.

As she stood patiently in the immigration queue, she picked up some of the conversations around her that revealed the expectations of a nation. In front of her were two middle-aged men who spoke softly of their plans. Not that it was possible for an African to speak softly anyway because their conversation was clearly audible to at least five people ahead and behind them.

"*Kwangu ku foreign affairs,*" – I'm going to work in foreign affairs – declared one of the men. "*Pa* information desk," he specified.

The second man responded quickly. *"Inga Smith apfidza. Kuti isu vanhu tisevenze mugovernment!"* – Smith has been cowed, to give top civil servant jobs to Africans? *Ini ndiri kuenda ku praiveti sector na Lonrho."* – I'm going into the private sector with Lonrho. He paused both for effect, and in anticipation of a reaction. It came.

"You're in money there. Tiny Rowlands is switching allegiance quickly," the first man answered in a know-it-all manner, befitting of his soon-to-be civil servant status.

"Tiny Rowlands interviewed me personally. When I dropped the name of my well-known political uncle, I was hired there and then. And the package!" he gasped.

They didn't realise they'd reached the immigration desk. Then the Lonrho man said, with a smile of triumph. *"Toonana"* – See you again.

Eriza was bemused by the word 'package'. She was soon to discover that it was a word central in the recruitment of African people into the positions that were once only open to the whites. In the circles she was to move in with her brother Naijo in the coming days, people were saying either, *"Ndine package yakanaka"* or *"Iwe wakawana package yakanaka"* – I have a good package or You were given a good package.

It was then her turn at the immigration desk which was manned by a young and pretty chatterbox. The chatterbox had not paid much attention to the civil servant and the Lonrho employee because she'd clearly heard their story long before they'd got to her. She just gave them a look that said, "I know all about you already," matched their photos with their faces then stamped their passports without a word.

With Eriza, the chatterbox was more involved. *"Ndipei passport yenyu sisi."* – Let me have your passport sister. *"Ko makadii?"* – How are you? she added the friendly greeting while simultaneously stamping Eriza's passport.

"Ndiripo hangu muningina" – I'm fine, young sister.

"Murikubva kuEngland. Kwakadii mhiri kwemakungwa nhai sis? Inga zvenyu mamboona London." She enquired about the well-being of England, full of admiration for Eriza for having been in London.

"Kwakanaka zvako muningina," – It's OK – Eriza replied with a broad smile and with her passport in hand.

"Muve nenguva yakanaka munyika yedu ino itswa" – Have a nice time in our new country. She wanted to chat more but the immigration line was long.

The chatterbox had been on the job for about a week. The instructions to the new recruits were to just quickly stamp the passport of any African who spoke Shona or Ndebele then check that the passport photo matched the face in front of them. But with Eriza, she'd been adventurous and forayed beyond those simple instructions. Eriza was grateful to have been greeted so warmly, in Shona, which was something she had missed while in England.

She followed her fellow passengers to the baggage section and positioned herself strategically by the conveyor belt. She recognised some of the suitcases that had caused problems for their owners at Heathrow. Just as her mind wandered to the reunion with her relatives, she spotted one of her own big suitcases and pounced on it.

"Bokisi renyu sisi rakakura, munotoda rubatsiro" – Sister, you will need help with that big suitcase of yours. It was one of the young men milling around to assist, for reward of course.

"Maita mukoma" – Thank you, brother. Eriza capitulated without argument, and the young man swept the suitcase from the conveyor belt in one fell swoop.

"Pane imwe yacho iyo yakutosvika pano" – The other suitcase is just here. Eriza called to the young man, who was dragging the first suitcase, before deftly placing it on 'his' luggage trolley.

He rushed back in seconds, trolley in tow, pulled the second case from the conveyor and without a word, swung it on top of the first case. It was clear to Eriza that these young and muscular young men were masters of their new trade. He led her to the customs section and as she was taking out two English pounds from her purse to tip the young porter, she heard someone call out her name in all the glory reminiscent of her childhood days.

"*Ndiwe Eriza Mukwesa?*" – Is that you Eriza Mukwesa?

She turned around to see a giant of a man looking straight at her expecting to be recgonised instantly. He did so as he took over the reins of the luggage trolley of the young porter, who didn't mind now that he had his two British pounds.

"*Uchandiziva?!*" – Do you remember me?! the customs man shouted.

"*Aaaah, ndiwe Joshua!*" Eriza exclaimed, as her 'aaaa' gave way to a broad smile. He was a former classmate in secondary school. They hugged briefly.

"I've seen so many of our schoolmates coming back that I've wondered whether I was the only one who had remained here," he added jokingly while gesticulating to Eriza to push her trolley behind him. He looked at Eriza's gigantic suitcases and joked, "*Mune ma siwiti here imomu?*" – Are there sweets in there?

Eriza laughed loudly as she thought of the lollipop encounter with Ndondo. Joshua ticked and signed the 'no duty' part of the form he was holding. He then helped her with her suitcases and escorted her out of customs to her waiting relatives. The others in the queue behind them would have to wait – after all, none of them were his old friends. They both scanned the crowd for Eriza's family and soon enough, Eriza spotted her clan. There was Prudence standing with her arms folded below her breasts. Eriza was amazed because when she left for England, they were just pimples on her chest and now they had outgrown the rest of her body, especially as she stood there with nervous abandon. Behind her stood Sekuru Fani. Just then, Joshua saw Naijo coming for the suitcases and the two of them just nodded at each other as Joshua handed over the luggage silently before bidding Eriza farewell.

"*Prudence, manyira mainini,*" – Prudence, go and hug your aunt – Sekuru Fani woke Prudence up, gently pushing her forward.

"Mainini! Mainini!" Prudence shoved herself forward, pushing aside Eriza's trolley to reach and embrace her. Sekuru Fani secured the trolley in amusement.

He and Naijo were focused on ensuring that there were no *matsotsi* nearby ready to grab their luggage; it was well known that they lurked about ready to take advantage of the owners being engrossed in the emotion of family reunions before quietly taking over the trolleys and walked with them out of the crowd. Satisfied that all was clear, uncle and nephew quickly pushed the trolleys out of the building. Eriza and Prudence were left entangled in each other's arms, dragging each other out with Prudence awash in tears of joy and Eriza happy but stoic in order to keep things under control as she remained mindful of her handbag. Sensing that the entanglement of aunt and niece could go on for some time, Sekuru Fani and Naijo let the two women be and pushed on to the car.

Once out in the car park, they finally released each other and followed Sekuru Fani and Naijo to the tune of Prudence's sniffles.

"*Ndiyo mota yasekuru iyo, mainini,*" – That's uncle's car, auntie – Prudence said with a smile and eyes red from the crying as she pointed to a white car a few metres ahead of them.

Eriza just looked at the car and Prudence helped her aunt out, chipping in with "*Ipejoti*" – It's a Peugeot.

"*Yakanaka chaizvo!*" – It's beautiful – Eriza exclaimed. Her eyes caught sight of a Cortina just pulling out of the car park. "*Iyo zvainenge mota ya Mr Kanyemba wani*" – That looks like Mr Kanyemba's car.

Both stared at the Cortina in silence before surveying the rest of the car park, watching families happily loading their cars and driving off.

Once all four of them had gathered around the Peugeot, Naijo instructed Eriza and Prudence to get in while they loaded the suitcases in the boot. At the same time, Naijo was accosted by a friend who he invited to his house later that day, telling him that he had to take his tired sister who had just arrived from England home. He and Sekuru Fani then got into the passenger and driver's seats.

Now that the luggage was safe in the car, Sekuru Fani was ready to greet his niece. *"Muzukuru wazokura wena. Chikafu chevarungu chinopindirana newe"* – My niece, you have grown big. English food agrees with you. Sekuru Fani had turned his head around to address Eriza and shake her hand through the gap between his and Naijo's seat. Naijo turned to do the same before starting the car. His mission to get out of the car park was not yet done.

"Sekuru makadii?" Eriza asked Sekuru Fani about his well-being.

"Tiripo wena muzukuru. Yatoopo Zimbabwe yedu and zvirikuita tantamount to heaven," – I'm well. Zimbabwe is almost here and it's tantamount to entering heaven – he answered in a very confident and jovial manner. He desperately wanted Eriza to recognise that he was dressed in a shirt and tie she'd sent him from England. However, Eriza missed the cue.

"Ko mukoma Naijo zvirikudii? Inga mafuta. Ya BP yamuri kutiira muno muZimbabwe!" – My brother, how are you? You've put on weight, attracting blood pressure to our Zimbabwe. Eriza greeted her brother in kindly concern about his bulging weight.

"Zvinenge zvoita wena hama," – It's good so far, my dear – Naijo replied as he prepared to zoom out of the car park. He ignored the comment about his blood pressure but conceded, silently, that his sister was truly a nurse and was right to point this out. However, he still leaned more towards excess weight being a culturally-positive social connotation of success

rather than a health concern – a view shared by many. Sekuru Fani and Prudence had no clue what BP was, but at that moment believed it to be a complimentary term.

They came up to a traffic jam as dozens of cars tried to squeeze into two lanes out of the car park. Eriza took the opportunity to survey her surroundings and see if she recognised anything from the time of her departure to England. Nothing. Everything was different – there were even more African faces than there were back then. Soon the bottleneck of cars loosened, their car picked up speed and made its way out of the airport grounds. To their right, Eriza spotted a wildlife park. In the distance, the green pastures and trees were graced by magnificent giraffe and jittery zebras whose stripes glistened in the morning sun.

Houses started to appear along the left side of the road. She spotted their occupants stepping out to start their day while others were already en route, on foot, towards their destinations. Some of the women balanced loads on their heads. Naijo's car then drove past a shopping centre where others had already set up stalls selling vegetables and dry goods. Then the big houses appeared. With their white bosses gone to work, housemaids and gardeners chatted across fences and hedges or in each other's front gardens. In some she spotted *mamisis* behind the leafy borders of houses strolling around in their gardens while their workers bustled around them.

Traffic was building up again as they approached the city centre. Naijo began to enlighten Eriza about some of the changes that were taking place.

"Many of these houses are vacant and will soon be up for sale. They are in the hands of estate agents as we speak,' Naijo said. "When we get to Mount Pleasant, you'll see all the *For Sale* signs."

"Things are changing into Zimbabwe even before Zimbabwe is born," Sekuru Fani chipped in as he turned his head to address Eriza. His eyes suggested to her that she shouldn't miss out.

"I have three African neighbours. One to my left, another to my right and the last one right opposite me. When I moved into my house that came with the job, the white owners of these three houses put their houses up for sale and within a week, *For Sale* signs sprung up here, there and everywhere." Naijo narrated this and the many manifestations of racial hatred that showed no signs of abating. "I call the signs Ouija boards," he joked.

"Naijo boards! Your name Sekuru?" Prudence asked laughing.

"No muzukuru. Ouija. You have much to learn," Naijo said, laughing with Sekuru Fani, who joined in on the laughter.

"Even I thought you'd said 'Naijo'," Eriza quipped.

"Ah, even you straight from England do not know that a Ouija board means a board that flashes messages from the dead?" He questioned with good humour.

"Ah! Naijo you must be joking. These white people of ours are not dying, they're just quitting," Eriza objected.

Sekuru Fani seized his moment. He had been perplexed by the term but waited for the right moment to jump in as if he knew all along what Ouija meant. "Eriza, their leaving this country is tantamount to them dying. They're not coming back. Even if they wanted to come back, we shall say 'NO' just as we did to the Pearce Commission years ago. Besides, we control guns now." He laughed victoriously.

"You Sekuru and your guns. I don't know!" Prudence said in despair.

"No mistake about it muzukuru. It's the gun which is driving them out," Sekuru Fani asserted.

"We're in Mount Pleasant now, Eriza. Look at that house to our right. I was assaulted by white schoolboys from this house as a student a few years ago. That sign wasn't there yesterday," Naijo said calmly.

"Ouijo!" Sekuru Fani shouted and everyone laughed. Naijo knew very well that his uncle was not sure what the word meant and had replaced the 'a' to mock Naijo while hiding his ignorance.

Eriza sat forward in her seat to take a closer look at this side of Salisbury that was way beyond the Mbare and Railway Avenue that she knew. Manicured gardens with flowers in full bloom. Roads straight and smooth. Avenues and streets lined with jacaranda trees.

"I've never seen houses as big and beautiful as these," she said in awe.

"Yes, the white people hid themselves in this paradise. But it's all over for them now." Sekuru Fani was about to launch into a tirade.

Naijo cut him short. "It's the same everywhere. Highlands, Greendale, Mabelreign, Borrowdale. If we turn left here, we'll end up in Alexandra Park. Same thing. We'll go another time and visit one of my friends there.

"Any of these houses are yours for the taking Eriza," Sekuru Fani stressed.

"They must be quite expensive though." Eriza was overwhelmed.

"Yes, but there is a stampede by whites to sell up and go and prices are falling like manna from heaven," Naijo said as they turned into a street called The Chase in suburban Mount Pleasant, now lined with Naijo's Ouija boards.

They then turned left into another street, but Eriza could not read the name because the sign was obscured by red bougainvillea. Suddenly, without warning, the car turned into the driveway of a big house. She didn't realise the gate to the house had opened under remote control because she was so mesmerised by her surroundings.

"*Waawu!* This is a mansion mukoma," Eriza exclaimed as she caught sight of the house. She remained glued to her seat with her eyes transfixed as the others climbed out of the car. When she eventually snapped out of her trance, she slowly scanned the front of the house. "Even the porch is spacious!" She slowly walked to the right side of the house. "*Maiwe!*" – Oh my! She walked around the back, leaving the others to deal with her suitcases.

She came up to what was the kitchen door; then out came a beautiful young woman. They looked at each other. Eriza wondered whether she was the maid. No, she was too smartly dressed to be the maid. The woman had a broad smile which exposed dimples. She was light-skinned and it seemed naturally so, as she could see no signs of the effects of skin-lightening creams. Then she realised this was the woman that featured in the photos that Naijo had sent to her in letters over the years. This had to be Nomsa in the flesh. Eriza looked at her in awe and admiration as she recalled the nightie set that Naijo had given her as a goodbye gift when she left for England all those years ago. Yes, only a woman like Nomsa could have picked such an exquisite item. They shook hands, though they wanted to hug each other. All along, Nomsa knew that the woman in front of her was the family's legend, Eriza. Eventually the silence was broken.

"How was your journey?" Nomsa asked with a shy smile.

"Very good. I slept most of the way," replied Eriza, admiring Nomsa's voice. *It was a lovely voice*, she thought to herself.

"You two seem to know each other by the looks of it," Naijo sort of ambushed them just as they were about to introduce themselves.

"*Ndiye Nomsa ka muroora wako*," – This is Nomsa, your sister-in-law – Naijo added lovingly. It was the first time that Nomsa had been elevated to the ranks of the Mukwesa family by Naijo himself, without a marriage certificate at that. It meant a lot to Nomsa.

"Aah!" Eriza was excited. She gave Nomsa a tight and possesive embrace.

Nomsa returned the embrace with "*Moroi* tete" – Hello sister-in-law.

Those phrases alone sealed one aspect of the traditional Zimbabwean marriage. The certificate was a formality for the benefit of the church and the authorities.

Naijo grinned as the two women started chattering loudly. Mai Eriza, who had gone to the front door to meet her daughter, raced to the back of the house, ululating for the arrival. The irony was that it was also the same adulation used to welcome a new bride. Sekuru Fani did not miss the irony.

"Nhai Gogo murikupururidza mwana kana kuti muroora?" – Are you welcoming your daughter or your daughter-in-law?

Schooled and skilled in rural diplomacy about these things, Mai Eriza replied, "For both." She was now laughing wildly.

Though Mai Eriza had known Nomsa for some time as Naijo's girlfriend, because Naijo had not yet made it clear that Nomsa was to be his future bride, she was not permitted to make any joyful sounds for Nomsa. Today she had broken protocol but it had been for a good cause – she had to make Nomsa feel special.

As Mai Eriza faced her daughter, she took hold of her hands, stepped back and said reverently *"Mwari wangu"* – My God. She momentarily freed her right hand to gesticulate the sign of the cross before throwing herself against Eriza who, like her mother, was now in tears.

There was silence as they both sobbed quietly. Soon that silence was broken by the shuffling of Mbuya Mukwesa's feet as she walked through the kitchen towards the excitement. Naijo was afraid that his grandmother might stumble down the steps outside the door even though Prudence was guiding her. He launched forward in front of her only to be rebuked humorously.

"You are not Eriza. Move over."

Everyone laughed loudly. Mbuya grinned as a wail roared out of her mouth.

"Eriza, Eriza! You have made it to us in our lifetime. I thank you Muchaida and those before you for keeping me to see this day. From now on feel free to take me to join you!" Her glassy eyes looked straight into

Eriza's teary ones. With both her hands she wiped away the tears from her granddaughter's eyes.

"*Zvaita*," – It is well – she uttered her spiritual gratitude. They then all walked around to the front of the house to enter through the living room.

There, Baba Eriza finally had his chance to embrace his daughter. He was calm, as he always was in moments of excitement but they all knew that he was the happiest father that day. He had remained in the background, while all the drama was unfolding by the kitchen door, patiently waiting his turn to welcome his only living daughter back home. His only daughter fell straight into his open arms.

❖❖❖

It was only Sekuru Fani who ate breakfast with gusto. In between mouthfuls, he revealed that he had to go back to Chena later that morning to see to 'things'. The others were too excited to eat much and just nibbled as they bombarded Eriza with questions. Since it was Mai Eriza who had prepared the breakfast and not Nomsa, there was no risk of offending anyone by not eating hearty mouthfuls like Sekuru Fani was.

"What are these things you are rushing to Sekuru? I want to do a medical examination on you," Eriza asked in a light mood. There was laughter.

"Ah! Your Sekuru has endless things these days. He does not even tell us," Mai Eriza interjected.

For once, Sekuru Fani kept quiet before excusing himself as soon as he had swallowed his last gulp of tea. Naijo did the same, as he had to drive Sekuru Fani to Mbare for his bus to Chena.

No one else rushed to get up except Prudence who was expected to clear the table. She wanted to get things done quickly so that she could persuade Eriza to open her suitcases. All the others just wanted to hear, blow by blow, about Eriza's life in England. Eriza, on the other hand, wanted to hear all that she had missed in the years she had been away. The conversations became an exciting tussle. Mbuya Mukwesa assumed, at times, the role of a very partial chairperson completely in favour of Eriza. On the other hand, she became frustrated because Eriza used the 'floor' that she was repeatedly given to ask them about Chena instead of telling them about her life in England.

Suddenly, out of nowhere, Mbuya Mukwesa suggested that perhaps Eriza might want to freshen up.

"The England perfume does not agree with you Mbuya!" Prudence laughed and everyone else joined in.

"Eriza just needs to wash off some sleep," Mbuya Mukwesa suggested calmly.

"Ehe Mainini Eriza. Do what Mbuya says," Prudence encouraged her aunt, seizing on a potential opportunity to get the suitcases opened. Eriza ignored Prudence but could not do the same with Mbuya, so she excused herself and allowed Nomsa to show her to the bathroom. Prudence was directed to the kitchen and ordered to leave Eriza in peace by both her grandmother and great-grandmother.

It was only after Naijo had returned from Mbare an hour or so later, and with some friends, that the Mukwesas, including a freshly washed Eriza ready for the next round of interrogation, finally shifted from the dining table to the sitting room. At that point Mbuya Mukwesa excused herself to go and lie down in the large bedroom, which she was to later share with Eriza and Prudence, just like they did in Chena, but now it was to be in more luxurious surroundings.

After Naijo introduced his friends and their wives, they all settled into talking about the new order in the country. That word 'package' featured from the get-go and was littered throughout the conversations.

"*Imi ana sisi Eriza ndimi murikuwana mapackage akanaka ne experience dzenyu dze overseas,*" – Sister Eriza, with your overseas experience you can get a very good package – Miriam, who had been introduced as Victor's wife, pointed out. Victor appeared to be Naijo's closest friend, because they addressed each other as *sawhira*, meaning a confidante.

Naijo could see that his sister had no idea what this package business was about, though it was clear that she was curious and fascinated by what it meant. He rescued her.

"A good package is a job offer whose trimmings are worth far more than the salary – a company car, a mortgage, a housing allowance, children's school fees and, for people like Eriza, a welcoming lump sum they call a 'resettlement sum'. Then there are other bits and pieces which different companies throw in to make themselves more attractive employers. Some people are getting rich before they even do a day's job." There were nods of agreement from the 'locals' and a gasp of awe from Eriza, the 'returnee'. Baba and Mai Eriza, who had never known that jobs could be as lucrative as was laid bare by Naijo, glanced discreetly at Eriza.

"At the moment it's Lonrho and Nestle who are the most generous," Victor added. "There are also many government jobs but they are not as good moneywise. Do you remember my brother Ernest? He was offered jobs in the ministries of heath, local government and finance all in one day. He could have walked into other ministries and got offers of good jobs in all of them if he hadn't taken a long lunch break."

Everyone including Eriza burst into loud laughter.

Soon it was lunchtime. Nomsa and Prudence had at some point sneaked out of the living toom to prepare a lunch of sadza, beef and cabbage. Mbuya

Mukwesa shuffled into the dining room. She was helped to the chair by Victor, whom she had come to know and love as another *muzukuru*. Naijo, who knew how his grandmother acquired relatives the moment she discovered if they had the totem of Musiyamwa, had warned Victor not to reveal this to her. But she had figured it out anyway the moment Victor said his surname was Dzengedza.

"Ah, Naijo should call you Sekuru then," Mbuya had told them.

The two young men had taken one look at each other and laughed so hard. Their friendship blossomed over the years, with Naijo being the best man at Victor and Miriam's wedding.

As Mbuya Mukwesa settled into her special and very opulent chair, she said "Thank you Musiyamwa" to Victor. By so doing, she alerted Eriza to the fact that Victor was a Sekuru, making Miriam their Mbuya.

"Eriza, do you still remember sadza?" Mbuya Mukwesa teased.

"Sadza! Mbuya, I missed it until I got fed up and just ate whatever was there without thinking about it." Eriza was waiting impatiently for everybody else except Prudence to dish out their food before she dug in.

"We hear that some people returning from overseas don't eat it any more and they call it 'shajha'," joked Victor.

"Aah, Baba Itai don't you lie!" reprimanded Miriam, even though she was giggling. Everyone else followed suit, with the loudest laughter coming from Mbuya Mukwesa. It was obvious that there was more to her laughter. She liked Miriam's bossy interjections, and this time confirmed it by saying *"Mazvinzwa ka vaMusiyamwa"* – You heard it from the boss Musiyamwa.

Eriza had warmed up to them now. "Where is Itai? How old is he? Does he have a school package?" she asked, looking at Baba Itai. More loud laughter.

"Mu-mu-zukuru, do you see what 'shajha' does to you?" Victor replied. The table rocked with raucous laughter.

"We are all going to choke today," Baba Eriza warned light-heartedly.

One by one, people began to focus on their plates, with the chewing and swallowing doing the talking. It would be an understatement to say that Eriza ate her sadza ferociously. All noticed her delight with each mouthful, but none dared interrupt her. This was a reverent moment for a returnee. However, Naijo and Victor eyed each other, satisfied that she would never call this dish 'shajha'.

The rest of the afternoon passed with more joviality and enlightenment for Eriza. By late afternoon, the excitement of Eriza's arrival had taken its toll. Victor and Miriam left, followed by the other couples. Mbuya Mukwesa settled down to watch television – her new favourite toy. Naijo had noticed that she needed glasses if she was to continue enjoying her new pastime, so he had taken the liberty of arranging an appointment with an optician the following week. Of course, the timing was such that Eriza would accompany them. Baba and Mai Eriza took a walk in the big garden then out on the avenue. Naijo followed them after finishing his telephone calls, and Eriza, Nomsa and Prudence saw to the dishes in the kitchen.

There was a little chatter along with the clutter and clatter of dishes. Though Eriza and Nomsa knew each other well through third party correspondence via Naijo, it was a different matter seeing each other in the flesh. However, they felt comfortable with each other and Eriza had a feeling that she may at last experience what it was like to have a big sister. Meanwhile, all Prudence was interested in was getting the dishes over and done with so that they could unpack Eriza's suitcases.

FOURTEEN

The first week of Eriza's return visit was full. Naijo had drafted in a distant aunt from his father's side of the family, Mai Murambiwa, to formally tell Baba and Mai Eriza and Mbuya Mukwesa about Eriza's wishes to get married. He had already told his grandmother weeks before Eriza's arrival, knowing how jittery she would be about talk of Eriza getting married. Once she had established that David was not white, she'd immediately calmed down and could focus on being one up against her son and daughter-in-law.

Meanwhile, Eriza and Mary's and Eriza and David's conversations were dominated by talk of wedding plans and packages – the former of Mary and Jemias and the latter of Eriza and David. It turned out that after the Christmas visit to Ireland, Jemias had returned on his own and asked Mary's parents for her hand in marriage. The family had fallen in love with him – clearly the Irish were a different breed of whites from Rhodesians. Things were moving fast and the plans for the nuptials were in full swing.

"Eriza, please hurry back so you can help me. I need my maid of honour. By the time your wedding comes we'll be professional wedding planners!' Mary had squealed in excitement.

"We need to be sure we get the best package when we return, you're right," David agreed with his future wife.

On his part, David had organised, with his parents in Bulawayo, that his *tete* – paternal aunt – would avail herself at Naijo's home to start linking up the upper echelons of the two families. The aunt lived in Salisbury and as it turned out, not very far from Naijo's home. She and her husband had quickly upgraded themselves from their location home. Her husband was a headteacher and had moved rapidly up the pay scale, making his salary shoot through the roof. The *tete's* husband, being a prudent man, had wasted no time in buying a dream home in Mount Pleasant.

David's *tete* and husband visited on the first Saturday and Eriza was put in charge of the lunch preparations, to show off whatever kitchen skills she'd acquired overseas. The visit was an all-round success. Mbuya Mukwesa liked David's *tete*. The post-mortem of the visit was that, judging by her exuberance and frankness, David's family had the right blood to mix with the Mukwesas. That was Mbuya Mukwesa's biological conclusion as, according to her, there was no hint of the Musiyamwa and the Mukwesa Garwe lineage in David's Shungu family. If she'd so much as caught a hint of any connection, she would have cried incest and put a stop to the proceedings. Above all, Mbuya Mukwesa was impressed by the fact that the *tete* spoke about the demise of Rhodesians with absolute conviction. The fact that her husband got on well with Baba Eriza was just the icing on the cake.

The subsequent days were spent at home catching up with her family, visiting Naijo's bosses and friends and touring Salisbury, mostly in the evenings with Naijo, Nomsa and Prudence. She was surprised that Naijo was not keen to take her to Chena. He kept saying that they will go and pick Sekuru Fani when he was ready to return to the city.

She got the hint when Prudence inadvertently said, "Ah, *Mainini, Sekuru vari muRadio Dar*". That was her euphemism for Sekuru Fani being in the armed struggle.

When they met with Naijo and friends, the talk was always about the momentous changes taking place. Central to these changes was… 'package'. This word constantly came between her and her wish to know what had happened during her absence. She tried to ask about Mr Kanyemba but almost everyone referred her to Sekuru Fani who, of course, was still in Chena. Then the conversation would quickly change to the new Zimbabwe that was emerging. At one point though, Mbuya Mukwesa bluntly said that "the white men killed him," but even she preferred to talk about how Naijo's home had become her halfway place to Kuwadzana and that excited her. Her own 'package' was the return to her ancestral home. At night in their bedroom with Eriza and Prudence, she spoke as if Kuwadzana had stood still and she would just walk into her home as soon as Naijo was ready to drive her there.

Little did Eriza know that a conspiracy for her and David to be entangled in this word 'package' was well afoot, and it included Lonrho. Clarence & Hayes, Naijo's employers, were the leading counsel for the giant that was Lonrho. In its mining subsidiary, Lonrho had set up a health and safety department and Naijo and his bosses saw Eriza in the centre of that department. Naijo strategically revealed the plans to his sister as he drove her back from the Avondale Shopping Centre where she had gone to pick up some items for that evening's meal.

"And the package, well, you will be making more money than I am," Naijo pointed out, after he'd finished coaxing Eriza to marry and settle in what would soon be Zimbabwe and forget about midwifery. He didn't stop there.

"Then with David in their agricultural sector, you'll be drinking water in crystal glasses."

Eriza had to laugh as she recalled the joke her brother had told her about his friend's wife, who vehemently demanded to drink, even water, from a crystal glass whenever she visited another friend in their clique.

"Does David know about this?" Eriza asked anxiously, concerned that he would not finish his degree.

Naijo had already anticipated Eriza's question. "Do you remember last week when I spoke on the phone with David?"

"I thought that was just about how my marriage plans were progressing!" Eriza protested.

"OK, listen. Calm down. He's excited about everything going on here. Mr Hayes had an informal chat with Lonrho and they have invited David to fly here next week for an interview." Naijo spoke firmly but delicately as he knew how his sister would react.

"What?!" Eriza exclaimed ferociously. "He hasn't finished his studies! He has some time to go before he even graduates!"

"Exactly! With such a short time left before he graduates, the more reason he should set himself up here. This is a fast-moving scenario my sister. Next year this time, these jobs loaded with packages will not be so abundant. The offer for David is right here in my bag. After the interview, the job offer will be made. He will fly back to Ian Smith's native land, complete his studies and fly back again. His package is huge, and he'll be paid a salary in absentia. Normally a person is sentenced to jail in absentia, but a salary in absentia...!" Naijo knew that to convince Eriza, you had to lay out a strategy piecemeal, saving the best for last.

"I'm not sure. Let me think about it," was Eriza's quiet response.

Sensing victory, Naijo sealed the deal by revealing the fortuitous border crossing into Botswana that he'd staged for David. Eriza turned slowly to face her brother, her eyes and mouth wide, unable to speak. Naijo could see her from the corners of his eyes but continued driving and talking steadily. He then gave Eriza a full account of his 'teaching' job in the south. In true lawyer fashion, Naijo completed his monologue dramatically with "...and that my sister is all that you missed when you were away."

The silence that followed confirmed that the deal was done and victory was his and his sister's, though she was yet to realise it.

"David never told me," was all Eriza could say.

"It was part of the contract not to tell people about our activities. I can tell you now because I am certain that the Zimbabwe is within sight."

"Naijo. Where are we really going?" Eriza asked.

It was a question that caught Naijo off guard. Did she mean where they were driving to at that moment or where their beloved country was headed?

ABOUT THE AUTHOR

Peter Molife was born in 1951 in Msengezi, near Zvimba, in Zimbabwe. He enjoyed his rural upbringing on his parents' farm which he shared with three brothers, five sisters and numerous cousins.

He studied History (Hons) at Leeds University, England, graduating in 1975, then went on to live with his wife and two daughters in Guyana, Jamaica and The Bahamas over a 15-year period. Whilst in Jamaica, he obtained an MA in Education from The University of the West Indies and worked as a teacher. He moved back to England in the early '90s and continued to teach, taking time out to study law, gaining an LLB (1998) and LLM (1999) from Essex University, before he retired in 2014.

Eriza is his first book.

Lightning Source UK Ltd.
Milton Keynes UK
UKHW010952140620
364911UK00001B/142